Reading and Study Skills

Book One

Second Edition

Ronald V. Schmelzer
Eastern Kentucky University

William L. Christen
President, The Dimension Group, Inc.
Mesa, Arizona

KENDALL/HUNT PUBLISHING COMPANY
2460 Kerper Boulevard P.O. Box 539 Dubuque, Iowa 52004-0539

The authors wish to thank the copyright holders for permission to reprint the articles in this text. An acknowledgment appears on the first page of each article.

Contents

Unit 3   Active Listening and Lecture Notetaking   55

PART 2   PROCESSING SKILLS   85

Unit 4   The Key to Reading Mastery: The PREP Study System   87

Unit 6   Applying the PREP System to Textbooks, Works of Literature and Newspapers 155

Preface

Reading and Study Skills meets two important needs of students. First, it can help them to improve their reading rate and comprehension. Second, it can help them to study more efficiently and effectively. To succeed in school, students must be both skillful readers and studiers.

In developing the two volumes of **Reading and Study Skills,** the authors have strived to accomplish certain key goals:

1. To provide for individual differences among students. For example, the reading-comprehension selections in Book Two cover a wide range of difficulty levels so that each student can begin at a comfortable level.
2. To give many opportunities for practicing the concepts and principles presented. Numerous exercises are included so that student can develop skill and confidence.
3. To provide easy material for rate improvement and challenging material for comprehension development. By dealing with a variety of materials, students can learn to become flexible readers, adapting to different kinds of reading material.

Reading and Study Skills is composed of two volumes. Book One concentrates on a variety of reading and study skills, and Book Two contains 41 readings selections divided into five difficulty levels. Each selection is followed by ten comprehension and ten vocabulary items. The two volumes together may be used in a coordinated reading and study skills program. Also, Book One may be used alone in a course that stresses study skills, or Book Two may be used in a course emphasizing reading improvement.

Many people worked hard to make these materials possible. The authors would like to thank Dr. Alton Raygor, Richard P. Thiel, Erika and Stephen Schmelzer, Claire Schmelzer and the many study skills specialists and students who have contributed their insights and criticisms.

Introduction to the Program

The material in the program is of two main types: information and practice. You first need to know what to do. Each unit is a source of valuable information on some aspect of reading or studying. You also need to know how to do it. In many cases you do not truly know something until you have experienced it. You can read about how to take notes, but without practicing the method, you cannot master it. Therefore, exercises and other activities are included to help you learn how to apply the suggestions.

How the Program is Organized

The material in this program is divided into two books. Book One covers aspects of reading and study skills, vocabulary development, skimming and scanning and reading rate improvement. Book Two contains numerous reading selections at five levels of difficulty, to be used for reading comprehension improvement. A comprehension exercise and vocabulary exercise accompanies each selection. Also in Book Two is a placement guide to aid the instructor in determining which difficulty level you should begin at. Your instructor will explain how these materials are to be used.

Introduction to Book One

Some ways of dealing with school can hinder your success. For example, if you habitually sit near the back of the classroom you may be greatly reducing your listening efficiency. If you postpone studying and try to cram at the last minute, you may be hurting your performance on course exams. If you read your textbooks without a clear purpose, you may be losing valuable comprehension. Other approaches can increase your chances of success. The units in Book One may help you develop the skills and habits needed to succeed in school.

One point needs to be stressed: there is no single set of reading and study methods that works best for everyone. Some books on study skills will tell you: "Use a three-ring notebook," or "Always take notes when you read textbooks." Our approach is more flexible. We try to allow for differences among individuals. The fact is that some students succeed by using methods that would make many study-skills specialists shudder. We believe that you must make the final decision about which suggestions to use, which to modify, and which to discard.

Overview of Book One

Here is a brief description of the topics covered in Book One:

1. Reading. Reading is not a single skill but a complex variety of skills and behaviors that interact with one another. Book One deals with a number of reading-related topics:
   a. Reading for ideas and details (Unit 5). To read effectively you should be able to pick out the main ideas and important details found in each paragraph.
   b. Using the PREP study system (Unit 4). Preview—Read activity for a specific purpose—Examine by questioning—Prompt to improve your memory. These are the parts of PREP, a framework for flexible, active reading.
   c. Reading textbooks, works of literature, and newspapers (Unit 6). Special techniques are discussed for dealing with each of these important reading tasks.
   d. Increasing your reading rate. You will learn about the reading process. Rate-boost articles are included in this section to help you reach your reading rate potential.
   e. Skimming and Scanning (Units 1–8). Skimming is the rapid processing of material to determine the main points. Scanning is the searching of material to find a specific piece of information. These are very useful in many kinds of reading situations. Each of the units contain exercise to help you develop these skills.
2. Concentration (Unit 1). You cannot perform any study-related activity if you cannot focus your attention on the tasks. Suggestions for improving your concentration are discussed.
3. Time management (Unit 2). Time management is important if you wish to use your energies most effectively and have time for recreation and relaxation as well.
4. Listening and note-taking (Unit 3). Although most of what we learn comes through our ears, many of us have had little or no training in how to listen actively. In this unit effective listening techniques are discussed and suggestions are given to help you establish a note-taking system for class lectures.
5. Preparing for exams (Unit 7). Much of what you do in a class should be aimed toward preparing for the course exams, yet the approach of many students to this important task is haphazard and unplanned. The suggestions in this unit may help you develop a plan of action.
6. Taking exams (Unit 8). The final step in your efforts, exams let you show the instructor what you know. But your performance may not reflect your true knowledge if you have inefficient test-taking skills.
7. Improving your vocabulary (Units 1–8). Having an adequate vocabulary is necessary for success in school and in many careers. Exercises throughout Book One help you add to your vocabulary.

While these units are mainly intended to help you succeed in school, many of the suggestions will be useful in other situations as well. Skills like time management, effective concentration, and efficient reading are important in careers and everyday living as well as in school.

How to Use Book One

Your instructor will give you specific direction on how to use Book One. In general, you should try to read the opening topic in each unit. As you read, ask yourself which information you could use to improve your skills. We suggest that you attempt each exercise unless you are told otherwise by the instructor or have a good reason not to. The supplemental activities can be used as you see fit. We strongly suggest that you diligently work through all the vocabulary, skim/scan, and rate-boost exercises. Improvement in these areas requires practice and does not come quickly.

You will probably want to study the units in numerical order. The authors have tried to organize the material in the sequence that students normally would need it. However, if you need some information before it is assigned, don't hesitate to read ahead. If you need some pointers on how to take exams, for example, read Unit 8 early even though it is the last unit.

PART 1

Input Skills

UNIT 1

Building Your Concentration

Unit 1: Building Your Concentration

In a survey by one of the authors concentration was r
lems experienced by students. How to improve cor
tion.

We define a concentration problem as the freq
tion. The key word in this definition is "frequent". E.
sionally. But if you find that your mind wanders so much ‚
your assignments, then you have a concentration problem.

Actually, concentration difficulties are symptoms of other pr
elevated temperature in your body may be a symptom of a more serious ṇ
concentration problems may be a symptom that something else is wrong.
if you want to improve your concentration, the first step should be to ask y
what is causing your mind to wander.

Personal Needs: Physiological and Psychological

In this era of "wellness" it is surprising that so many students pay so little attention
to their personal health. Health scientists tell us that the human body is a highly
integrated organism. If one part is not functioning properly, the whole organism may
be negatively affected.

The psychologist Abraham Maslow developed a concept about the hierarchy of
human needs. Understanding this hierarchy can be helpful in understanding yourself.
A representation of this hierarchy (as modified by the authors) appears in Figure 1.0.

Supporters of Maslow's hierarchy say that each lower need must be satisfied before
a person can expect to deal with the higher level needs. For example, your physiological needs must be met before you can attend to your psychological needs. That is, if
you have an inadequate diet, are thirsty, or are ill, then all (or most) of your motivation
and following behavior will tend to be directed toward correcting these basic needs.
Once satisfied at this level, you will tend to seek out satisfaction at the next higher
level of needs, and so on.

There are, of course, exceptions to this hierarchy. People may strive for the higher
levels without satisfying the lower needs; however, this is more the exception than the
rule.

Exercise 1.0 is an exercise that you can use to help yourself become aware of how
well you are handling your total life as a student. It focuses on five important areas
that can be inferred from Maslow's hierarchy of needs. They are physical exercise;
education and work; family (intimacy); social relations; and, the philosophical and
religious needs.

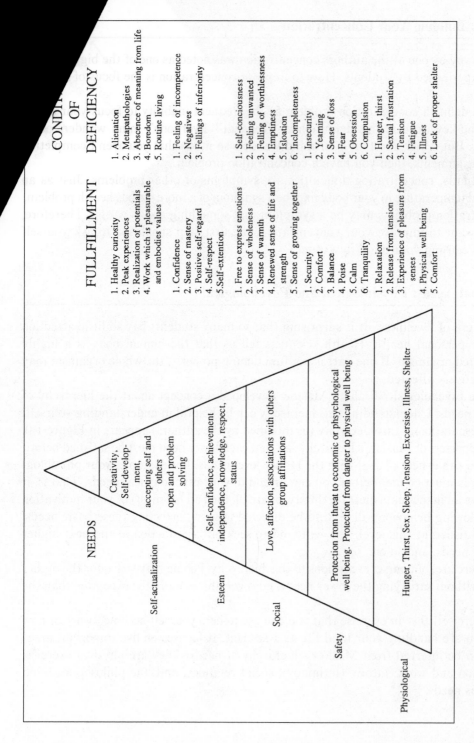

Figure 1.0 Human needs and the effect they have on our well-being.

Every person needs to be doing something in the area of **physical exercise.** You will remember that we are an integrated whole; in order for our brain to function at its best it needs to be in a body that is aerobically fit.

We all need to have some meaningful activity—something to strive for, something to challenge us. **Education and work** can serve this need.

We also need a person or group of people around us with whom we can be ourselves and be accepted. This person or group has traditionally been identified as our **family.** We should try to foster our relationships in this area.

Too, all of us need friends outside of our family. People that we can have fun with, talk with, do things with and that care about us (although we can't expect them to care about us as much as family). These people fulfill our **social needs.**

Finally, all of us need to discover the important things in life: where we fit into the scheme of things. This is discovered in the **philosophical or religious** area.

EXERCISE 1.0 *Balance in Life*

Directions: Think about each of the below listed areas. Write down what you are presently doing that is important to you in each of the below listed areas. If one or more of these categories have nothing significant in them, this could cause you not to do your best or have trouble concentrating.

Physical Exercise	Education/ Work	Family	Social	Philosophical/ Religious
1	1	1	1	1
2	2	2	2	2
3	3	3	3	3
4	4	4	4	4
5	5	5	5	5

Your personal profile developed from exercise 1.0 may make you aware of some changes that may be necessary to be made in your present lifestyle. Perhaps some of your basic needs are not presently being met, or perhaps you do not have a solid balance between all the demands in your life. (Balance does not mean that you should have an equal number of items under each category. At different stages in our lives we can expect to have a different number of items in one or another category. It is important, however, to have at least one personally significant item in each of the categories. Upon reflection, you may decide that there should be more or less items in a particular category). Change does not come easily. Many people work hard to change themselves. Developing an Action Plan can provide a systematic approach to helping ourselves change. Exercise 1.6 at the end of this section, contains a blank Action Plan for you to complete. Directions on how to complete it are also given.

General Suggestions to Improve Concentration

1. Try to have one or two special study areas. Have you ever noticed that you feel different in different physical settings? Ideally, you should have one special place where you do most of your studying because the location itself tends to become associated with study. A bed, because you sleep in it night after night, becomes associated with sleep. If you try to study in bed, you will probably fall asleep. If, however, you study at the same desk every night, the desk will become associated with studying. Eventually, when you sit down at that desk, your mind will automatically click into its study mode.
2. Become actively involved in your studying. Nobody can do more than one thing at a time. Therefore, the more involved you are in your studying, the less likely it is that you will start thinking of something else. Later in this book we will be offering you a variety of suggestions regarding how you can get involved more in your work.
3. Take a short break when you begin to feel tired. How long a person can study before he or she begins to feel mentally tired varies with the individual. The difficulty of the task will also have an effect on how long you can study. When you begin to feel your energy fading, take a short break. Even a five-minute stretch to walk around and get a drink of water can help a lot.
4. Keep physically and mentally fit. We have already discussed the need to have balance in our lives but it is also true that besides physical exercise we need to eat right, get enough sleep and make sure that we are physically sound. In a recent study by one of the authors it was discovered that fully 20 percent of students in his "efficient learning" classes had previously undiagnosed eye problems that needed to be corrected by an eye care specialist.

Some Specific Causes and Remedies for Concentration Problems

To better understand your concentration problem, ask yourself, "When my mind wanders, where does it tend to wander?" Does it wander more when I am in a particular location or during a certain time of day? Does it wander more when I am studying certain subjects? This kind of self-analysis may help you identify the causes of the problem. Remedies for some typical causes include:

1. Habitual mind-wandering. Do you repeatedly discover that you have read several pages without realizing that you even read them? That your eyes have been moving over the words but your mind has been elsewhere? Sometimes this kind of mind-wandering can be just a habit. If this is the case you can overcome the problem by gradually reducing the frequency of mind-wanderings. One way is by turning away from the material for a moment each time you realize that you haven't been concentrating. This method helps you to break the association between mind-wandering and the material. A second way is to put a check mark in the margin of the page each time you discover your attention wavering. Your goal will be to reduce the number of check marks. This technique is designed to make you aware that you are losing concentration—awareness leads to control. A final technique is to keep a note pad next to you. If your mind tends to wander to errands you must do or some other issues that keep cropping up, writing them down (with the understanding that you will deal with them later) helps to get back on track. In essence, you have then dealt with the distracting problem.

2. Worries about "keeping up". It's a vicious circle: You start to fall behind in your assignments. Then you begin to worry about the fact that you're behind, so you have trouble concentrating on your studies. And, the inability to concentrate makes you fall further behind. Soon you spend more time worrying and delaying your study than you do studying.

   To avoid this trap try to avoid falling behind. Clearly this is easier said then done but if you set reasonable goals for yourself it is possible. Use the time management techniques that are discussed later in this book to help yourself. If you find yourself starting to fall behind, catch yourself as soon as possible.

3. Physical distractions. Earlier we mentioned that you should choose one or two places that are your special study areas. When choosing these spots, you should consider in what kinds of places you study best. Some people concentrate best when they are alone, while other people prefer to have some people around them. Some people like quiet, while others like background noise or music. Once you have decided what distracts you, choose study areas that minimize those distractions.

EXERCISE 1.1 *Distraction Analysis*

Directions: To help locate a suitable study area, fill out this distraction analysis. For each of the locations you list put a check mark in the column if the numbered statement is true for that location. The location for which there are the least checks probably will have the fewest distractions.

Situation	Locations (write in)		
	SMALL Room	WITH Television	
1. Other people frequently disturb me when I study here.			
2. I take too many breaks when I study here.			
3. I seem to be especially bothered by distractions here.			
4. My breaks tend to be too long when I study here.			
5. I tend to start conversations with people when I study here.			
6. I spend time on the phone here that I should be using for study.			
7. Temperature conditions here are not very good for studying.			
8. Chair, table, and lighting arrangements here are not very helpful for studying.			
9. When I study here, I am often distracted by certain people, i.e., people watching.			

TOTAL CHECKS _____ _____ _____

Exercises to Help Concentration

Breaks in concentration often occur when you are not prepared for unexpected interferences such as noise or mind wandering discoveries. The following exercises, modified from Gestalt psychology, attempt to prepare you for accepting and identifying possible distractions and thus make them a part of your consciousness rather than a hindrance to your concentration.

EXERCISE 1.2 *Listening for Sounds in the Environment*

1. Situate yourself in any location. A relatively out-of-the-way room where you are not likely to be disturbed might be best at first.

2. Sit quietly, close your eyes and simply listen to the sounds that surround you. Try to identify the various sounds.

3. Do this for as long as possible several times each week. Change locations whenever possible. Listen carefully for every sound in each location. Spend enough time to assure that you hear and identify all noises likely to occur in that location.

EXERCISE 1.3 *Observing a Common Object*

1. Pick a common object, i.e., pencil, flower, cup.

2. Observe it carefully. Note such features as its texture, color, how the light effects it, shadows; note everything about it.

3. Do this whenever you have a few extra minutes and a convenient object.

EXERCISE 1.4 *Mind Setting Exercise*

Before sitting down to study, close your eyes, take a few deep breaths and say to yourself, "I am ready to study. I am going to concentrate. Extraneous noises will not bother me. My mind will be clear of distracting thoughts. I will focus on the material and understand it thoroughly. I will remember the information and soak it up like a sponge. During the test, I will remember the material".

Summary

Improving your concentration involves learning to recognize the factors both within yourself as well as within the environment that take you away from staying focused on your studies. Some of the distractions that are within you include unfulfilled physiological and psychological needs. An external factor is your location for study.

The Action Plan was introduced as a method that you can use to help yourself become a more effective learner. In order for the Action Plan to be effective, you should make the desired changes as soon as you decide that they will help.

Unit Comprehension Check

1. How does the text define a concentration problem?

2. How can we improve our concentration if one or more of our "basic needs" are not being met?

3. What are the five areas that a person should be attempting to do something significant within?

4. Why did the authors include an Action Plan to be completed at the end of each of the units in the text?

5. List one activity that you can do to avoid habitual mind wandering.

Study Questions

1. Involving yourself in "significant" activities are mentioned as important to balance in life. Review what you are presently doing under each of the five categories (see exercise 1.0) and discuss those that you believe are significant and how they help you in your life.

2. Choose an area in your life that you believe is important. Try to use Maslow's Hierarchy to define what more basic areas may need to be fulfilled before you can devote your full attention to achieving the identified area.

How to Develop an Action Plan

Action Plans, as used in this book, are designed to provide you with a method of putting into action some of the suggestions that are presented in each of the units. It's easy to think, "This is a good idea, I think I will use it", only to delay putting the idea into practice, sometimes until it is forgotten. Maximum benefit can be obtained from a plan only if the ideas are put into action willingly and right away—preferably within 24 hours.

Goals	Strategies to Complete Goal	Completion Date	Evaluation Procedure
To become more physically fit	a. Purchase and read a book on Yoga	3 weeks from today	at the end of the term see if I feel more relaxed
	b. Practice Yoga 15 minutes daily		
	c. Practice after I get home in the afternoon		

Figure 1.1 Action Plan: Balance in Life.

Exercise 1.5 involves establishing an Action Plan from your Balance in Life profile. To help you get started, some example statements have already been included. Use the following steps to complete the Action Plan for yourself:

1. Consider what it is that you want to do. Write this in a very brief statement under *Goals*.
2. Plan in detail the steps needed to accomplish your goal. Note that in the example the hypothetical person developed two steps to accomplish the goal of "becoming more physically fit". Write these steps in the order in which you will do them under *Strategies to Complete Goal*.
3. Decide when you plan to complete the steps. Put this date under *Completion Date*. Sometimes a specific completion date will not be appropriate. Nevertheless, set a goal for when you hope to complete the steps.

4. Determine how you will evaluate yourself (whether or not you successfully followed the steps you set for yourself). Sometimes your evaluation will be self-evident. Other times you will gauge your success according to specific criteria. Write this information under the heading, *Evaluation Procedure.* For example, you may want to plan on asking someone, a friend or instructor, to evaluate how they think you are doing.

By following through with the Action Plans, thinking about what, how and when you plan on improving yourself, you are taking control of your life. The more of these Action Plans you complete the greater the probability that you will accomplish your study goals.

EXERCISE 1.5 *Action Plan: Concentration*

Directions: Fill out this Action Plan for improving your concentration. You may want to use some of the suggestions offered in this unit, or you may have thought of a technique not mentioned but one you want to try.

Goals	Strategies to Complete Goal	Completion Date	Evaluation Procedure

Vocabulary Development

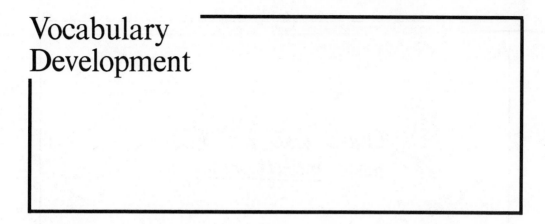

Educators generally agree that an adequate vocabulary is important for success in school and in many careers. If you have a good knowledge of word meanings, you can better understand what you hear and read. You can express yourself more clearly when you speak or write. And, psychologists tell us, you even can think more precisely. Every worker has tools important for a particular job, and word knowledge is one of the tools students need.

Some Ways of Improving Your Vocabulary

We learn most of our words in two main ways. In the first case, we read and hear a word a number of times in different contexts and gradually develop a feeling for the meaning of the word. In the second case, we find out directly what the word means. Most vocabulary-building materials are based on one or both of these learning methods.

There are a number of ways that you can increase your vocabulary:

1. *Look up and drill on words that interest you.* When you read or hear a word whose meaning interests you, look up the word in the dictionary. If you do nothing else you will have at least made a start. But if you really want to master the word, go one step further and make up a vocabulary card. A 3 × 5-inch index card (or half of one, to save money) works well. On one side write the word, along with the sentence in which you found it. On the other side, write the definition. Also, if the dictionary tells how the word was derived, you might include that information to help you remember the meaning of the word. Figure 1.2 shows an example of such a card.

2. *Learn meanings of words provided by someone else.* There are many sources of words that you can use to build up your word knowledge. For example, lists of words with definitions often are published in the *Reader's Digest*. And many books that include such lists are available at bookstores and libraries. In some cases, the lists are designed for a particular group, such as college students, medical personnel, or

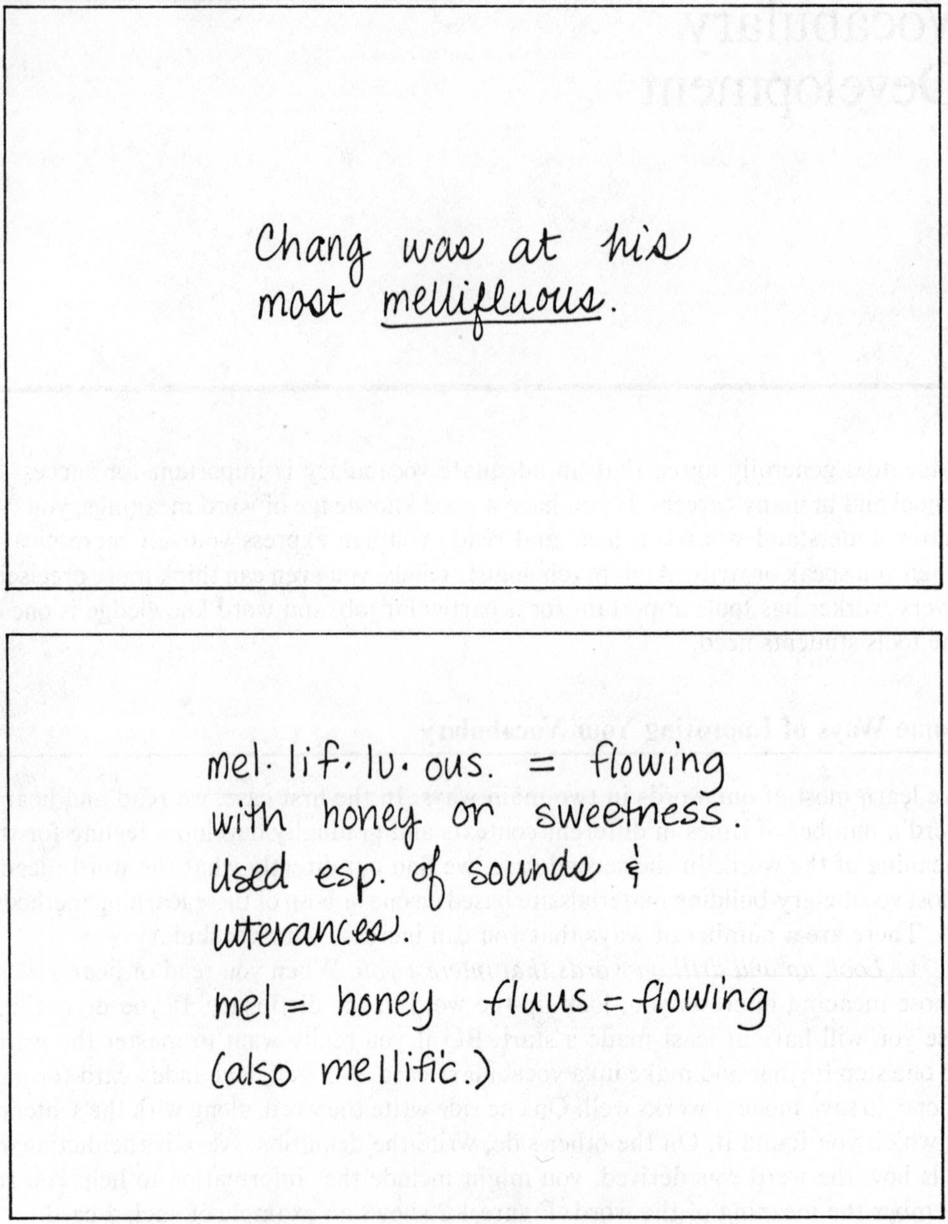

Chang was at his most <u>mellifluous</u>.

mel·lif·lu·ous. = flowing
with honey or sweetness.
Used esp. of sounds &
utterances.
mel = honey fluus = flowing
(also mellific.)

Figure 1.2 Sample Vocabulary Card.

real estate salespeople. Memorizing such lists of words is one of the quickest ways to increase your vocabulary. One drawback, however, is that words gain meaning from their association with other words, and you may be learning words as isolated units.

3. *Determine the meanings of words from their contexts.* Suppose you started reading an adventure story about sailing ships and you had no knowledge about how a sailing ship operates. You would soon find yourself reading unfamiliar words and phrases like *lee shore, reef the sails, gig,* and *tops' clew lines.* Rather than trying to look these words up, you probably would guess their meanings from the surrounding words. You would not always have an exact understanding, but usually you would know enough to follow the story. You would be learning words from their *context.*

Although this method is often suggested as a way of increasing vocabulary, there is virtually no verifiable evidence that it works. People tend to skip over words they don't understand, and unless a conscious effort is made to write down the word—as in the vocabulary card method—little vocabulary growth can be expected. Even learning the typical context clues, such as looking for a definition after the word, seems to be of little use for vocabulary growth. However, if you decide to use this method occasionally to try to figure out a word's meaning, do it the following way:

a. When you come across an unknown word while reading, stop and look at the words that precede and follow it. See if these words will cue you to the word's meaning. If that doesn't work,
b. Read the section that contains the unknown word again, taking another run at it, as it were.

If you still cannot determine the meaning of the word, and the definition is important, then you'll have to resort to a dictionary.

The vocabulary exercises and information in this and later units are designed to make you familiar with some common prefixes, suffixes, and roots. By learning these common affixes and roots you increase the probability that you will be able to unlock the meaning of an unknown word. Of course, learning affixes and roots is only one way to improve your word knowledge. You should take every opportunity to learn and to use less familiar words. Vocabulary development is more than a ten- or fifteen-week course; it is a lifelong activity.

Prefixes: Introduction

Each word in the English language has a root or basic meaning. Sometimes the root is a complete word, such as *zip* or *worthy;* however, a root may also be a unit that does not stand by itself, such as *cede* (yield), as in the word *precede.*

A prefix is a word part placed at the beginning of a root to change the meaning. Examples are *preview* (pre + view), which means "to view in advance," or *renew* (re + new), which means "to make new again." Look at other examples below:

A. Root Words	B. Prefixes Added	C. New Meaning
happy	unhappy	not feeling happy
exact	inexact	not precisely correct
loyal	disloyal	lacking in loyalty
legal	illegal	not lawful

The words in column B have different meanings from the words in column A because prefixes have been added. Underline the prefixes in column B. Then check your answers with the correct ones found in the next paragraph.

You should have underlined the words in column B as follows: <u>un</u>happy, <u>in</u>exact, <u>dis</u>loyal, and <u>il</u>legal.

Four Prefixes

in   A Latin prefix meaning *in, into, within;* it is found in words like inhabit, interior, and inroad.

pre   A Latin prefix meaning *before;* it is found in words like preview, preside, and premonition.

post   Latin prefix meaning *after, following, later;* it is found in words such as postscript, postwar, and postgraduate.

ab   A Latin prefix meaning *away, from,* and *from off;* it is found in words like absent, abnormal, and absolution.

Vocabulary Exercise

Study the four prefixes presented above. In the eleven sentences below, find a word that begins with one of these prefixes and underline it. In the blank space in each sentence, fill in a meaning for the prefix. Study the examples before you begin the exercise.

A <u>post</u>war conference is a meeting held <u>after</u> the war is over.

To <u>in</u>flate a bicycle tire is to put air <u>into</u> it.

1. A person who is abducted is someone taken ___AWAY___ by force.

2. Postnatal care of a baby is care ___AFTER___ birth.

IN SIDE

3. John had a premonition of a terrible accident; he knew something would happen

   WHEN it took place.

4. The senate committee postponed a decision on the energy bill until a LATER date.

5. Aborigines are a primitive tribe of people who have existed BEFORE the start in that locale.

6. Someone taking postdoctoral courses takes them AFTER he or she has completed the doctoral degree.

7. A prefix is a word part placed BEFORE a root.

8. Animals who inhabit a territory are said to live WITHIN a specific boundary of land.

9. A child who is absent from school because of illness is AWAY from school that day.

10. To preempt means to seize or act LEGAL others do.

11. The doctor will inject the serum with a needle INTO the patient's arm.

Here are some cases where context can help you determine the missing word. Try to fill in the missing words.

12. A "know-it-all" is a person who knows more and more about LESS and less.

13. The gunsmith was asked to repair the GUN .

14. The teacher was having a difficult time explaining the idea to his STUDENT

15. You may memorize but still not KNOW the material.

16. Books are ordered in a certain way at the LIBRARY.

17. The police brought in several SUSPECTS for questioning.

18. She whispered sweet nothings to her BOY FRIEND

Skim/Scan
Exercise 1

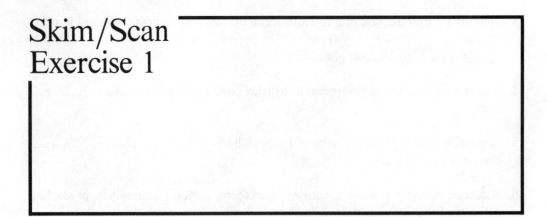

Beginning with this unit there will be one skim/scan exercise per unit. Both skimming and scanning are useful techniques for students.

Skimming

When you read, you can be as selective as your purpose and the difficulty of the material dictate. Reading rates can range from one extreme to the other. At the lowest end of the scale is word-by-word reading. You might use this rate when reading a chemistry textbook or directions for assembling a bicycle. As the material becomes progressively less demanding or as you require a less complete understanding of it, you can increase your rate and become more selective. As your selectivity increases, resulting in higher and higher rates, you are not so much reading as skimming.

There is no definite dividing line between reading and skimming. The one blends into the other. But skimming might be defined as the processing of material at a rate higher than that required to comprehend it completely for most purposes. In other words, when you skim you miss some information that you would need in order to understand the author's message fully.

Uses of Skimming

If skimming results in less than complete comprehension, what use is it? Skimming is to reading as an outline is to writing. A writer makes an outline to have an overview of the topic. The outline is a skeleton that omits everything but the essentials. Skimming serves a similar purpose for the reader, allowing him or her to get the gist of a piece of writing in a relatively short period of time.

Skimming can be used for three purposes: (1) previewing before careful reading, (2) getting an overview of the content, with no intention of a later and more careful reading, and (3) reviewing something you have already read.

How to Skim

You probably will want to experiment with various ways of skimming until you find a method that suits you. One method recommended by Edward Fry, a noted reading specialist, is to read the first paragraph or two more slowly to get an idea of the topic and a feel for the author's style. Then skim through the rest of the material at 800 or more words per minute to pick out the main points.*

Preview skimming and overview skimming are similar, but the goals are different. When previewing, you are planning to read the material later in more detail. When overviewing, you are not planning a later reading. Therefore, overviewing tends to be somewhat slower and is usually not appropriate for difficult material. In an earlier part of this unit the concept of paragraph patterns is discussed. When previewing or overviewing, you concentrate on locating a main-idea statement in each paragraph. Then you move on quickly to the next paragraph. Supporting details are largely overlooked in the interest of speed. Previewing is discussed further in Units 5 and 6.

Review skimming is used when you have already read the material. To do this type of skimming you might look quickly over portions of the selection to study its organization, fill in gaps, and look for specific information. Reviewing can be the most rapid type of skimming.

Scanning

Scanning is the process of searching for a specific piece of information in printed material. While not as important as some other skills, scanning can be a very useful technique in certain situations. For example, suppose you remember that somewhere in a book you read was a reference to Alexander the Great. You would like to reread the reference but it is not listed in the index. Instead of searching by reading every word or even by skimming, you probably would want to scan the sections where the reference is likely to be.

Uses of Scanning

Scanning can be used any time you want to find one item among many. For example, you might scan:

1. a table of atomic weights
2. a passage for mention of a specific person, date, event, etc.
3. a directory for a specific name

---

*Edward Fry, Skimming and Scanning (Providence, R.I.: Jamestown Publishers, 1978), p. 12.

How to Scan

Of course, the scanning strategy you use depends on the circumstances. For example, if you are using an alphabetical listing, you can narrow your search to a small area. A general scanning technique is first to visualize as vividly as you can the specific words or numbers that you are searching for. Then, as you scan, let the type go slightly out of focus. And keep repeating in your mind the desired piece of information. The item then will often "jump out at you" when you locate it.

Let's review what we know about skimming and scanning:

1. Skimming and scanning are techniques used for definite purposes.
2. Scanning is used to locate specific facts.
3. Skimming is used to preview material, to get a general overview, and to review after a more careful reading.
4. In both skimming and scanning you need to be constantly aware of time and force yourself to work rapidly.
5. Do not try to read every word.
6. Look for opportunities to skim and scan.
7. Carefully consider your purposes before deciding to use skimming and scanning.

How to Prepare for the Skimming and Scanning Exercises

Since you must pay close attention to the tasks that are required of you in the exercises, it will help you to take a few minutes to relax prior to each session. These steps may help:

1. Get into a relaxing sitting position and close your eyes.
2. Relax and remain quiet, perhaps for two or three minutes.
3. Then move into your practice in a relaxed but attentive manner.
4. Be confident that you can succeed.

Instructions

This section is divided into two parts that are to be used together: the skim/scan selection and the accompanying questions.

Look first at the numbered directions below and then at the questions that follow the skim/scan selection. You will be asked to make several kinds of responses to the material you read. In some cases, you will be required to answer multiple-choice questions; in others you will have to fill in the correct responses. To benefit most from these exercises, carefully follow the directions in the book and others that may be given by your instructor.

1. Record your starting time in the space provided at the beginning of the selection.
2. Using the suggested skimming techniques, rapidly preview-skim the entire selection.
3. Record your ending time in the space provided.
4. Answer the skimming questions.
5. Go on to the scanning questions, using the suggested scanning technique to find the answers.
6. Use the answer key at the end of the unit to determine your skimming and scanning scores.
7. Subtract your starting time from your ending time, and record the answer (your skimming time) in the space provided.
8. Use the conversion chart that follows the scanning questions to determine your skimming words-per-minute rate.
9. Record your score on the skimming questions and your skimming rate on the progress graph in the appendix at the end of this book.

the strategy of course is to separate
the idea of the essue but continued to
accomplish the dub that was in prospect
circumstances
strategy course

The White-Collar Worker

	Hour	Min.	Secs.
A. Ending time:	___	___	___
B. Starting time:	___	___	___
C. A − B = Reading time:		___	___

As our industrial technology has grown in the last century, so has the size of our business organizations. A business may have a small office with a handful of employees and one boss, or it may have several far-flung branches around the world employing thousands of office workers. In all such offices most of the employees are called white-collar workers. Their jobs and responsibilities revolve around "paperwork"—producing, recording, classifying, and storing information. (Today the term *paperwork* is only partly descriptive. Computers, using magnetic or electrical impulses rather than paper to convey information, have become essential to all large and many small organizations.)

Percentage of White-Collar Workers	
Year	**Percentage of Work Force**
1950	37.5
1955	39.0
1960	43.4
1965	44.8
1970	48.3
1972	47.8
1973	47.8
1974	48.8

Sources: United States Department of Commerce, Bureau of the Census, *Current Population Reports,* series P-50 (Washington, D.C.: U.S. Government Printing Office, 1950–74); United States Department of Labor, Bureau of Labor Statistics, *Employment and Earnings* (Washington, D.C.: U.S. Government Printing Office, monthly since 1960).

White-collar workers are now the largest percentage of the work force in our society. White-collar positions range from low-paid file clerk to executive secretary, computer programmer, and office manager. The tasks range from routine and tedious work, such as filing invoices, to responsible and varied problems, such as maintaining confidential records or responding to clients and visitors.

We have seen that semiskilled workers on the automobile assembly line have little control over their work. Office workers too are usually closely regulated within a definite hierarchy of authority, although not quite as much controlled as assembly-line workers. Secretaries, file clerks, and bookkeepers often have to produce a certain output continually. These white-collar workers usually do not have strong trade unions looking out for their interests in such matters as working conditions, salaries, health and pension plans, and other fringe benefits. An employee who protests may well be fired, because, like semiskilled factory workers, most white-collar workers can be quickly replaced.

Secretaries and other office workers learn that certain attitudes are an important part of their work roles. They must accept norms about dress, manner, and attitude toward work, as well as learning skills of stenography, typing, bookkeeping, or office management. Although there is a great variation in norms from office to office, white-collar workers are socialized to expect more pleasant and clean surroundings, more varied tasks, and more prestige than factory workers. At the same time, they learn that they are not the major decision-makers in the office and are usually supervised carefully in their work.

Costs and Rewards

Depending on the temperament, values, and norms of the worker and the conditions on the job, white-collar work can be rewarding or frustrating or a combination of the two. For example, a secretary to two physicians in England described her hectic schedule and overcrowded conditions at work. Although she was unhappy about the tiring pace and the variety of tasks she had to do, she was very satisfied with her job. "The reason, quite briefly, is that I feel I am doing a necessary job. But even that wouldn't be sufficient if I weren't lucky enough to be working for two such good doctors."*

In order to succeed at this job, the secretary had to learn to keep track of appointments, answer phone calls, make children in the waiting room comfortable, attend to correspondence, handle contacts with the hospital, and file records. In mastering both the secretarial skills and the ability to get along with a variety of people in the clinic, she gained respect and therefore self-esteem from her job.

One of the chief attractions of the job for me is the feeling of being in charge, feeling that I matter. Patients often comment that without me the surgery [clinic] would

*Catherine Dracup, "The Secretary," in *Work,* ed. Ronald Fraser (Harmondsworth, England: Penguin Books, 1969), 2:288.

be in chaos. . . . I'd find it difficult to be just a small part of some large organization. In the four years I have worked at the surgery I have never been late, although in previous jobs I was never on time.†

Clearly, this woman found recognition and satisfaction in her job. Where these do not exist in white-collar jobs, tensions and frustrations can arise. Consider the following description by one dissatisfied secretary in a pamphlet by a Massachusetts feminist group:

The secretaries seem to control what is going on and do not seem easily intimidated. . . . But [this] does not change the nature of our work: boring, painful, degrading . . . the role of the secretary is the role of a servant. . . . [For example, you find yourself] being bugged on the intercom by an administrator who gives you a phone number which you are to dial while he waits at his desk. . . .

If a secretary should find herself mentally composing a letter without having first placed her fingers firmly on the typewriter keys and adopted an expression of intense readiness to type, she will also find that she is being watched disapprovingly by some superior who has been observing his servant-children for signs of idleness. A secretary is not evaluated by the amount or quality of the work she does so much as by her ability to look respectful, bland, and moderately busy at all times.

Skimming Questions: *Circle the letter of the best answer.*

1. According to the author, secretaries learn that certain ___PEOPLE___ are an important part of their work roles.
   a. skills
   b. abilities
   c. training experience
   d. attitudes

2. 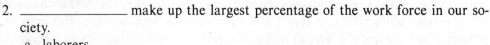 _____ make up the largest percentage of the work force in our society.
   a. laborers
   b. white-collar workers
   c. secretaries
   d. blue-collar workers

3. _____ have little control over their work.
   a. executives
   b. semiskilled workers
   c. secretaries
   d. white-collar workers

4. One secretary describes her work as:
   a. boring, painful, and degrading
   b. fun
   c. lucrative
   d. much too easy

5. The secretary states that when mentally composing a letter secretaries should:
   a. hold a pencil
   b. leave the office
   c. ask permission from their supervisor
   d. put their fingers on the typewriter and look ready to type

Scanning Questions

1. According to the selection, a secretary is not evaluated by the amount or ___QUALATY___ of the work she does.

2. In ___72 ↓73___ white-collar workers made up 47.8% of the work force (see table).

3. Most white-collar workers can be quickly ___REPLACE___ .

4. White-collar workers' jobs revolve around ___THAM___ .

5. According to the table, in 1974 ___WAS___ percent of the work force was made up of white-collar workers.

Time-Rate Conversion Chart

Min:Sec	WPM	Min:Sec	WPM	Min:Sec	WPM	Min:Sec	WPM
1:00	805	3:00	268	5:00	161	7:00	115
1:10	690	3:10	254	5:10	156	7:10	112
1:20	604	3:20	242	5:20	151	7:20	110
1:30	537	3:30	230	5:30	146	7:30	107
1:40	483	3:40	220	5:40	142	7:40	105
1:50	439	3:50	210	5:50	138	7:50	103
2:00	403	4:00	201	6:00	134	8:00	101
2:10	372	4:10	193	6:10	131	8:10	99
2:20	345	4:20	186	6:20	127		
2:30	322	4:30	179	6:30	124		
2:40	302	4:40	173	6:40	121		
2:50	284	4:50	167	6:50	118		

Unit 1 Answer Key

Unit Comprehension Check

1. Inability to focus attention
2. Try to meet our basic needs
3. Social; Physical; Philosophical/Religious; Family; Education/Work
4. In order for a person to make a change it should be started as soon as possible
5. answers will vary

Vocabulary Development

1. abducted, away
2. postnatal, after
3. premonition, before
4. postponed, later
5. aborigines, from
6. postdoctoral, after
7. prefix, before
8. inhabit, within
9. absent, away
10. preoccupy, before
11. inject, into
12. less
13. gun
14. student
15. know/understand
16. library
17. suspects
18. sweetheart/boyfriend

Skim/Scan Exercise

Skim
1. d 2. b 3. b 4. a 5. d

Scan
1. Quality 2. 1972–1973 3. replaced 4. paperwork 5. 48.8

UNIT 2

Improving Your Time Management

Chapter 2: Improving Your Time Management

The way that we view time is a very personal matter. To a large extent our cultural background and individual circumstances influence how we view time. People in some cultures (our own among them) tend to be schedule-oriented. However, in other cultures time is often viewed differently. In some American Indian cultures time is seen to vary with the growing seasons; in others, with the time of year. Recently, one of the authors taught a learning effectiveness course to a group of men who were in prison. When we discussed how they viewed time, time was seen as a function of how long they were to be incarcerated. For those who had long sentences to serve, the basic unit of time was seen as the seasons (Fall, Winter, Spring, Summer), rather than as days and hours; for those with less "time" to serve, the basic unit of time was the month.

Even within the so called "majority" culture there are different ways of perceiving time. Our individual personalities may affect the way we view it.

Some psychologists have divided personality types into two broad categories, labeling them Type A and Type B. The Type A person, is very conscious of time, and tends to write and follow schedules and lists scrupulously. The Type B person, on the other hand, likes to let events happen as they may, with only loose control.

We like to view students as falling somewhere on the continuum below.

Prophets   Super
of Doom _____ Heroes

While the two ends of the continuum are quite different, both are, in their own way, self-defeating.

The Super Heroes look at their syllabi, their stack of books and their class notes and say to themselves, "I'm going to learn it all." They begin to study without rest. They cut down on sleep, they either eliminate or severely reduce any social life and recreation; and some even study when they are eating. The Super Heroes deny that they are human beings with basic needs and limitations. Eventually, they burn-out, lose interest, become resentful, or become ineffective learners.

The Prophets of Doom, on the other hand, react to all of the work they need to accomplish by saying to themselves, "There is too much to do; I'll never learn it all; I'll probably flunk out". Their ever-present belief in failure, the impossibility of mastering the course work, often becomes self-fulfilling. The Prophets of Doom say they will fail, so they fail. Because they believe that there is no way to succeed, they accept defeat by not even trying to study.

Few of us are at the extremes; but both can be avoided by establishing a sensible time management program for your studies and for your entire life-style. At the end of this section you will have the opportunity to complete an Action Plan. Be alert to which of the suggestions you can incorporate into your study system.

Before beginning to manage your time, you must first develop the proper point of view. Any effective time management strategy must evolve from a realistic compromise between your limitations and the demands of your course work. The principles discussed in this section should help you establish this realistic compromise.

Basic Principles

1. You are a human being. All people have limitations and basic needs (see page 6, Maslow's Hierarchy of Needs).
2. It is possible to succeed. You would not have been admitted unless the college or university believed you could succeed. Further, even in the most demanding curricula, the vast majority of students succeed. Those who do fail are usually those who do not accept their limitations or who do not use the resources available to them.
3. You do not have to learn everything. Your instructors may tell you that you must learn everything because everything is important. They are right. But everything is not going to be on the test, and you do not need to know everything that is on the test to pass. The trick, which most can master, is to determine what is important.

EXERCISE 2.0 *Self-Assessment of Basic Needs and Limitations*

Directions: Before you begin to make a schedule, you need to understand your individual needs and limitations. To do so, fill out the questionnaire.

1. How many hours of sleep do you need each night?

2. How often do you need to get exercise to remain fit and alert?

   _5.0_ hours per day

   _3.5_ hours per week

3. How much time do you need to socialize with friends? _15 M_ per day.

4. List the major commitments you have outside of school (e.g., church, clubs, work, etc.)

CHURCH _____ __1__ hours per week

CLUB _____ __1__ hours per week

WORKING AT HOME __2__ hours per week

_____ _____ hours per week

5. List three activities you enjoy.

WALK 3 HURS _____ _____ hours per week

LIFTING WHEI _____ _____ hours per week

PLAYNG SOCCAR 2.0 _____ hours per week

Setting Priorities

It is important to set priorities, to decide what is essential and what is less important. Your instructors may give you a lot of work and they will tell you that all of the information is important. Though all of the information is important, not all of it is equally important. For example, your instructor may take ninety percent of the test questions from the class lectures and only ten percent from the textbook. If so, you can concentrate on learning the material in the class notes.

Think of this example and how it may affect your time management. Let us assume that seventy percent of the test comes from your class notes. It will take you ten hours to thoroughly learn your class notes and fifteen hours to thoroughly learn the material in the textbook. If you had only ten hours to study for a test, how would you spend those hours?

How many hours would you spend on your notes?

How many hours would you spend on your textbooks?

There is no perfect answer, but if you spend eight hours on your textbook or even equal time on your textbook and notes, you would not be dividing time in the best manner.

Remember, we have been discussing an example. Not all instructors take seventy percent of their test questions from class notes. This example illustrates one principle of how to set priorities in any college curricula.

The following are priority setting principles that can be applied to your program.

1. Concentrate on the source from which most of the questions will be taken, e.g., class notes, textbooks, etc. Use other sources as supplement or for reference when the first source is unclear.
2. Do not spread yourself too thin. The first time you go over your book or notes is relatively time consuming; later reviews are quicker. Focus on the important materials and go over them several times. The more repetition the more thoroughly you will learn it.
3. Concentrate on the most basic material first. If you must learn something that is prerequisite to learning something else make sure you learn the prerequisite information first, don't try to avoid the inevitable, it just wastes time.
4. Follow the 80/20 rule. Figure out how much time it will take to do the task 80 percent perfect; then, figure out how much time it will take to do it the additional 20 percent perfect. For example, you may be able to do a term paper 80 percent perfect (and receive a B or an A−) in 20 hours, but would have to spend an additional 20 hours to receive an A+. You may, therefore, decide that a B or an A− is good enough and save yourself 20 hours of work. Sometimes, of course, you will want to strive for perfection, but the 80/20 rule helps you to be flexible.

The Process of Making a Schedule

Making a schedule is a flexible process. You cannot make a schedule one day and then follow it for the rest of your life. You will have to make changes in your schedule because it may be unrealistic, it may not fit your lifestyle, your goals may change, or you may want to change it simply because you are in a rut. The step-by-step procedure we will use to develop a schedule follows these principles.

Step One: Centralize Goals and Objectives

In most college curriculums, you may have four or five courses per term and each course may have a syllabus of 4 to 10 pages (some may have more or less).

At the beginning of each term, you should take the time to organize all of the requirements for each of your courses. If you already have your syllabi, go through them and list all of your courses' requirements (readings, papers, reports, tests, etc.) on a sheet of paper as they are listed below.

Subject	Task	Due Date
History	Text, pp. 1–25	Sept. 28
Chemistry	Exam	Nov. 23
English	Paper, 8–10 pages	Nov. 15
Study Skills	Oral report	Oct. 15
Math	Problem set	Oct. 5

Step Two: Transfer Goals and Objectives to a Calendar

Your master list of goals and objectives may make you feel more organized already. At least, you should have a better notion of what is expected.

But you can make your master list more useful by transferring it to a calendar—one with large spaces in which to write.

Transfer one month of your master list to the calendar on page 37.

EXERCISE 2.1 *Calendar*

Now you can visualize your tasks and you can see exactly when they must be completed. Even more importantly, you can begin to plan ahead.

If you notice that many of your requirements fall closely together, for example several tests during one week or two or three papers all due within the space of a week or so, you will probably want to adjust for this by beginning to work on the papers during an earlier time when there isn't so much to do.

Another important technique to use with your calendar is "backtracking". If you think that you need two weeks to work on an oral report, begin at the date of the report, backtrack two weeks, and insert a reminder on your calendar, such as "Begin Oral Report". This will help prevent you from forgetting important assignments, only to realize too late that it must be done and possibly doing less than your best work.

Go over your calendar, find the possible trouble areas, and decide how you will plan ahead for those difficult periods in the term.

CALENDAR

Sunday	Monday	Tuesday	Wednesday	Thursday	Friday	Saturday

Weekly and Daily Schedules

Once you have finished your term calendar, you can begin to make a weekly or daily schedule. Some people like to make weekly schedules; others a daily schedule. Some like to use both.

To make a weekly schedule, use the form on page 39. The process you need to follow is:

1. Using a pencil, fill in all fixed times. Fixed times include going to class, the time you meet with a study group, work, and so forth.
2. Look at your calendar and begin to fill in flexible times. When will you prepare for your test? When will you study chemistry? When will you work on your paper? When will you get exercise? Fill in the most important tasks first.

To make a daily schedule, use your calendar to make a list of the goals you want to accomplish today. Your list may look like this:

TO DO

Research paper, 1 hour

Study Chemistry, 1 chapter

Review History Notes, 20 minutes

Exercise, 45 minutes

Prepare for Chem. Lab., 1 hour

Then organize the list placing the most important tasks at the top.

TO DO

1. Prepare for Chem. Lab., 1 hour

2. Study Chemistry, 1 chapter

3. Research paper, 1 hour

4. Excersise, 45 minutes

5. Review History Notes, 20 minutes

Weekly Schedule

NAME: _____

DATE: _____

Time	Monday	Tuesday	Wednesday	Thursday	Friday	Saturday	Sunday
6:30–7:30							
7:30–8:30							
8:30–9:30							
9:30–10:30							
10:30–11:30							
11:30–12:30							
12:30–1:30							
1:30–2:30							
2:30–3:30							
3:30–4:30							
4:30–5:30							
5:30–6:30							
6:30–7:30							
7:30–8:30							
8:30–9:30							
9:30–10:30							
10:30–11:30							
11:30–12:30							

Summary	Monday	Tuesday	Wednesday	Thursday	Friday	Saturday	Sunday
Sleep							
Eat							
Study							
Personal							
Work							
Classes							
Travel							
Social							
Lost Hrs.							

Begin with the top of the list and work to the bottom. As you complete each goal, cross it off your list. If you fail to complete all of your tasks, you need not be concerned. Since you have set priorities for yourself, the most important tasks will be completed first.

If you make out a daily schedule, try making it out the night before. This can help your motivation because you will go to bed thinking of and preparing for the day ahead. You will wake up more prepared to begin the day.

Evaluation

Finally, you need to evaluate your schedule. You need to find out if it is working for you and if it isn't change it. The best way to analyze your schedule is to ask yourself questions. Look at your schedule, and answer the following questions:

1. Am I scheduling my most difficult tasks at my most alert times? Am I scheduling less difficult tasks, such as exercise or typing, at my less alert times?

2. Do I need to take more breaks? Fewer breaks? Am I taking breaks before I become too tired?

3. Do I have a reward system built into my schedule? Am I rewarding myself for sticking to my schedule?

4. Am I spending too much time planning? Too little?

5. Am I getting enough sleep?

6. Can I combine any of my activities? Which ones?

7. Am I spending too much time with low priority tasks? Am I staying busy but still avoiding high priority tasks?

8. Am I neglecting long-term tasks?

9. Am I avoiding unpleasant tasks?

10. Am I controlling my schedule, or am I letting others control it?

How to Stick to Your Time Schedule

Developing a time schedule is one thing and sticking to it is another. Unfortunately, this step is not easy. Some students will spend a lot of time developing a schedule and then let it sit unused and forgotten. One reason for not following a schedule is habitual procrastination. Some students have developed a habit of putting off school work until the last possible minute. Another common reason is pressure from friends and relatives. Some students have trouble saying "no" when an alternative to studying is offered.

If you are having trouble keeping up with your studies, these suggestions may help:

1. Keep a low profile. In other words, don't make yourself readily available to temptation. For example, if you are studying at home, you might take the phone off the hook or leave instructions not to be disturbed. Better yet, if possible, go someplace where you're not so easily found, like the library.
2. Learn to say "no" when someone tries to lure you away from studying. Believe it or not, you won't lose friends by telling them you have to study. In fact, they probably will respect you for it.
3. Study with conscientious students. This is an especially useful technique if you like company when studying but find yourself gabbing away the time. Who knows? By studying with good students, you may pick up some helpful study habits.
4. Make a contract with yourself or with someone else. This technique is used in many situations where certain specific behaviors are desired. For example, the authors have had success using contracting to help students in academic motivation groups. The technique has three basic parts: (a) Set a goal for small improvement over your present behavior; (b) establish incentives for reaching your goal; (c) put your contract in writing, and sign it.

When making a goal, it is important that you try for small improvements rather than ones that might require too much of a change. For instance, if you are not reading any material for your psychology course now, it may be unreasonable to make your first goal a chapter a night. Instead, your first goal might be to read two or three pages a night. After some successes, you can gradually increase the amount.

There are three main kinds of incentives. First there is peer pressure. Once you have told a peer (friend, roommate, spouse) that you have set a goal for yourself, you will want to reach the goal so that you won't feel like a slob. Second, there are rewards that you can give yourself. Generally, keep the rewards small and simple so that they are easy to give when you reach your goal. Third, there are penalties you can give yourself for not reaching your goal. Some people are more affected by punishments than by rewards. You will have to decide which works best for you. Below is a list of some typical rewards and penalties.

```
                    Study Contract

        Period: Feb. 19-25
        What: Spend 3 hours this week
              reading History assignments

        When: 1 hour each, Mon., Wed., & Thurs.
              nights.

        Where: Library.

        Ways to avoid problems: I'll use the
              library study carrels, where no
        one will spot me.

        Reward: Soft drink when I'm
                finished each night.

                    signed    Pat Jones

                    witness   Jan Stewart
```

Figure 2.0 Study Contract.

Rewards

1. Eating (ice cream, candy, fruit, cookies)
2. Drinking (water, milk, soft drinks, tea, coffee)
3. Playing a game (crossword puzzles, solitaire)
4. Listening to music
5. Reading for enjoyment
6. Doing something else (sewing, "people watching")

Penalties

1. Going without dessert, or some other treat you usually have.
2. Not exercising (assuming that you enjoy it).
3. Eating a little less (this may actually be good for some of us!)
4. Not doing any of the above rewards.

Once you have decided on a goal and a reward or penalty, write out a contract and, if possible, have someone witness it. Figure 2.0 gives an example of a study contract that a student made for one week.

Summary

Managing time is one of the most important skills that a person can learn. To manage your time effectively, you should keep track of important upcoming events and make commitments to study at definite times. On the other hand, a time schedule should be flexible enough to allow for the unexpected.

Unit Comprehension Check

If you can answer these questions, you have retained many of the main points of this Unit at the literal level.

1. Type A and Type B personalities were mentioned as examples for what main idea or general concept being discussed?

2. Should you plan every minute when scheduling your time?

3. What is meant by "backtracking" in your study schedule?

4. What are three incentives to use when making a study schedule?

5. What is the value of centralizing your goals and objectives?

Study Questions

1. Can you think of situations other than a school setting where careful time management would be important?

2. The statement was made, "The fact that you're in school does mean you have agreed to limit your freedom somewhat." What are some ways that your freedom is limited in school?

EXERCISE 2.2 *Action Plan: Time Management*

Directions: Fill out the Action Plan for improving your control of time. Follow the directions on page 12.

Goals	Strategies to Complete Goal	Completion Date	Evaluation Procedure

The ability to effectively manage our time is a key ingredient to a successful student. Good time management involves setting goals and priorities and realistically deciding what is needed to do in order to accomplish our goals.

Vocabulary Development

Three Prefixes

bi   A Latin prefix meaning *two*. E.g.: bicycle (a two-wheeled vehicle).

super   A Latin prefix meaning *over, above,* or *extra*. E.g.: supervise, superior.

inter   A Latin prefix meaning *between* or *among*. E.g.: interrupt, interfere, interject.

Vocabulary Exercise

Study the three prefixes presented above. In the following sentences add the appropriate prefix to the italicized word in each sentence. Write the word on the line following the sentence. Study the examples before you begin the exercise.

A *sonic* aircraft flies at speeds above the speed of sound. supersonic
Spaceships in the future may conduct *planetary* travel as we search for new life. interplanetary

1. John, who speaks English and German fluently, is said to be *lingual*.

    bilingual

2. People believed that we had an *abundance* of oil in the world. SUPER ABUNDANCE

3. The Air Force has built *ceptor* missiles to protect our nation against attack.

    INTER CEPTOR

4. Small-town newspapers are often *monthly* publications. bi *monthly*

5. The ruling of the president *seded* the order of his predecessor. INTENSEded

6. People who wear eyeglasses that have one part for near vision and the other for

   distant vision are using *focal* lenses. bifocal

7. Truckers who transport goods between states are engaged in *state* commerce.

   INTER State

8. The art director taught the class how to *impose* one color on top of another.

   SEPERIMPOSE

9. During the football game an *mission* will take place after the second quarter of

   play. ETERMISSION

Skim/Scan
Exercise 2

1. Record your starting time in the space provided at the beginning of the selection.
2. Using the suggested skimming techniques, rapidly preview-skim the entire selection.
3. Record your ending time in the space provided.
4. Answer the skimming questions.
5. Go on to the scanning questions, using the suggested scanning technique to find the answers.
6. Determine your skimming and scanning scores and your skimming words-per-minute rate as described in Unit 3.
7. Enter your skimming score and rate on the progress graph in the appendix at the end of this book.

Inflation and Stagflation

by Roger LeRoy Miller

	Hour	Min.	Secs.
A. Ending time:	____	____	____
B. Starting time:	____	____	____
C. A − B = Reading time:		____	____

The persistent increase in the cost of living in the United States has affected all of us. Rising prices now seem as inevitable as death and taxes. We are continually reminded by newspaper and magazine articles that today's dollar is only worth 30 percent of the 1939 dollar. Although prices have not always gone up at a rate of 5 to 15 percent a year, they rose at a compounded rate of almost 1 percent per year from 1867 to the 1960s. The pace of inflation (defined as a *sustained* rise in the general price level), however, has not been even.

Inflation and the History of Prices

The behavior of prices has been erratic. After shooting up at a rate of 25 percent per year during and after the Civil War, the price index *fell* at the rate of 5.4 percent from 1867 to 1879. That is equivalent to a halving of the price level in less than 15 years. Farmers and businesspersons during those years of falling prices cried out, strangely enough, for higher prices—*greenbackism* as it was later called. Farmers thought that inflation would cause the prices of the products they sold to rise faster than those of the products they bought. Politicians apparently didn't listen very well, however, for prices kept falling, averaging a decline of 1 percent per year from 1879 to 1897. Prices then rose 6 percent a year continually until a few years after World War I. For a year or so after the war, prices fell drastically and then remained fairly stable until the Great Depression. Wholesale prices dropped at an average rate of 8 percent a year from the stock market crash in 1929 until Roosevelt declared a "banking holiday" in March 1933. Roosevelt's attempts to raise prices were moderately successful, and there was general inflation until 1937. Then prices leveled off until the beginning of World War II.

From pp. 147–150 in ECONOMICS TODAY: THE MACRO VIEW, 2nd Ed. by Roger LeRoy Miller. Copyright © 1973, 1976 by Roger LeRoy Miller. Courtesy of Harper & Row, Publishers, Inc.

The rate of price increases during World War II was less than it had been during both the Civil War and World War I. The wholesale price index rose 118 percent from August 1939 through August 1948—about 9 percent per year. From 1948 until the mid-1960s, prices remained quite stable except for a jump during the Korean conflict. Since the Vietnam involvement, inflation has accelerated.

Inflation in Other Countries

The United States is not alone in its history of rising prices. Inflation seems to be a worldwide problem. In fact our rate of inflation has been mild relative to inflation in many other countries. Some countries have had waves of hyperinflation that make our wartime episodes look like ripples. In 1939, Hungary had a price index set at 100; by January 1946, it was almost 5,500,000. A half a year later it was 20,000,000,000,000, or 2×10^{13}! This means that a commodity with a 1939 price tag of 100 forints would have cost 5,500,000 forints in January 1946, and by August of the same year it would have cost 20,000,000,000,000 forints. Imagine having to carry a wheelbarrow full of money to the store just to buy a loaf of dark bread!

How We Measure Inflation

If inflation is defined as a sustained rise in the general price level, how do we come up with a measure of the rate of inflation? This is indeed a thorny problem for government statisticians. It is easy to determine how much the price of an individual commodity has risen: If last year a light bulb cost 10¢ and this year it costs 15¢, there has been a 50 percent rise in the price of that light bulb over a 1-year period.

Let's construct a hypothetical price index for light bulbs, using the information in Table 1. In the first column we show the year, where year 3 has been singled out as the base year, or period against which all comparisons will be made. Column 2 gives the number of light bulbs sold, and column 3 gives the price per light bulb. The fourth column presents a price index, which is merely the price per light bulb each year expressed as a percentage of the base year's price. We created columns 5 and 6 to express the output of light bulbs in current dollars, that is, column 2 times column 3, and the value of light bulb output in constant (year 3) dollars. Column 6 is merely a simplification of what real GNP is all about, except here we are talking about "real" light bulbs. All that we have to do to obtain real GNP is correct for price changes, just as we have done in Table 1.

Now you should have a little better idea about the difference between *current* dollar or nominal GNP, which is expressed in today's dollars, and *constant* dollar or real GNP, which is expressed in the dollars of some base period. Part of the growth in current dollar GNP has been growth in real output and part has been due to inflation. The real part is obtained by correcting for inflation as in the above simplified example.

Table 1. Converting the Value of Output in Current Dollars to the Value of Output in Constant Dollars

We arbitrarily choose year 3 as our base period. We construct a price index in column 4. When we correct for price changes with this index, we obtain output expressed in constant, year-3 dollars in column 6.

(1)	(2)	(3)	(4)	(5)	(6)
Year	Production of Light Bulbs	Price ($ per Bulb)	Price Index = Each Year's Price as a Percent of the Base-Year Price	Value of Output in Current Dollars (2) × (3)	Output in Constant (Year 3) Dollars (5) ÷ (4)
1	5	$0.10	50%	$0.50	$1.00
2	10	0.15	75%	1.50	2.00
3 = base year	11	0.20	100%	2.20	2.20
4	13	0.22	110%	2.86	2.60

A formal definition of a price index, which may be used for an entire economy, is as follows:

$$\text{Price index} = \frac{\text{quantities of outputs in the current year valued at their current year prices}}{\text{quantities of outputs in the current year valued at their base year prices}}$$

That is exactly the formula we use in column 4 in Table 1, except there the price index is for light bulbs only, not the entire economy.

Skimming Questions: *Circle the letter of the best answer.*

1. _____ is defined as a sustained rise in the general price level.
   a. stagflation
   b. depression
   c. inflation
   d. recession

2. The CPI and the WPI are both:
   a. price indices
   b. sales indices
   c. measures to combat inflation
   d. measures to combat stagflation

3. WPI stands for:
   a. wholesale price index
   b. world price index
   c. world progress indicator
   d. wholesale progress indicator

4. The author constructs a hypothetical price index for:
   a. corn
   b. tissue paper
   c. light bulbs
   d. hamburger

5. The nominal GNP is also referred to as the:
   a. current price index
   b. current dollar GNP
   c. constant dollar GNP
   d. real GNP

Scanning Questions

1. If last year's light bulb cost 10¢ and this year's costs 15¢, there has been a

   _____50%_____ rise in the price of a light bulb.

2. In Table 1, column 2 gives the _____ of light bulbs sold.

3. The stock market crash was in _____ .

4. From Table 1, _____ light bulbs were produced in year 3.

5. Roosevelt declared a _____ _____ in March 1933.

Time-Rate Conversion Chart

Min:Sec	WPM	Min:Sec	WPM	Min:Sec	WPM	Min:Sec	WPM	Min:Sec	WPM
1:00	1770	4:30	393	7:50	226	11:10	159	14:30	122
1:10	1517	4:40	379	8:00	221	11:20	156	14:40	121
1:20	1328	4:50	366	8:10	217	11:30	154	14:50	119
1:30	1180	5:00	354	8:20	212	11:40	152	15:00	118
1:40	1062	5:10	343	8:30	208	11:50	150	15:10	117
1:50	965	5:20	332	8:40	204	12:00	148	15:20	115
2:00	885	5:30	322	8:50	200	12:10	145	15:30	114
2:10	817	5:40	312	9:00	197	12:20	144	15:40	113
2:20	759	5:50	303	9:10	193	12:30	142	15:50	112
2:30	708	6:00	295	9:20	190	12:40	140	16:00	111
2:40	664	6:10	287	9:30	186	12:50	138	16:10	109
2:50	625	6:20	279	9:40	183	13:00	136	16:20	108
3:00	590	6:30	272	9:50	180	13:10	134	16:30	107
3:10	559	6:40	266	10:00	177	13:20	133	16:40	106
3:20	531	6:50	259	10:10	174	13:30	131	16:50	105
3:30	506	7:00	253	10:20	171	13:40	130	17:00	104
3:40	483	7:10	247	10:30	169	13:50	128	17:10	103
3:50	462	7:20	241	10:40	166	14:00	126	17:20	102
4:00	443	7:30	236	10:50	163	14:10	125	17:30	101
4:10	425	7:40	231	11:00	161	14:20	123	17:40	100
4:20	408								

Unit 2 Answer Key

Unit Comprehension Check

1. People perceive time in different ways; therefore, each individual needs to manage time differently. The main goal is to accomplish our goals.
2. No
3. Determining when to start a project
4. (a) Peer pressure (b) rewards (c) penalties
5. We are able to see at a glance what needs to be done and when it needs to be done.

Vocabulary Development

1. bilingual
2. superabundance
3. interceptor
4. bimonthly
5. superseded
6. bifocal
7. interstate
8. superimpose
9. intermission

Skim/Scan Exercise

Skim
1. c   2. a   3. a   4. c   5. b

Scan
1. 50 percent
2. number
3. 1929
4. 11
5. banking holiday

Unit 3

Active Listening and Lecture Notetaking

If you do not take adequate lecture notes you are at a genuine disadvantage. Without some way to review lecture material, you may remember as little as 2 percent of the information one month after hearing it. Yet students often are poor note-takers, for a number of reasons. First, they may be untrained listeners. The quality of their notes is limited by their listening ability. Second, they may have had little practice taking notes. Third, they may not have a note-taking system. Without some kind of system, students frequently use inefficient trial-and-error methods. And fourth, some students may be under the false impression that they are able to listen better if they don't take notes.

Should you audio-tape your lectures? Generally not. Listening and note-taking skills can, with practice, be quickly developed. And, reviewing audio tapes requires a lot of extra listening time. There are some exceptions to this rule, however. For example, in a highly technical class where the instructor tends to speak rapidly, audio tapes might be used to supplement your notes. You could play the tapes for clarification where your notes are inadequate. But tapes should never be used as a crutch to avoid taking lecture notes.

Become an Active Listener

What do we mean by "active" listening? You're sitting (preferably in the front row) as the instructor starts to speak. Your attention is focused on the lecturer. You are sitting slightly forward, pen ready to take notes. Your mind is working: What is she going to discuss? What is the point she is trying to make? What is the new idea? What is she doing? Giving an example? Generalizing? Showing how the idea developed? Digressing? What's he putting on the board? How does it fit in? Should I write it in my notes now or wait . . . ?

By the time the lecture is over, you'll feel mentally wrung out. But you will not have been bored. And you will have a good understanding of what was said. You'll have exercised your mind.

Techniques for Effective Listening

Active involvement is necessary if you want to overcome the many barriers to listening. These barriers may be external, coming from outside; or internal, from within you. Some external barriers are noises, movements, poor acoustics, uncomfortable physical conditions, or poorly organized lectures. Some internal barriers are fatigue, negative feelings about the speaker, negative feelings about the ideas being expressed, and lack of vocabulary to understand the ideas.

There are several techniques to reduce both external and internal barriers. Some of them are listed here (as you read try to identify if the suggestion is for an internal or external barrier):

1. Prepare ahead of time. Learn as much as possible. If there is related reading material, at least skim it before the lecture. ✕

2. Have questions in mind. By developing some questions ahead of time, you are more likely to pay attention to what is said because you will be trying to find out if your questions are being answered.

3. Have a desire to listen. Some students make the mistake of mentally preparing themselves to be bored. Instead, focus on the message, not the speaker. Challenge yourself to concentrate on what is being said.

4. Don't let personal feelings interfere. Get the message while you can. You can let your feelings come through later. You need the information. Psychologists tell us that we tend to forget information that we disagree with much quicker than information that we agree with so make sure that you write down information you don't like!

5. Sit close to the speaker. This suggestion is important! Research shows that your listening efficiency improves greatly when you sit closer to the speaker. Sit in the middle in the first three rows if possible. If not, at least sit on the outside row in order to avoid as many distractions as possible from other people.

6. Listen for main ideas. In studies of good and poor listeners, poor listeners were found to focus their attention on details: facts, names, and dates. Effective listeners, on the other hand, concentrated on main ideas. What was the speaker "getting at"? Certainly you should also note important supporting details, but always ask yourself how they relate to the main ideas.

7. Listen for signal words. Your instructor isn't going to shout and bang on the podium when he states an important new idea but he will give verbal signals. Some common signal words include: "There are two reasons why . . ." "And most importantly" "On the other hand" "For example" "In conclusion" "Finally" "The causes of . . ." "The types of . . ." Also, listen for a pause. An instructor will often make a slight pause just before saying something important. Repetition. If the instructor says the same thing more than once it is probably important. Use of the chalkboard. Anytime the instructor writes or draws something on the board, the more a student should pay attention. The instructor uses the board to help explain what she is saying.

8. Stop the speaker if necessary. What? Stop the speaker? Yes. You have the right to act if there is something you don't understand. Most instructors are happy to stop and answer questions or in some other way to help you understand. If, for example, the speaker is talking too fast or too softly, or if you cannot read the notes on the board, raise your hand and say so. Be polite—but give the speaker feedback.

The Speaker's Organization

Students quickly learn that not all lectures are created equal. Unfortunately, many instructors have had little or no training in giving lectures. Most have a good knowledge of their subject, but they vary as to how well they can present it. A well-organized speaker can make your job of listening and note-taking much easier. As the presentation becomes less well-organized, your job becomes harder.

EXERCISE 3.0. *Speaker Evaluation*

If you are having trouble taking notes in a class, part of the problem may be the way the lectures are presented. Evaluate the lecturing style of one of your instructors by answering the questions below. The more "No's" you marked, the harder you probably will have to work at listening and note-taking.

Speaker Evalation

Yes   No   1. The speaker usually begins a lecture by introducing the topic of the day.

Yes   No   2. Each main idea is clearly stated.

Yes   No   3. Examples, illustrations, and other specific details are clearly related to main ideas.

Yes   No   4. Digressions—stories told for the sake of storytelling—are kept to a minimum.

Yes   No   5. The pace is about right, neither too slow nor too fast.

Yes   No   6. Pronunciation and voice level are satisfactory

Yes   No   7. Distracting gestures or movements are kept to a minimum.

Yes   No   8. The level of vocabulary is appropriate.

Yes   No   9. If humor is used, it helps the listener's concentration on the topic instead of detracting from it.

Yes   No   10. The audience is treated with respect.

Yes   No   11. The speaker usually tries to summarize the main points at the end of the lecture.

Developing Your Lecture-Note-taking Skills

The main purpose of your lecture notes is to provide an accurate, complete record of important class events for later study. If taking notes helps you concentrate on the speaker, that's an added benefit. But don't forget the main purpose of taking notes.

What Note-taking System?

You will want to choose a note-taking system that fits your needs, personal preferences, and lecture style of the instructor. This discussion may help you make that choice. The decision is yours.

Notebooks come in all sizes. The smaller the notebook, the easier it is to carry around. But remember that your notes are likely to be more cramped on smaller pages. If you want some flexibility in your note-taking, a larger format is probably better.

You will also have to choose a notebook style. The two most common ones are the spiral type and the three-ring, loose-leaf type. Each kind has certain advantages. For example, the spiral notebooks usually are a bit cheaper than the three-ring kind. On the other hand, the three-ring types tend to be more flexible to use because you can add, remove, and shift pages. The spiral notebooks usually are a little easier to carry and to take notes in, while the three-ring types allow you to have notes for several different classes under one cover.

If you choose spiral notebooks, use one notebook per class. Write only on the right-hand sheet so that additions can be made later on the facing page when the notebook lies open.

If you choose the three-ring type, you may want to buy one lightweight notebook for each course. Obviously, you would use the same notebooks term after term—only the loose-leaf pages would be replaced. Make sure you have notebooks thick enough to hold all the notes for a term. Since a three-ring notebook cannot be folded back the way a spiral can, a clip-board is useful for taking the actual notes. Then, after the lecture, the pages are placed in the notebook. If you wish to save your loose-leaf notes at the end of the term, transfer them to an inexpensive folder with fasteners to hold the pages together.

What Note-taking Style?

Exactly how you take notes is a personal matter, but one suggestion is strongly made: Whatever style you use, divide the note page into two parts by a vertical line about one-and-a-half to two inches from the left-hand margin. The wider part of the page to the right of this line is for your lecture notes. The narrow column to the left of the line is called the recall column (see Figure 3.0). The purpose of this column is discussed later.

Recall colum
(Filled in after
the lecture)

Main topics are underlined

Biorhythms

3 biorhythm cycles?

3 main cycles:

1. Physical Cycle

Numbers used sparingly

- 23 days long
- strength, disease, etc.

What ea. cycle affects

2. Emotional Cycle

- 28 days long
- Creativity, sensitivity
  Mntl health, etc.

The cues do not give away the answers

3. Intellctl Cycle

Space left between main ideas

- 33 days
- Memory, alertness, etc.

Ideas are written as briefly as possible

Define "Critical day."

Critical Days
- When 1 or more rhythms cross baseline.
- ↑ chance for colds, disease, accdnts.

Cues are kept very short

Personal symbols are used

Some words are abbreviated

E.g. Japanese bus drivers receive warnings.

A summing up of the day's lecture

Standard symbols used

Summary: Biorhythms can have an effect on how we think, feel, and behave, especially on critical days.

Figure 3.0 Sample Lecture Notes.

A myth persists that all notes should be taken in outline form. An outline has a series of very general categories under which is grouped related, more specific information. Thus, an outline of a lecture might follow this format:

I. First topic
   A. First main-idea statement
      1. First example
      2. Second example
   B. Second main-idea statement
      1. First example
      2. Second example
II. Second topic
   (and so forth)

There are at least two problems with using this note-taking style. First, many lecturers do not present their material in a form well enough organized to be outlined this way. Second, a student may become so concerned with getting the outline just right that listening suffers. While trying to decide whether to use capital letter "B" or number "1", the student may miss some important information.

Instead, you might try the following system: First of all, don't use numbers or letters unless the speaker is giving you a list organized that way. Do, however, categorize information by indenting and spacing. Main topics are written to the far left and underlined to make them stand out, main-idea statements are indented about an inch to the right, and supporting details are indented to the right under the related main-idea statements. If you cannot figure out at first what the topic is, leave space to fill in later. If you are getting a series of facts without any main idea to tie them together, leave space to fill in the main idea when it becomes clear later.

When there is a major break between topics or main ideas, leave two or three lines of space between them to signal the break. This space also is useful if later on you need to add some information. Figure 3.0 shows a sample page of notes.

Abbreviating

Notes should be an accurate record of the important information given in class. But they do not have to be an exact record, or even close. Anything you can do to shorten your writing time is worthwhile, as long as you can understand later what you have written. There are four main ways to abbreviate your notes: 1. Be selective; only include useful and important information. 2. Abbreviate sentences; either leave out unnecessary words or shorten an idea by using your own words. 3. Abbreviate words by leaving out unnecessary letters. 4. Use symbols whenever possible.

With some practice, you can learn to translate a speaker's words into short, concise sentences and phrases. For example, the speaker might say, "Freud worked with hypnosis for a while, but he decided that it did not tell him anything about the causes of his patients' problems." You might write:

Hypnosis
    Freud stopped using:
        It didn't get to causes.

Thus, through indenting and condensing, you would have written nine words in place of the twenty-four used by the speaker.

EXERCISE 3.1. *Abbreviation*

Practice abbreviating the following sentences. Try to cut the number of words at least in half. See the answer key at the end of this unit for examples of abbreviations.

1. "Small businesses often fail because of cash-flow problems. The owner begins with too little capital and does not forsee all the expenses."

    Your Notes:

2. "The Employment Act of 1946 stated that it was the responsibility of the Federal Government to take measures to prevent recessions and to minimize the harm caused by any recessions that take place.

    Your Notes

You can also shorten your writing time by abbreviating words and using symbols. Here are some suggestions:

1. Leave out vowels whenever possible. Example: Lve out vwls whenevr psslbe.
2. Sometimes you can eliminate the ends of words. Examples: Biology = bio, subject = subj; introduction = intro
3. Shorten "ing" to g. Examples walking = walkg; wishing = wishg.

4. Make use of standard symbols. Here are some common ones:

=	equals	>	greater than
≠	does not equal	<	less than
e.g.	for example	⊙	individual
i.e.	in other words	≡	identical to
&	and	∴	therefore
w/	with	w/o	without
c.f.	see also	etc.	and so forth

5. Develop your personal set of symbols, especially for words or phrases that occur frequently. For example:

increasing ↑   before B4
decreasing ↓

Other Hints

If you have trouble writing notes that are complete enough, set a goal to write a certain amount during the lecture period. For example, you might decide to write at least one page per fifty-minute lecture. You may not think the lecturer has that much information, but you can be sure the instructor thinks so. Also, in most cases write down anything the instructor puts on the board. That usually is the information the instructor thinks is especially important. One excellent habit is to make sure you have written a summary at the end of each day's notes. If the instructor makes a summary, record that. If not, take a minute to write your own just a few sentences that try to make sense out of the idea (see Figure 3.0). Weeks later, these summaries will help you as you prepare for the exam. If you cannot write a sensible summary, it may be a danger signal that you did not understand the lecture.

Reviewing the Day's Notes

Too often notes are written and then ignored until weeks (or months) later, when exam time is close. Actually, the few hours after you have made notes are precious—your memory of the content of the lecture will never be as good as it is then. During those hours, while the words of the instructor are still echoing in your mind, review and edit your notes. Here are some suggestions:

1. Clarify any unclear notes and fill in gaps in the information.
2. Highlight information that seems important to you or that the instructor stress. (For example, did the instructor repeat something or write it on the board?)

3. Fill in the recall column (mentioned earlier). The recall column is used for self-test cues to help with later recitation. Recitation is discussed in more detail in Unit Four. Briefly, it is a powerful memory technique that involves saying information aloud from memory. The cues you write in the recall column tell you what ideas and facts need to be learned. When writing a cue in the recall column, write just enough information to provide a cue but not enough to give away the answer.

Should you completely rewrite your notes instead of simply editing them? This is a very time-consuming process, but some students claim that it helps them learn the material. On the other hand, study-skills specialists generally recommend against taking the time to rewrite notes. The decision is yours. Ask yourself, however, whether your time might be better spent thinking about the information and reciting it instead of rewriting it. If you want to rewrite your notes because they are hard to read, consider that using the methods discussed in this unit may help you make your notes more readable.

EXERCISE 3.2 *Note-taking Evaluation*

Use the questionnaire below to evaluate the way you take notes now.

Evaluation

Yes No   1. My notes are easy to read (legible) long after they've been written.

Yes No   2. My notes are complete enough for me to understand long after they have been written.

Yes No   3. I manage to leave out most of the unnecessary words.

Yes No   4. I make good use of symbols.

Yes No   5. I abbreviate words whenever possible.

Yes No   6. My notes usually include the important main ideas that are presented.

Yes No   7. Important examples and other details also are included.

Yes No   8. The relationship between main ideas and their associated details usually is clearly shown.

You might want to work at improving your notes in the areas you responded "No".

Summary

Listening to a lecture is much more demanding than listening under ordinary circumstances. For example, in polite conversation you are not usually expected to have a detailed memory of what you hear. In order to grasp what the lecturer is saying, you should listen actively, focusing your full attention on the message. But active listening is only half the job. Unless you take accurate, complete, readable notes, you will not have a record later on, when you will have forgotten most of the original lecture. Once the notes are made, they should be reviewed and edited shortly thereafter, while the information is still fresh in your memory.

Unit Comprehension Check

If you can answer these questions, you have retained many of the main ideas at the literal level.

1. Why is audio-taping generally not recommended?

2. List some examples of external barriers to listening; some internal barriers.

3. Should you focus on your personal feelings while listening to a lecture? Why?

4. Where is the best place to sit in a classroom for effective listening? Why?

5. Do effective listeners tend to focus more on main ideas or on details? Why?

6. If the speaker is speaking too softly, what should you do?

7. What is the purpose of a "recall column"?

8. Should you try to use the outline format for all your notes? Why?

9. What should you write at the bottom of each day's notes? Why?

10. What are three activities recommended when you review your day's notes?

11. Define the term "recitation". Why is this an important activity?

Study Questions

1. Which suggestions for effective listening are most valuable for you?

2. What is your reason for using the notebook system you now have? How might you improve your system?

Supplemental Activities

1. Below are three topics an instructor might lecture about. Write down at least five questions that you might ask yourself ahead of time to prepare for each topic. (The first topic is done for you.) See the answer key at the end of this unit for examples.

Introduction to Business Law

    a. What does law have to do with business?

    b. What are some common unlawful business practices?

    c. How does law relate to business ethics?

    d. What topics are included under Business Law?

    e. What kinds of work does a business lawyer do?

Computer Applications in Business

    a.

    b.

    c.

    d.

    e.

The Psychology of Selling

    a.

    b.

    c.

    d.

    e.

2. Shorten the following passages, using any abbreviation technique that is appropriate (rephrasing, leaving out words, abbreviating words, and using symbols).

    a. "A revolution is any occurrence that affects other aspects of life, such as economic life, social life, and so forth. Therefore revolutions cause change."

Your Notes:

    b. "In the canyon and mesa country of the Pajarito Plateau in New Mexico are found the ruined dwellings of one of the most extensive prehistoric Indian populations of the Southwest."

Your Notes:

    c. "The people have a right to clean air, pure water, and to the preservation of the natural, scenic, historic, and aesthetic values of the environment."

Your Notes:

    d. Recall column entries should provide just enough information to help recitation self-testing. But the entries should not give away answers. In the spaces below, write recall column entries for each of the three notes in supplemental activity 2 above.

EXERCISE 3.3 *Action Plan: Listening and Note-taking*

Directions: Identify at least one idea in this Unit that you think you can incorporate into your notetaking. Develop an Action Plan for that idea.

Goals	Strategies to Complete Goal	Completion Date	Evaluation Procedure

Vocabulary Development

Five Prefixes

de   A Latin prefix meaning *down* or *from*. E.g.: descend, degrade, demote.

non   A Latin prefix meaning *not*. E.g.: nonviolent, nonsense.

un   An Old English prefix meaning *not*. E.g.: unnatural, unusual.

ex   A Latin prefix meaning *out of* or *from*. E.g.: expel, extend.

anti A prefix that has Greek origins, meaning *against*. E.g.: antisocial, antiaircraft.

Vocabulary Exercise

Study the five prefixes presented above. In each of the following sentences, underline the word beginning with one of the prefixes and fill in the blank with the best meaning for that prefix.

1. Unfit water is ___NOT___ fit to drink.

2. Using an antiseptic mouthwash protects ___AGAINST___ bad breath.

3. A student who demonstrates bad conduct will be expelled ___FROM___ school for three days.

CAH DOWN

4. The mountain climbers will descend __Down__ the peak once the weather gets better.

5. The nondelivery of the generator will __NOT__ help the construction of the new plant.

6. Antinuclear demonstrators are voicing their opinion __AGAINST__ the building of nuclear generating facilities.

7. Automobile exhaust emissions __FROM__ cars are a major source of air pollution.

8. A nonsense phrase is a phrase that makes __NO__ sense.

9. The soldier was demoted __FROM__ sergeant to private because of a fight with another soldier.

10. The unexpected blizzard was __NOT__ forecasted by the weatherman.

11. Nonfiction writing is about real events, people, and things; it is __NOT__ imaginary.

12. Antiaircraft carriers are naval ships that are used for defense __AGAINST__ air attacks.

13. When buying a new car the buyer must deposit a __DOWN__ payment in order to complete the purchase.

14. The exit sign in the theatre shows you the way __OUT__ of the building in case of an emergency.

15. An unqualified race car driver did __NOT__ attain the minimum speed necessary to race in the final event.

Common Prefixes

Prefix	Meaning	Examples
1. *ab*	away or from	absent, abnormal
2. *ad*	to or toward	advance
3. *anti*	against	antilabor, anticolonial
4. *bi*	two	bifocal, bicycle
5. *com, con*	with or together	combine, congregate
6. *de*	down or from	descend, demean
7. *dis*	apart	disbar, disconnect
8. *ex*	out of	exit, expel
9. *in, il, ir*	not	invalid, illegal, irregular
10. *non*	not	nonavailable
11. *ob*	against	obstruct, object
12. *per*	through	pervade
13. *post*	after	postpone, postmortem
14. *pre*	before	precede, predispose
15. *pro*	forward	proceed, promoter
16. *re*	back or again	return, retreat
17. *semi*	half or partly	semiconscious
18. *sub*	under or below	subway, subsoil
19. *super*	over or above	superpower, superior
20. *un*	not or no	unnatural, unlimited

Skim/Scan
Exercise 3

1. Record your starting time.
2. Rapidly preview-skim the entire selection.
3. Record your ending time.
4. Answer the skimming questions.
5. Go on to the scanning questions.
6. Determine your skimming and scanning scores and your skimming words-per-minute rate.
7. Enter your skimming score and rate on the progress graph in the appendix at the end of this book.

Overcoming Sales Objections

by Stan Kossen

	Hour	Min.	Secs.
A. Ending time:	____	____	____
B. Starting time:	____	____	____
C. A − B = Reading time:		____	____

"I can't afford it right now." "I'm really not interested." "The one we have still works okay." "It wouldn't work for us; our needs are different." Statements like these don't surprise experienced salespeople. They know that objections are a normal part of the selling process.

As a salesperson, should you feel threatened if prospects resist your sales messages or react negatively to them? Not at all. In fact, prospective buyers who don't object may be thinking about a weekend skiing trip instead of listening to your presentation. So don't be afraid of objections—welcome them as opportunities for learning more about the prospect's attitudes toward you, your company, and its products.

Objections can be looked at as opportunities to convert resistance into sales. In fact, long-run success in selling hinges strongly on your ability to turn buyer objections into sales opportunities. Objections may arise at any time during a sales presentation, and you have to be ready for them. In this chapter we explore some of the proven techniques used for overcoming objections and then examine the more common types of objections you are likely to be faced with as a salesperson.

Reasons Prospective Customers Object

Psychologists believe that resisting change is a natural human tendency. For many individuals, the old, familiar methods and products are better or more useful than the new ones, which are sometimes viewed as threatening or less predictable. As a salesperson, you are the force opposing a prospective customer's desires for stability and certainty. Your goal is to modify the behavior of potential buyers, and, therefore, every time you persuade them to purchase your products, you are an instrument of change.

The Desire to Be Persuaded

If you could get into the minds of prospective buyers, you might discover that frequently they have a genuine interest in your product, may even have the urge to make a purchase, but that they want to be convinced or at least reassured that their decisions will be right ones. Some objections that appear genuine are merely indirect requests for more information. When a prospect says, "I can't afford it," he or she may actually mean, "Tell me why it's worth that price." In some instances, objections are intended to test the salesperson's ability and knowledge. Objections, which often are used by prospects as protective shields, can be persuasively and gently removed by the deft activities of creative salespeople.

Common Types of Objections

Learn the typical types of objections you are likely to be faced with as a salesperson. By anticipating and preparing for them, you'll discover that you can develop the necessary skills quite rapidly. You may even find that you enjoy the experience of overcoming objections, an activity that can give you strong feelings of personal satisfaction and self-worth.

Objections typically fall into one of six principal categories. These are:

1. Price
2. Product
3. Source and service
4. Salesperson
5. Poor-time-to-buy
6. Inherent suspicion

Understanding these types of objections can help you answer them more skillfully. A little later we'll discuss each of them in detail.

How to Overcome Objections

Resistance to any sales message is a somewhat natural tendency. In order to guide a customer into accepting your proposal, you need a tremendous degree of empathy: you must continually try to put yourself in your prospect's shoes. Try to classify your prospect's objections. Ask yourself if they're genuine or merely a coverup for other feelings. When developing methods for handling objections you should carefully consider how your prospect really feels about your product or service. A prospect's stated reason for resisting your sales presentation could simply be a reaction to the changes you're trying to effect. Ask probing questions and listen—then you'll have a better idea of how to conduct your presentation.

Let's look at some of the techniques regularly used by professional salespeople to overcome objections. (See Figure 1 for a graphic summary of the major techniques.)

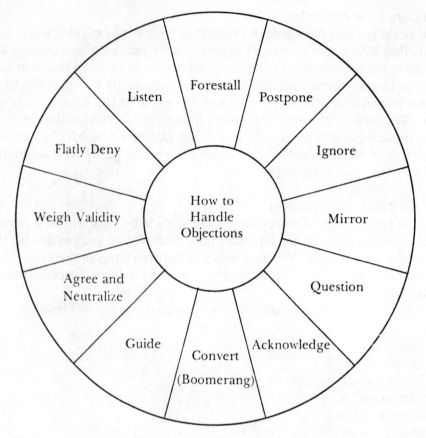

Figure 3.1 Techniques for Overcoming Objections.

Listen to Objections

Although talking is a necessary ingredient to selling, during the early stages of your sales interview *listening* is of far greater importance—particularly if you sincerely want to learn about your prospect's needs and attitudes. Effective listening, accompanied by creative probing, helps both you and your prospect. It helps you learn, for example, why your prospect may be resisting your sales message, and it helps the prospect get out into the open any negative feelings he or she might have.

Customers who are listened to are more likely to feel that you have a sincere interest in their needs and problems. When objections are brought out into the open, they frequently seem less real to the prospect. Also, people don't generally like to be contradicted. If you argue with or insult the intelligence of your prospect, you are almost certain to lose the sale—even if you win the argument. Your techniques should subtly guide—not push—your prospects into positive agreement.

Forestall the Objection

Although objections are not to be feared, the creative salesperson tries to anticipate specific objections and, in effect, answer them before they arise, an activity termed *forestalling*. By anticipating negative reactions, the salesperson stops prospects from being put in a position where they feel compelled to defend their objections. Customers don't have to bring up or defend objections that have already been covered to their satisfaction.

For example, you may have learned during your preapproach that your prospect, Ms. Schmidt, a buyer for a large janitorial service company, prefers to deal with firms that allow her at least sixty days to pay for purchases. Your company, however, requires payment within thirty days. During your sales presentation, you could forestall her objections to a shorter credit period by saying something like, "Ms. Schmidt, you can see that our supplies are not only of high quality, but are competitively priced, factors certainly of importance to you in your operations. As a businessperson, you realize that one of the ways we are able to maintain reasonable prices is by operating efficiently and using businesslike practices, such as asking our customers for payment within thirty days. We've received few complaints on this policy since, by supplying better products at lower prices, we can help customers increase their profits."

Postpone the Objection

Part of your task as a creative, professional salesperson is to sort out real from stated objections, realizing, of course, that they are not always one and the same. You should not, however, regard any customer's objections as trivial since to him or her they may be quite genuine and of great significance. In some instances, though, it's better to postpone an objection, at least until you've had an opportunity to offer sufficient evidence of your product's value and its benefits to your customer.

One technique for *postponing* objections is to say, "Ms. Balsham, you've brought up a valid point. I'll be discussing that specific subject later in my presentation. If you don't mind, I'll just go on until then, at which time I think you'll find the answer far more meaningful."

Price is one topic that many salespeople feel should be postponed until value and benefits have been established. For example, there is a substantial difference in the handling characteristics and durability between fiberglass belted and steel-belted radial automobile tires. There is also a substantial difference in price. Customers who are unaware of the quality differences might feel that the price of radials is completely out of line with more conventional tires. Some radials, however, are useful for 50,000 miles or more, while ordinary tires may last only 20,000 miles.

When involved in a field where repeat customers are desired, selling on the basis of price rather than value can be a costly mistake, even when your prices are generally lower than those of your competitors. Say, for example, that you sell auto insurance, and that your policy is $20 less expensive than the expiring policy of your prospect.

If you try to sell the $20 savings instead of your policy's *features,* chances are you'll find later that another agent took the account away from you, either by stressing quality or maybe even by having a price lower than yours. Instead of price, you should stress the policy's coverage and the quality of service offered by your company in relation to the customer's needs.

Ignore the Objection

A technique for handling objections that some sales managers have determined to be dangerous to your selling health if not used with caution is the act of simply *ignoring* the objection. It certainly isn't a method you want to use frequently with the same prospect. Some salespeople use this method when they feel the objections are a bit weak. The salesperson may pretend not to hear the objection and move immediately on to the next point.

Mirror the Objection

You have studied various listening responses. One of these, the *mirror response,* is the act of restating to the prospect what you think he or she has just said. *Mirroring* a response clarifies your own understanding and also allows prospects to reconsider their own words. Frequently an objection doesn't have the same validity when it has been restated by another person. Ways in which you can phrase the mirror response include: "Mr. Prospect, are you saying that . . . ?" or "If I understand you, you're saying . . . ." or "Then you are worried about . . . ."

Question the Objection

Questioning objections can also be of considerable benefit in overcoming them. For example, assume a prospect says, "Based on what I've been hearing from my associates, I don't feel that I can depend on a regular supply from you people." You might respond with, "I'm certainly concerned about what you're implying. Specifically what have you heard about our shipments?"

In effect, by questioning the prospect, you are asking him or her to move from the general to the specific. When this method is used, especially when it's in conjunction with other techniques, the objection often appears less significant to the prospect. Let's look at another example:

Mr. Hitch (a prospect): I hear that Household Mutual doesn't pay its insurance claims.

Mr. Ouvert (insurance agent for Household Mutual): Household Mutual doesn't pay its claims (mirror)? Why do you say that (open question)?

Mr. Hitch: I know of a man who had his insurance with Household three years and for *no reason* at all he was cancelled.

Mr. Ouvert: Would you agree, Mr. Hitch, that Household Mutual is in business to make a profit? We don't make it by *not selling* insurance. Mustn't there have been some good reason for Household to decide it no longer wanted to accept premiums from the person you've mentioned (closed question with likely affirmative response)?

Acknowledge the Objection

A low-key response to sales resistance is *acknowledging* the objection. This relatively soft approach can be used to show your prospect that you feel he or she brought up a logical point. In this manner, you show the person that you understand and sympathize with what was said. You aren't conceding anything, however, but are merely acknowledging that you understand the prospect's point of view.

The Conversion (Boomerang) Process

A fairly common technique for overcoming objections is the *conversion process,* or the *boomerang technique;* this involves converting objections into selling features. For example, assume that you work for the KaiCan Aluminum Company, and that your customer, Mr. P. C. Ristantz, has just informed you that his firm is no longer going to use your aluminum products. Mr. Ristantz has explained, "We've decided to discontinue the use of aluminum in our products in favor of other raw materials. We've discovered that we have to reduce the weight of our materials, yet maintain strength. I really doubt that any of your products can meet our needs."

Your response could be, "Mr. Ristantz, I can certainly understand your needs for both reduced weight and adequate strength. Here's what we've recently done to overcome that problem. We have broadened our lower gauge limit from .020 to .008. This has resulted in a 60 percent potential savings in weight over the .020 sheet you presently use. And, it doesn't significantly alter the integrity or strength of your particular product. So you can see that our sheet aluminum eliminates your need to switch to raw materials you may not be as familiar with."

Guide the Objector

Related to the conversion method is the *guiding* technique of handling objections. This method can be used when the prospect has made both positive *and* negative comments about your product. With this technique, you try to guide your prospect's thought toward those parts of your proposal he or she has already agreed with. For example, a prospect might say, "I can see several advantages of your photocopying machine over the one I'm presently leasing, but I'm not sure if it's worth the extra cost." You could ask, "What are some of the advantages of our machine that you feel would be most helpful to you?" Through the use of the guiding technique, you can focus on the positive aspects of the interview and, in a sense, sidestep the negative portions.

Agree and Neutralize the Objection

A method long used by salespeople when facing objections has been termed the *agreeing and neutralizing* technique. Referred to also as the *agree and counterattack* or the *yes, but* technique, this method tends to "disarm" prospects since the salesperson appears to be agreeing with their responses. The salesperson shows sympathy for their points of view, which relaxes them, but then shows how the objections are actually unfounded.

You must be careful with this technique also, since people generally don't like to be contradicted or proven wrong. If you appear contradictory, your prospect is likely to become defensive and resist your efforts.

The 3M Corporation recommends that its sales personnel use a modification of the *yes, but* approach. 3M salespeople are advised to drop the "but" and in its place use a *pause*. For example, instead of saying, "I don't blame you for doubting that this procedure will work for you, but Mr. Dent at Arrowhead Offset . . .", a salesperson might say, "I don't blame you . . . (pause) Mr. Dent at Arrowhead Offset . . .".

Some salespeople use the word "however" instead of "but," feeling that it's a gentler term. For example, a customer might say, "That's one heck of a lot of money to pay for a car." The automobile salesperson then could say, "You're right. It is a lot of money. However, have you considered the low maintenance, high mileage, and extremely favorable resale price you'll get at trade-in time with this automobile?"

Weigh the Validity of the Objection
Assume that your prospect has made nothing but negative comments about your products. In such cases, you could use the *weighing* technique, a method that involves your listing on one side of a sheet of paper all the disadvantages cited by the prospect and on the other side the advantages. No product is perfect, but a visual comparison that shows how the advantages far outweigh the disadvantages can often overcome customer resistance.

Flatly, but Politely, Deny the Objection
The *denying* method for handling objections is another technique used by some salespeople. A major problem with this method, however, is that it can appear to be argumentative. The salesperson is hitting the prospect head-on with a contradiction. There are some instances, however, when a direct denial may be called for. For example, if a prospect had accused your company of engaging in unethical practices, and you know that the charges are untrue, a definitive and sincere denial is a very convincing response. If the accusation about your company is true, however, your future credibility will be adversely affected by your denial.

Skimming Questions: *Circle the letter of the best answer.*

1. Customers who are ____PEOPLE____ are more likely to feel that you have a sincere interest in their needs and problems.
   a. tired
   b. ready to buy
   c. wealthy
   d. listened to

2. Answering objections before they arise is called:
   a. postponing
   b. forestalling
   c. converting
   d. questioning

3. Many salespeople feel that discussion of ___tHE CAR___ should be postponed until value and benefits have been established.
   a. price
   b. expected life of the article to be sold
   c. discussions of the quality of the article to be sold
   d. discussion of the customer's needs

4. The act of restating to the prospect what you think he or she has said is called:
   a. questioning
   b. postponing
   c. mirroring
   d. forestalling

5. The conversion process is also called the ___A GOSHIETING___ technique.
   a. questioning
   b. boomerang
   c. guiding
   d. neutralizing

Scanning Questions

1. As a salesperson, your goal is to ___SALE___ the behavior of potential buyers.

2. From the list of common objections, objection number three is _____ .

3. From the figure on how to handle objections, _____ is between Listen and Postpone.

4. If you _____ with your prospect you are almost sure to lose the sale.

5. _____ a response clarifies your own understanding and also allows prospects to reconsider their own words.

Time-Rate Conversion Chart

Min:Sec	WPM	Min:Sec	WPM	Min:Sec	WPM	Min:Sec	WPM	Min:Sec	WPM
1.00	3255	7:00	465	13:00	250	19:00	171	25:00	130
1:10	2790	7:10	454	13:10	247	19:10	170	25:10	129
1:20	2441	7:20	444	13:20	244	19:20	168	25:20	128
1:30	2170	7:30	434	13:30	241	19:30	167	25:30	128
1:40	1953	7:40	425	13:40	238	19:40	166	25:40	127
1:50	1775	7:50	416	13:50	235	19:50	164	25:50	126
2:00	1628	8:00	407	14:00	233	20:00	163	26:00	125
2:10	1502	8:10	399	14:10	230	20:10	161	26:10	124
2:20	1395	8:20	391	14:20	227	20:20	160	26:20	124
2:30	1302	8:30	383	14:30	224	20:30	159	26:30	123
2:40	1221	8:40	376	14:40	222	20:40	158	26:40	122
2:50	1149	8:50	368	14:50	219	20:50	156	26:50	121
3:00	1085	9:00	362	15:00	217	21:00	155	27:00	121
3:10	1028	9:10	355	15:10	215	21:10	154	27:10	120
3:20	977	9:20	349	15:20	212	21:20	153	27:20	119
3:30	930	9:30	343	15:30	210	21:30	151	27:30	118
3:40	888	9:40	337	15:40	208	21:40	150	27:40	118
3:50	849	9:50	331	15:50	206	21:50	149	27:50	117
4:00	814	10:00	326	16:00	203	22:00	148	28:00	116
4:10	781	10:10	320	16:10	201	22:10	147	28:10	116
4:20	751	10:20	315	16:20	199	22:20	146	28:20	115
4:30	723	10:30	310	16:30	197	22:30	145	28:30	114
4:40	698	10:40	305	16:40	195	22:40	144	28:50	113
4:50	673	10:50	300	16:50	193	22:50	143	29:00	112
5:00	651	11:00	296	17:00	191	23:00	142	29:20	111
5:10	630	11:10	291	17:10	190	23:10	141	29:30	110
5:20	610	11:20	287	17:20	188	23:20	140	29:50	109
5:30	592	11:30	283	17:30	186	23:30	139	30:10	108
5:40	574	11:40	279	17:40	184	23:40	138	30:20	107
5:50	558	11:50	275	17:50	183	23:50	137	30:40	106
6:00	543	12:00	271	18:00	181	24:00	136	31:00	105
6:10	528	12:10	268	18:10	179	24:10	135	31:10	104
6:20	514	12:20	264	18:20	178	24:20	134	31:30	103
6:30	501	12:30	260	18:30	176	24:30	133	31:50	102
6:40	488	12:40	257	18:40	174	24:40	132	32:10	101
6:50	476	12:50	254	18:50	173	24:50	131	32:30	100

Unit 3 Answer Key

Exercise 4.0

1. Small businesses often fail because owner has not enough capital.
2. Employment act of 1946: Federal Government should try to prevent recessions and minimize harm.

Unit Comprehension Check

1. Because tapes are time-consuming to review and good note-taking methods can be learned.
2. External: noises, movements, poorly organized lectures, etc. Internal: fatigue, negative feelings, etc.
3. No, because you will not listen as well
4. As near to the speaker as possible
5. more on main ideas
6. Raise your hand and inform the speaker.
7. for later self-testing from memory
8. No, because it may slow you down, and not all lectures are in outline form
9. A brief summary. It ties the ideas together and shows you that you understand the general concepts being presented.
10. (a) underline important information
    (b) fill in the recall column
    (c) clarify any unclear points
11. Self-testing from memory, aloud, if possible, and checking the accuracy of your answer.

Supplemental Activities

1. Computer Application in business
   a. How can a computer be used in business?
   b. What is some typical equipment?
   c. What is "software"?
   d. How expensive is a computer?
   e. Can computers be used in all kinds of business?
   The Psychology of Selling
   a. How is the psychology of selling different from regular psychology?
   b. Can I be manipulated into buying something I don't want?
   c. What type of psychologist studies this?
   d. What are some techniques to improve my selling?
   e. Do many salesmen use psychology in their pitches?

2. (a) Revltn affets life, e.g , econmc, social, etc. Revs cause chnge
   (b) Pajarito Plateau, N. Mex-canyon & mesa cntry: ruined homes of greatest prehist Indian pops in S.W.
   (c) Pple have rt to clearn air, pure wtr, and beautiful ctry
3. (a) Revolution causes What?
   (b) Where found largest prehist Indian ruins in S.W.?
   (c) Peoples Rights?

Vocabulary Development

1. unfit, not
2. antiseptic, against
3. expelled, from
4. descend, from
5. nondelivery, not
6. antinuclear, against
7. exhaust, from
8. nonsense, no
9. demoted, from
10. unexpected, not
11. nonfiction, not
12. antiaircraft, against

Skim/Scan Exercise

Skim
1. d   2. b   3. a   4. c   5. b

Scan
1. modify
2. source and service
3. forestall
4. argue
5. mirroring

PART 2

Processing Skills

The Key to Reading Mastery:
The PREP Study System

Unit 4: *The Key to Mastery: The PREP Study System*

According to a survey done by the authors, college students at a large Southern University, majoring in business, and taking twelve semester hours had to read a minimum of 1,650 pages per semester. While lectures and discussions are important sources of information, assigned readings play an important role in most courses. Therefore, being able to understand and remember what you read is an essential ability in school. In this Unit you will be introduced to the PREP study system. The four parts of the system—previewing, active reading, examine, and prompting, will be covered in detail.

A System like PREP is necessary because study-type reading is more demanding than regular reading. For example, although previewing would not be necessary for less demanding reading, it is a helpful tool when you need additional power to understand and remember material.

The PREP Study System

Reading for study purposes involves a variety of skills. If learning is to be efficient, you must apply these skills appropriately to different types of material. PREP is a study system which provides you with a number of techniques to use in reading. It provides you with a framework around which you can place these skills in order to maximize your reading and learning effectiveness.

The PREP study system provides a framework for flexible reading and studying. The parts of the system are based on the research findings of how we most effectively learn from reading material. The letters in PREP stand for:

Preview the material to determine its contents, importance, organization and to develop a purpose for reading.
Read Actively to achieve your purpose(s).
Examine the material by formulating and answering relevant questions.
Prompt yourself to remember the material by using various techniques.

Two points about the PREP system must be emphasized. First, instead of being rigidly separate, the parts of the PREP system often blend together and overlap. For example, you might be framing questions (examining) as you preview. Or, you might be prompting your memory at the same time as you read. Second, you would not use every part of the PREP system for every reading task. To do so would be as inappropriate as using your car's heater on a hot day or air conditioner when the temperature is below zero. To be an assertive, flexible reader, you choose the parts you need to use at the time, based on your purpose for reading. Table 4.1 shows how one reader might select to use different parts of the system for some typical reading tasks.

The imaginary reader previewed only the more demanding material or, in the case of the newspaper, when trying to get a general impression of certain articles. The

Table 4.1.
Applying PREP to Different Reading Tasks

	Preview	Read	Examine	Prompt
Newspaper	X	X		
Novel for Entertainment		X		
Course textbook	X	X	X	X
Poem	X	X	X	
Difficult Journal Article	X	X	X	

Examine step was used where a deeper understanding was desired, such as for the textbook. And the Prompt step was used in only one case where the reader needed to remember the material for a longer period of time.

Previewing

Previewing serves three main purposes for most reading situations. First, it provides a warm-up for your later, more careful reading. There is evidence that we need a warm-up period before we reach our full reading efficiency. Just as an athlete or musician warms up before a performance, a reader needs to prepare before attempting reading important materials. Second, previewing helps increase your reading speed. One study found that a group of students that previewed took less total time to read than a group that didn't preview. This result may be hard to believe when you consider you will be reading the same passage twice. But by previewing you are able to eliminate distractions and focus your thinking to the material to be read. Third, previewing can help your understanding of the material. To jump right into a textbook chapter or difficult selection without previewing is like beginning a trip without looking at a road map. Each part of a chapter makes more sense when you know how it fits into the larger structure. Previewing gets you actively involved, reducing the mind-wandering and day dreaming that often occur when you study.

There are five basic steps to a good preview. They are: 1. read the title; 2. look at any pictures, graphs, or charts; 3. read the introduction or opening paragraph(s) or chapter summary in order to predict what will be included in the chapter; 5. use headings and subheadings as a clue to organization. Once you become used to using these steps you will be able to preview most textbook chapters in just a few minutes. You will quickly learn that your time is well spent.

Read the Title

Titles are designed to announce the topic or subject, attract the reader and start the reader thinking. When you preview you should call to mind what you already know about the subject from past experience. Such a recall will help because recall promotes concentration and because associating new information with previous ideas is a useful learning technique.

The title may be a catch-line designed to attract your attention. Sometimes, the title may give a clue to the author's stand on the subject. For example, the title "Let's Support Vouchers for Education" tells you how the author feels about freedom of choice in education. Thus, reading the title may help you mentally prepare for the reading selection.

EXERCISE 4.0. *Making Predictions About Content Based on the Title*

Choose the topic that is most likely to be discussed in the titles listed below. Check your answers against the answer key at the end of this unit.

1. "Reaching a Decision" (psychology textbooks)
   a. The uses of decision making
   b. The steps to follow to reach a decision
   c. A short story about a problem

2. "The Steps to Success" (article from a business magazine)
   a. An article about failure in business
   b. An article on successful marketing
   c. The steps to follow to achieve success

3. "Smith Vs. the State" (law book)
   a. A case study of the legal proceedings between Smith and the State.
   b. A list of the legal rules followed in court
   c. An example of the steps to follow to sue Smith

4. "The Early South American Indians" (history book)
   a. A description of the early South American Indians
   b. A description of one South American Indian tribe
   c. A discussion of the customs of the South American Indians that are living today

Look at Any Pictures, Graphs, or Charts

The saying "a good picture is worth a thousand words" is especially true in previewing. An illustration accompanying an article can tell you much about the content. It can tell you **where** (a farm, the arctic, the sea, Mexico); **who** (children, philosophers, ethnic groups); or **when** (the present, the Renaissance, prehistory).

Pictures, illustrations, or captions may help you clarify ideas and give direction to your thinking. An article titled "The Office of the Future" might be accompanied by an artist's idea of such an office. This type of illustration would certainly contribute to your understanding of the article. A chart or graph in a textbook illustrating a complex idea serves the same purpose.

EXERCISE 4.1 *Examining Graphs and Charts*

Look at Figures 4.0 and 4.1. Try to determine what kind of information they would provide during a preview. Check the answer key for the responses to the questions below the figures.

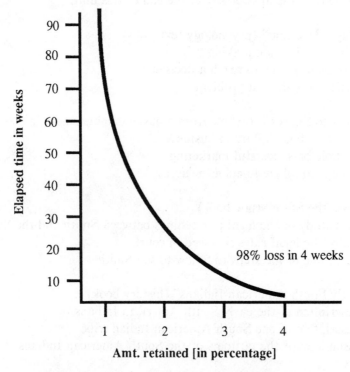

Figure 4.0 Rate of forgetting for meaningful material.

1. What do the numbers on the left side of the graph represent?

2. What do the numbers along the bottom of the graph represent?

3. What does the graph tell you about forgetting?

4. If this was an illustration in a chapter, what do you think the information surrounding the illustration would be about?

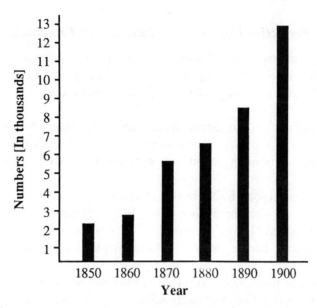

Figure 4.1 Membership in professional societies in the United States.

1. What do the numbers on the left side of the graph represent?

2. What do the numbers along the bottom of the graph represent?

3. What years are covered in this graph?

4. What is the main idea represented by this graph?

Read the Introduction or Opening Paragraph(s)

The third step of the preview is to read the introduction or lacking one, the first paragraph or two. In a magazine article, read the first paragraph. In a text, read the introduction if there is one. This section is the author's first opportunity to communicate with the reader. An experienced author will use the opening paragraph or chapter introduction for three purposes: first, to acquaint you with background facts or events needed to understand what is coming; second, to give the reason for writing—that is, what the writer is trying to accomplish in the article or chapter; and third, to give you a brief preview of what is to follow.

EXERCISE 4.2 *Predicting Content From Introductory Paragraphs*

Below are two examples of introductory paragraphs similar to ones found in introductory textbooks. Read each paragraph and decide what would most likely be found in that chapter. Check your responses against the answer key.

> The richness of one's life is largely measured by the extent of his or her personal experiences. A person with a limited perspective, a limited ability to experience the surrounding world, will necessarily have a narrow existence.

1. What would you expect to find in this chapter?
   a. A discussion of the importance of our life experiences
   b. A mathematical view of the world
   c. A discussion of the importance of becoming aware of yourself

> We live on one of nine planets orbiting around one of millions of stars in the universe. Our perspective is strongly affected by the fact that we see everything in terms of this planet that we call home. To properly study the universe, we must try to lift ourselves above this earth-bound view.

2. What would you expect to find in this chapter?
   a. A broad overview of the solar system with the earth as only one of a number of planets
   b. A view of the solar system with the earth as the center and then moving outward
   c. A progression through the planets starting with the sun
   d. Both a and b

Read the Closing Paragraph or Chapter Summary

Skip to the end of the selection, and read the last paragraph or the chapter summary. These sections are often used to draw conclusions based on the facts that have been presented, to restate the main ideas or purposes, or to summarize the important facts in the article or chapter as a brief review. Reading the first and last paragraphs will show you what the author thought was important.

EXERCISE 4.3 *Predicting Content from Ending Paragraphs*

Below are two passages from the ends of textbook chapters. Read each passage; then complete the statement that follows it. Check your responses against the answer key.

Studying for and taking tests are two highly related activities. How well you do when taking a test will depend largely on how well you studied the material. When studying, you should carefully organize your efforts, always looking for your weak areas. You should become as active as possible instead of being passive. Taking a test also requires a system. You should read instructions and questions carefully and budget your time. Essay questions are especially hard for many students; therefore, a plan of action should be developed ahead of time.

1. This chapter was about:
   a. How to study for a test
   b. How to take tests
   c. How to write essay questions
   d. all of the above

The forms we call constellations are groups of stars that seem to form various shapes. The people of Mesopotamia saw many of these shapes 5,000 years ago and named them after animals, occupations, and the like.

2. This chapter was about:
   a. The constellations, the stars and their patterns
   b. A history of Mesopotamia astronomy
   c. A description of the various occupation of people who lived 5,000 years ago

Use Headings and Subheadings as a Clue to Organization

The last step of the preview in the PREP system is to discover how the information in the material is organized. The chapter headings and subheadings, often in bold or italic type, separate the chapter into its main divisions. It is common for a reader to feel "lost" or confused even when the reading is fairly easy. This problem can be partially or even totally eliminated by looking at the organization of the material. For example, the reader may discover that the chapter is divided into four main topics, each topic containing three divisions or subheadings.

Research shows that if a reader is aware of the organization and general approach the author is going to adopt, it will be easier to understand the material and you will remember it longer. You will have some general categories to which you can relate the various facts in the chapter. Therefore, as you preview a chapter or an article, you should note, mentally or on paper, the organization used by the author.

EXERCISE 4.4 *Discovering Organization*

Below is a chapter headings and subheadings taken from a book on general aeronautics. Examine the list and answer the questions that follow. Check your responses against the answer key at the end of this unit.

A Short History of Human Flight

Bird Flight
Lighter-Than-Air Flight
  Ballooning
  Dirigibles
Heavier-Than-Air Flight
  Gliders
  The Wright Brothers
  Other Pioneers
World Wars I and II
  Aviation after World War I
  Aviation after World War II

1. What is the chapter about?

2. How many main topics are covered?

3. What are the subtopics under "Heavier-than-Air Flight?

4. What general organizational approach is the author following?
   a. A random organization
   b. A time chronology, going from the earliest development of flight to the present time
   c. A simple listing of the important milestones in the history of aviation

5. Which topic is treated more extensively, the Wright Brothers or Bird flight?

EXERCISE 4.5 *Categorizing Topics*

Below is a list of subtopics. Study the list and arrange the items by number under the main topics that follow. Check your responses against the answer key at the end of this unit.

1. Deviant Behavior and Social Control
2. Functions of the Family
3. Organization and Social Functions of Religion
4. Social Responses of Minority Group Members

5. Ethnic and Racial Minorities
6. The Nature of Deviance
7. Educational Organization and Change
8. Religion as an Institution
9. Family Structure
10. Patterns of Ethnic Relations
11. Causes of Deviance
12. Marriage, Divorce and Widowhood
13. Religion and Society in the United States
14. Education and Society
15. Ethnic and Racial Groups
16. Social Functions and Dysfunctions of Deviance
17. The Changing American Family
18. The Deviant Career
19. Prejudice and Discrimination Against Minorities
20. Religion and Social Change
21. The Social Functions of Education

Education   **Religion**   **The Family**   **Social Control**

A final word on previewing: It is useful but there are instances when it isn't necessary. Previewing is used for studying—reading that is normally done slowly, with attention to details.

Active Reading

The next step in the PREP study system is active reading. The extent of your involvement will affect how well you understand and, to a large degree, remember the material. An English instructor once gave a class some excellent advice. He said, "If you want to understand a book, you must live it." If you are reading a history textbook about the Roman conquest of northern Africa, you should "feel" the hot sun on your head and the burning sand on your feet, "smell" the sweat and leather, "hear" the swearing and grunting of the soldiers, and "see" the rough, unshaven faces of the men.

In short, you must become part of the text, not just a disinterested scanner of words. You must try to visualize that which is being written about. Sometimes this is very difficult but can be accomplished.

The kind of involvement you will have depends on the content of the material as well as your purpose for reading. In most courses you will need to become involved enough to be able to recall the important information on the different topics discussed. Your involvement begins with the preview step, when you determine the content and organization of the material. Then, once you begin to read in detail, several study techniques are available to help you become more involved.

The word "active" involves doing. When you read actively, often you use more than your eyes. You use your hands, ears and vocal cords as well. You use your hands to mark important material. You can recite what you've read using your vocal cords, mouth and ears. In short, active reading is total involvement.

Methods for Recording and Condensing the Information

Marking, notetaking, underlining, marginal notes, concept and semantic mapping and developing flash cards are some of the techniques that are used in active reading. The three main purposes of these techniques are: 1. to condense the content to its essence, 2. to help you become more actively involved with the material, and 3. to prepare the material for later review before an examination. If you keep these purposes in mind, you are more likely to use the techniques effectively. Remember that these methods, by themselves, are not likely to greatly increase your long-term memory of course material. If you only mark the material or take notes, you still will probably forget a lot of the information by exam time. These markings and note-taking techniques are tools to be used during later reviews.

Recitation is one of the most effective ways to use these tools. Briefly, recitation is self-testing. You use a cue to indicate an important piece of information. Then you try to recite—aloud, if practical, the information from memory, after which you check the accuracy of your recitation. Recitation is discussed in more detail later.

Numerous methods are available to aid in this active involvement, as well as to condense and record the information for later use. These methods can be divided into two main categories: marking the text itself and recording important information elsewhere.

Marking the Material

Underlining

Underlining is defined as any method used to emphasize key parts of a text. Usually words are either underlined with pen or pencil, or highlighted with a special marker called a highlighter. A highlighter covers the type with a transparent band of pastel ink.

A number of underlining techniques are recommended by study-skills experts. All seem to work quite well. One quick, easy-to-use technique involves highlighting (underlining) important main-idea statements and any supporting details needed to clarify those main ideas. Thus, when rereading the material, you would be able to quickly review the key points in each paragraph. Below is an example of how a paragraph might be underlined:

<u>Words have both denotative and connotative meanings</u>. The word <u>vulture denotes a large, scavenging bird</u>. But for most of us, the <u>word has</u> an <u>unappealing connotation</u>. Hence the word may be used figuratively to describe someone who lives off the misfortunes of others. On the other hand, the <u>word eagle</u>, which <u>denotes a large bird of prey</u>, usually <u>has</u> a <u>positive connotation</u> of strength and nobility. Thus, we have Eagle Scouts and the Eagle Squadron. Because there is a definitional and emotional level for many words, you should <u>be careful about your choice of words when trying to communicate</u>.

Rules for Underlining

1. Read the material to be underlined **before** underlining it.
2. Summarize the important ideas in your mind.
3. Underline just those words that convey these important ideas.
4. Review your underlining regularly.

Thus, one main-idea sentence is underlined completely and another partially; and one supporting-detail example (the vulture) is included for clarification.

Underlining is one of the fastest ways to condense textual material. It also helps you focus on the important ideas. But unlike the case with recitation, there is no strong evidence that underlining **causes** one to remember the material better. So underlining is useful for future reviews; but to help you remember the content, some kind of active recitation also is recommended.

Marginal Notes

Marginal notes are another way of marking material. Various kinds of notes can be used, such as:

1. Summary statements. The main points of the text can be condensed in the margin. For instance, a summary statement for the previous sample passage might be: connotation = feeling, denotation = meaning
2. Recitation cues. Marginal notes can also be in the form of cues to stimulate later recitation from memory. In the previous sample paragraph, a recitation cue might

be "connotative-denotative?" These words pinpoint what needs to be known in the paragraph. This type of note usually is more appropriate even when you expect to be examined on the material.

3. Symbols. Other marginal notes can be supplemented by symbols. For example, you might use a "?" when you don't understand something, a "*" for especially important points, and a "!" when you have a very interesting idea.

Recording Information Elsewhere

Numerous methods can be used to record and condense information somewhere other than on the text itself. A few of the more useful ones will be discussed.

Summary Sheets

One of the most common ways to take notes is by using some kind of summary sheet. Often the notes are either in outline form, with numerals and letters, or in some kind of indention form, where subpoints are indented under main points.

When writing summary sheets, remember that they are supposed to condense the information, not reproduce it. A summary sheet should give you a skeletal organization of the main points.

One summary sheet method very popular with students who have tried it uses two columns. It is similar to the two column note-taking strategy we discussed in Unit 3. In the left-hand column are recorded the more specific details related to the recall column entries. Part of a sample summary sheet is reproduced in Figure 4.2. The sample summary sheet has these features:

1. It is very brief. One page of a summary sheet should cover a number of pages of original material.
2. The writer uses his or her own words. This habit may help to eliminate unnecessary words and also may help the summary sheet writer to think about the material instead of slavishly copying it.
3. Abbreviations are used. Words are shortened and symbols are used to save space and writing time.
4. Indenting is used. For example, the subordinate information concerning "text norms" is indented under that heading to show the relationship.

By covering the material on the right-hand side of the summary sheet with a card or piece of paper, you can see the recitation cues only. These cues do not "give away" any answers; therefore, you must provide the missing information from memory. Then, by moving the cover sheet down a bit, you can check the accuracy of each recitation. A final point: work rapidly. By working quickly you force yourself to concentrate better and improve your chances of isolating and noting on paper the important ideas.

"Baloney Science"	Lies using scientific terms.
Eye-span	30% clarity ½" either side Av. rdr = 1.1 wds/pause Very gd. rdr = 2.7 wds/pause
Fixations	When eyes are stopped Nec. to see wds clearly Evidence: Watch someone rdg. Look in mirror

Upper rdg-rate limits	Eye-movement res:
	   Avrge = 264 wpm
	   Very gd = 810 wpm

Test norms	Rdg-test norms
	   Avrge = 260 wpm
	   V.g. = 400-500 wpm
	   Excellent = 650+ wpm

Skipping wds.	Can help ↑ rate 30% O.K. ; 50% too much (Bassin)
Regressing	Backtracking Av. coll. rdr = 15 per 100 wds.

Figure 4.2 Sample Summary Sheet.

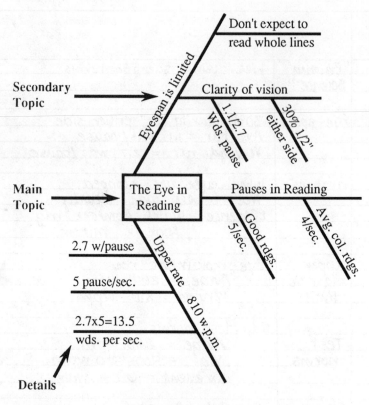

Figure 4.3 Sample map.

Semantic Mapping

A variation of summary sheets is a method called semantic mapping. This note-taking technique is likely to be used by a person who is graphically oriented. It is also useful for those people who dislike outlining or where the material doesn't lend itself to the outline format. For example, part of the information in the summary sheet example might have been mapped as shown in Figure 4.3. Lines are used to connect specific details with the related, more general pieces of information.

How To Make a Semantic Map

Step 1 Quickly skim through the section to be mapped in order to determine the main topic.

Step 2 Write the topic in the middle of a sheet of paper and put a box around it.

Step 3 Briefly think about what you already know about the topic and make some guesses about what you think might be discussed in the selection. This does three things: (a) sets the mental "stage" for reading (b) revives past experience for understanding, and (c) prepares you to actively read the material.

Step 4 Quickly read the selection to determine what secondary categories make up the main topic. An alternative to this method is to use the chapter subsection titles as the secondary categories. The maximum number of secondary categories that seem to be effective are six or seven.

Step 5 With this larger view of the selection's content in mind—and on paper, you now read the selection carefully for details. After this reading the map is completed (details added) from memory. This step provides you with immediate feedback of how well you understood and what parts of it need to be re-read (If you can't fill in the details obviously you don't know the material well enough.).

Concept Mapping

Concept mapping is a method of diagramming the meaning in an article, book, lecture, or interview. It breaks down the content of the material into a smaller number of ideas that can be focused on in order to understand the material. It helps the learner to see and understand relationships and how ideas interrelate with one another.

Similar to semantic mapping, concept maps are visual, thus we tend to remember the ideas better than we would by reading or hearing (it seems humans have the tendency to remember visual information better than most other kinds of "input", e.g., most people can remember a face better than a name. Also, the process of concept mapping helps us to understand relationships that are not easily recognized by any other method. It forces you to focus on just the key concepts or principles in an article or chapter.

Figure 4.4 is how the following paragraph might be concept mapped.

> Reading comprehension is a two-way process: The author's task is to communicate with the reader, and the reader's task, in turn, is to understand the author. Imagine the writer of a book as a football quarterback, and you, the reader, as the pass receiver. The message the author wants to get to you is the football. The quarterback throws the ball and you try to catch it. Both activities, throwing and catching, are very active processes. On a football team the quarterback and receiver work together. The same should be true of the relationship between the author of a book and the reader. The author uses certain techniques to get the message as clearly as possible to the reader. The reader should take advantage of these techniques in order to get the message as efficiently as possible.

Directions for concept mapping.

Step 1 Read the passage and underline the most important concepts.

Step 2 On a sheet of paper list the important concepts.

Step 3 Reorder the concepts from most to least general (some concepts may be equal).

Step 4 Construct the map using the rank ordered list as a guide. You may need to reorder the list as you develop your map. Choose appropriate linking words to form statements.

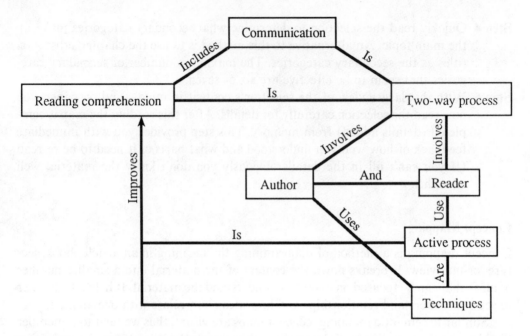

Figure 4.4 Concept map.

Step 5 Review your concept map and, if necessary, reorder some of the ideas. During the first several times that you try to develop a concept map you will probably need to re-draw it several times before you are satisfied with it.

You may want to attempt to re-draw the concept map.

Flash Cards

When very detailed knowledge of material is required, such as for some examinations, flash cards are an excellent note-taking technique. A flash card is simply a small card or piece of paper with a term, name, concept, fact, etc., on one side and the definition or explanation on the other side.

For example, a flash card could be made with *fixation* written on one side and *pauses necessary for reading* written on the other side.

Students who try this method for learning detailed information are generally enthusiastic about the results. Flash cards encourage recitation because the answers are hidden from view. The recommended method is to first try to say an answer from memory, and then turn the card over to check the answer.

Two other advantages of flash cards are their portability and flexibility. A pack of flash cards can be carried in pocket or purse. Also, the cards can be shuffled from time to time so that your memory of items is not dependent on their occurrence in a particular sequence. And as cards are learned, they can be removed from the pack so that efforts can be focused on the ones still to be learned.

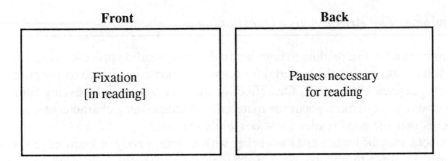

Front	**Back**
Fixation [in reading]	Pauses necessary for reading

Figure 4.5 Flash cards.

Tips About Using Flashcards

Once you have constructed a number of vocabulary flashcards, here are some suggestions for using them.

1. Carry as many as you can in your shirt pocket or handbag so that they will be on hand for review. You will find time to look at them when waiting for class, standing in line at the cafeteria or bank, waiting for a bus, sitting outside an office waiting for an appointment, and so on.
2. Look at the front of the card and try to recall as much of the information on the back as you can. You will be able to learn the information more quickly if you only try to study about seven cards at once.
3. If you are not satisfied with what you can recall, put a small check mark above the word or term. The next time you review your cards the check mark will remind you that you had trouble with that one on your previous review. When a card has more than two checks on it, it is probably time to study the card some more.
4. After a group of cards has been mastered, file them away and introduce new flashcards to your stack.
5. Whenever possible, recite the information to be learned on the card out loud. Saying the information aloud reinforces the memory trace because we hear it as well as see it.
6. Shuffle cards to avoid sequence learning (learn cards by themselves, not triggered by previous ones).

Figure 4.6

Examining: *The Art of Active Questioning*

Examining and active reading to together in the study reading process. As you actively read you are examining the material for relevant information, based on the purpose(s) you have defined for yourself. One effective way to examine is by asking yourself— and answering—questions about the material. A distinguishing characteristic of a good reader is that the good reader questions while reading.

A book may be looked at as a teacher with a certain body of knowledge you need to learn. In order to understand a teacher in the classroom, you often need to ask questions. You must also ask the "book-teacher" questions. If you become actively involved in the material you can usually find the answers, or you may discover that the book does not have the answer to your questions, in which case you must look elsewhere.

Be careful about making up questions after only briefly previewing the material; they may be too narrow and restricted. Research studies indicate that readers who make up "pre-questions" tend to mainly focus on the information that answers those questions. Thus, if your questions are too narrow, you may overlook important information in a passage. It is, therefore, recommended that you make up the questions as you read the text instead of during a preview.

By questions as you read, you are turning your reading purpose into action, into something concrete. The kinds of questions you ask will depend on the level(s) at which you are reading. Here are some examples:

1. At the literal level:
   a. What is the main idea of this paragraph?
   b. What is the main idea of this chapter?
   c. What examples are used to clarify the main idea(s)?
2. At the Interpretive level:
   a. Is the writer for or against the issue being discussed?
   b. (in fiction) What can you tell about a character from his actions?
   c. What symbols or images are used and what do they mean?
   d. How well organized is the argument?
3. At the Applied level:
   a. Can I use what I've learned?
   b. Can I apply this information to other situations?
   c. Do I understand the directions well enough to follow them?

Questions call for answers. Answers require action. And action enhances learning. If someone asks you what time it is, you respond automatically. When you formulate questions about information, you are forcing yourself to act, to learn.

The following example should help to clarify the idea of questioning at different levels of understanding. Below is a passage from *A Modest Proposal,* by Jonathan Swift:

> It is a melancholy object to those who walk through this great town or travel in the country, when they see the streets, the roads, and cabin doors, crowed with beggars of the female sex, followed by three, four or six children all in rags. . . . Whoever could find out a fair, cheap, and easy method of making these children sound, useful members of the commonwealth would deserve so well of the public as to have his statue set up for a preserver of the nation. . . .
>
> I have been assured by a very knowing American of my acquaintance in London, that a young healthy child well nursed is at a year old a most delicious, nourishing, and wholesome food, whether stewed, roasted, baked or broiled; and I make no doubt that it will equally serve in a fricassee or a ragout.
>
> I do therefore humbly offer it to public consideration that of the hundred and twenty thousand children, already computed, twenty thousand may be reserved for breed, whereof only one fourth part be males, which is more than we allow to sheep, black cattle, or swine. . . .

1. Literal Level:
   Q. What is the main idea of the first paragraph?
   A. A solution is needed for the poverty described.
   Q. What example is used to support the idea that poverty exists?
   A. Mothers begging, with numerous children, all in rags.
2. Interpretive Level:
   Q. Is the author really proposing to use children as food?
   A. Clues in this passage and elsewhere indicate that he isn't. For example, the reference to "London" may connect the cold-blooded attitude with the English authorities.
   Q. How effective is the author's cold, detached use of words like "computed" and "breed"?
   A. Each reader must answer this question based on his or her own reaction. Most critics feel that Swift's essay is a masterpiece of satire.
3. Applied Level
   Q. Can I relate the theme of this essay to present-day events?
   A. The issue of overpopulation might be one example of a present-day case where a similar essay could be written.

The Types of Questions

Literal (What does the author say?)
1. Who?
2. What?
3. When?
4. Where?
5. Why (if cause is given)?

Interpretive (What does the author mean?)
1. Define fricassee)
2. Describe (what happened?)
3. How are (these two essays alike? Different?)
4. What is (a satire)?
5. Classify (a conversion reaction)
6. What evidence can you find to support (the principle that air expands when it is heated)?
7. How can you solve (this problem)?
8. What will happen (if the ozone is depleted)?
9. What do you predict would happen (if the situation remains the same)?

Applied (How can the meaning be used?)
1. Do you agree (with the instructor)?
2. Do you believe (that this is the best way to do it)?
3. Would it be better (to do it this way)?
4. Which (procedure) is best?

Prompting: *Improving Your Memory*

A good memory is important both in school and out. In school you want to recall information for exams, and (hopefully) for a while afterwards. On a job you need to remember details related to your work. For a hobby you might need to remember certain relevant information. In fact, you use your memory in almost every facet of your life.

Forgetting

Have you ever been in trouble by realizing that right after reading a chapter from a book you could barely recall any of the points covered? Have you wondered whether you have an unusually poor memory? Well, you might want to know that such an experience is very common. In fact, studies have found that the average college reader can recall only about half of a textbook chapter immediately after reading it. Some of us naturally have better memories than others, but we all tend to forget a lot at first and then forget the rest more gradually.

The interference theory may help to explain why we forget much of what we read. One part of this theory says that we forget one piece of information because of interference from something learned afterwards. The later information "wipes out" what came before it. When you read through a chapter without pausing, the second bit of information is likely to interfere with your memory of the first, the third is likely to interfere with the second, and so forth. The same can happen, by the way, when you are listening to a lecture. Even though you understand what you read or hear at that instant, you may not be able to retain it because your attention switches to something else right away.

Memory Aids

There are a number of ways you can slow down the forgetting process. Some of the most useful methods are mentioned in this section. As you read these suggestions, ask yourself which ones you now use and which ones you might try in the future.

1. Have an Intent to Remember. Have you ever been introduced to someone and, because of nervousness or some other reason, not paid any attention to the person's name? Then, a moment later, you were embarrassed to realize you could not remember the name. In order to remember something, you should have the intent to remember; otherwise, the information is not likely to register. For example, when studying a textbook, remind yourself that you will have to remember the material in the future.

2. Organize information into logical groups. G. A. Miller of Harvard University found that the average adult can only keep about seven separate pieces of information in the immediate memory. Miller then observed it is probably not by chance that the number seven comes up often, as in the seven days of the week and the seven wonders of the world. You can use this knowledge to your advantage by grouping what you need to learn into no more than seven categories. Usually this grouping can be done by looking at how pieces of information are related to each other. Chapter headings and subheadings can be used to help divide information into chunks. Paying attention to these divisions can increase your retention, while saving time and effort. A brief exercise can show you the effectiveness of this technique. Below is a list of foods. You probably would have trouble remembering them when shopping, but organizing them into a few groups might help. Divide these foods into three logical groups.

EXERCISE 4.6. *Organizing*

steak	carrots	pork
pears	oranges	peaches
veal	beans	chicken
peas	apples	celery

Group Names: _____ _____ _____

_____ _____ _____

_____ _____ _____

_____ _____ _____

_____ _____ _____

3. Overlearn. One coat of paint may last for a while, but two coats (if done well) will last longer. Similarly, if you want to reduce forgetting, go beyond the stage of just barely learning something. Overlearn. Drill until the information is part of you. This technique is especially useful for hard-to-remember information that you need to know well.

4. Space our learning sessions. Sometimes you may have to cram all your studying into one or two long sessions right before an exam. But for the most efficient learning, space a number of shorter sessions over a longer period of time.

5. Recite. If you want to remember something, repeat it over and over again. Time and again, research has confirmed that self-testing, often called recitation, is one of the most powerful memory aids. People often recognize this fact intuitively. For example, if you are told a phone number and must remember it long enough to dial it, your natural tendency is to repeat the number aloud. Someone looking up the spelling of a word in a dictionary might say the spelling to fix it in their memory.

The recitation step is as simple as it is effective. At convenient, frequent intervals while reading, you pause and try to recite to ourselves from memory, aloud if possible, any information that you feel is worth remembering. You then quickly review the section to see whether you missed any important points, and repeat these points to yourself.

Each part of the recitation technique is based on current knowledge about the learning process. Recitations should be done at frequent intervals since the memory can generally hold only about seven new pieces (actually, seven plus or minus 2—5 to 9) at one time. Recitations should be from memory to force the information from short- to long-term storage. Recitations should be done aloud to take advantage of the hearing sense. And they should be checked for accuracy because immediate feedback about errors and omissions is very important.

Recitation is a logical step to use after the "examine" part of the PREP system. While reading material, you *examine* it by framing the important questions. To recite, use the cues you have written in the margins or in the recall column of your notes to trigger the questions and answers. You may also find recitation cues in the subheading divisions that often appear in textbook chapters. Look at a subheading and say the information contained in that section. This method works best when the section under a subheading is not too long.

Mnemonic Systems

Mnemonic Systems are memory systems that can be used to learn items that require recall but little understanding. Remembering lists of dates, names of people, or series of numbers are examples of items that can be remembered using these systems.

Before going into detail on the three basic mnemonic systems, try the three tests that follow. You will need assistance from someone who can read the test material to you at a slow and steady rate. Do not look at the test beforehand.

EXERCISE 4.7 *Memory Test*

Directions: Below are 3 lists of ten words. Have an assistant read the first list, saying first the number, then the word; after the first list has been read, write down as many words as you can remember in the order in which they were presented.

Test 1
1. barrel
2. dome
3. sunflower
4. gorilla
5. daffodil
6. zoo
7. anchor
8. bacon
9. measles
10. vinegar

Test 2

Directions: Follow the same procedure as you did in test 1 except this time, after the number and words have been read to you, write them down in reverse order.

1. moss
2. germ
3. armpit
4. mansion
5. freckle
6. ammonia
7. saucer
8. pickle
9. sardine
10. snail

If you managed to get more than 6 correct in this third test, you should skip this section. For the rest of you, there are some training techniques that can increase your performance.

The Basic Mnemonic Systems

The first system is very old, approximately 2500 years. It is called the Visual-symbol. This system works by making irrational or ridiculous pairings of two objects, forcing them into a relationship. To remember lists you develop peg words—words or images you can remember easily. You make a relationship with them to the new material. Here is a set of peg words that were developed by the British professor, Ian Hunter:

 1. bun
 2. shoe
 3. tree
 4. door
 5. hive
 6. sticks
 7. heaven
 8. gate
 9. line
10. hen

Go back to Test 3. Number 1 is a bun. One way to make the association with "cat" would be to imagine a bun sticking out of the cat's eye. Once this image has been made, develop an image with number 2 (shoe-revolver) and so on through the series of ten words. The more outrageous the relationship, the better. Do this for each number pair.

The second mnemonic system has an advantage over the first because you don't have to memorize a list of "peg" words. This system is called the *Successive-Comparison System*. It is based on the principle that if two items are fundamentally related to each other in some way, the recall of one automatically triggers the recall of the other. For example, if you can recall the name of a married friend, you may also be able to recall your friend's spouse's name as well.

The object in this system is to develop the strangest possible relationship between two words in a sequence. You might relate them visually, in terms of sound, throughout intermediate words, or through some absurd relationship. Use whatever works best for you. The only rule is that no more than two words can be related at a time. Below are examples of possible linking-thought connections for all the planets in our solar system.

Planet	Mediator Image	Connection
Mercury	Thermometer	(None)
Venus	Goddess	Thermometer falling on Venus, the Goddess
Earth	A globe of Earth	Venus holding a Globe
Mars	Marshmallow	Globe bumping into a marshmallow
Jupiter	Juke box	Marshmallow being put into a jukebox slot
Saturn	Satan	Juke box being played by Satan
Uranus	Uranium (atom bomb)	Satan standing next to an atomic bomb
Neptune	Tune	Atomic bomb transmitting a musical tune
Pluto	Cartoon dog "Pluto"	Pluto singing a tune

The final mnemonic system is the *Digit-Letter System*. In this system, you create sentences or develop words out of the items that must be memorized. For example, physicians can remember the treatments for patients with severe heart problems, in order of use, by the term MOST DAMP. These stand for:

M orphine
O xygen
S it patient up
T ourniquets
D iuretics
A minophyllin
M ore diuretics
P hlebotomy

There are only three kinds of mnemonics. All others are either variations or combinations of these three. Are they necessary? They will be helpful on occasion, but they also have limitations. We think that having some knowledge of them does have its value. Just don't overrely on them.

Summary

The PREP study system is a flexible approach that can be used to master textual material. The steps include: Preview, which involves reading the material to determine it's contents, importance, and organization. Active Reading is done to accomplish your purpose(s). This may involve either marking the text or writing notes; Examine the material by predicting and answering important questions, and; Prompting yourself to remember the material by using various techniques, the most important of which is review.

Unit Comprehension Check

1. Name three things to look at when previewing.

2. When underlining material, you should mark _____ and any important _____ needed for clarity.

3. Which note-taking method is recommended by learning and remembering very detailed, factual information?

4. What are the three levels of understanding at which you might read?

5. This unit and the other units in this book contain exercises. At what level of understanding are you working when trying to complete them?

6. Define the term "recitation."

7. How can you use chapter subheadings during the examining stage of PREP?

8. About how many separate bits of information can the average adult remember?

9. Most mnemonic devices make use of what two facts about human memory?

10. Before using a mnemonic device, you should try to find a _____ association instead.

Study Questions

1. Are you taking any courses in which mnemonics could be used?

2. Focus on one course you are taking now. What should be your reading purposes (levels of understanding) in that course?

3. For the information in this book to help you, what reading levels do you need to use?

Supplemental Activities

1. Practice forming clear, vivid mental images that can be easily associated with the object or person or term to be remembered. For example, you want to learn the meaning of electroencephalogram. The abbreviation EEG: you might then picture an egg sitting on top of a person's head, perhaps being etched with wave patterns. Recalling this image (an egg-head), remember that it had to do with the brain, and specifically with brain wave patterns.

2. Try remembering by making up sentences and stories. One can take a number of words that sound like the key words and construct a sentence or story about them.

3. Make up at least one question on each of the three comprehension levels about this unit.

EXERCISE 4.8. *Action Plan: The PREP System*

Directions: Select one or more of the ideas discussed in this Unit that you think you could incorporate into your study. Develop an Action Plan that will help you use these ideas.

Goals	Strategies to Complete Goal	Completion Date	Evaluation Procedure

Vocabulary
Development

Four Prefixes

bio   A Greek prefix meaning *life* or *live*. E.g.: biology, the study of animal and plant life.

mini   A Latin prefix meaning *less, little,* or *small*. E.g.: miniature.

poly   A Greek prefix meaning *many*. E.g.: polygons, many-sided geometric figures used in designs.

mon or *mono*   A Greek prefix meaning *one* or *single*. E.g.: monorail, a train that runs on a single rail.

Vocabulary Exercise

Study the four prefixes presented above. In the sentences below, underline the prefix and then fill in the missing word. Study the examples before you begin the exercise.

A <u>bio</u>psy is the removal of cells or tissues from a __live__ body for examination.

A <u>poly</u>glot is a person who can speak or write __many__ languages.

1. A biography on the _____ of John F. Kennedy was published last week.

2. A miniature painting is a very _____ one.

3. Biological warfare, using _____ organisms as weapons, was outlawed in the two world wars.

4. A monologue is delivered by a _____ speaker.

5. A polygamist is a man who has _____ wives.

6. The minimum wage set by Congress is the _____ amount of money that may be paid to an employee.

7. A monogamous marriage is with _____ person at a time.

8. A polyclinic is a medical facility treating diseases of _____ sorts.

9. The salesman spoke in a monotone, using only _____ unvaried pitch during the presentation.

10. Biochemistry includes the study of chemical _____ in plants and animals.

Skim/Scan
Exericse 4

1. Record your starting time.
2. Rapidly preview-skim the entire selection.
3. Record your ending time.
4. Answer the skimming questions.
5. Go on to the scanning questions.
6. Determine your skimming and scanning scores and your skimming words-per-minute rate.
7. Enter your skimming score and rate on the progress graph in the appendix at the end of this book.

Successful Jogging

	Hour	Min.	Secs.
A. Ending time:	___	___	___
B. Starting time:	___	___	___
C. A − B = Reading time:		___	___

It is simple and serene, and for a rare moment I am quiet, without a thousand thoughts in my head. My heart beats, I sweat in this adventure, this challenge. It is a statement against fumes and noise and crowds. It is joy and play—and work, too.

Becoming a successful jogger means becoming fit, incorporating regular endurance exercise into your life. Unfortunate as it may seem to the new jogger, good health and fitness cannot be stored, or even maintained, without very regular discipline and sweat, the same discipline and sweat that intimidates and defeats many new joggers, but leads to tremendous success and exhilaration in others.

The fact is, it takes work—especially at first—hard work. But not all that hard. You'll be surprised as you develop the discipline necessary to make it through the first 8, 12 weeks; jogging isn't a sport only for supermen, but for the many men and women, similar to yourself, you see jogging every day. Why jogging? Because of all the fitness activities commonly available, jogging is the cheapest, quickest and most efficient way for most people to achieve physical fitness.

The Heart of Fitness

The President's Council on Physical Fitness and Sports, the National Jogging Association and the American Medical Jogger's Association (over 1,500 jogging doctors) agree that fitness must emphasize heart, lung, and circulatory systems. *Without cardiopulmonary fitness you are not fit.*

Are you fit? Only if you are actively training your heart, lungs, and circulatory system to deliver large quantities of oxygen to all parts of your body for a minimum of thirty minutes at least four times a week. This active training is the *only* type of exercise associated with reducing heart disease, the number one killer in America, and is exercise that will lead you to feel and look better since it pumps blood, trains the heart, and burns calories.

Published by the National Jogging Association in cooperation with the President's Council on Physical Fitness and Sports and the Consumer Information Center.

The ability to perform endurance work is achieved through long-slow-gentle-progressive training that causes you to sweat and get your heart beating for regular, sustained periods of time. With proper training and patience nearly everyone can achieve this level of physical fitness by jogging. Walking is an excellent way to train, but since it is less demanding than jogging; it requires more time to obtain equal benefits. Other sports that get your heart pumping are also excellent ways to train: cycling, swimming, rowing, cross-country skiing, dancing, etc. Not everyone will discover the satisfaction they're looking for from jogging; the key to success is finding a sport that you enjoy doing, and then doing it regularly, not only for recreation, but with the intention of getting vigorous exericse.

Is Jogging for You?

Jogging is the most democratic, least expensive, quickest way to achieve physical fitness. Is it for you? Only a number of weeks and months of jogging exploration can begin to answer that question. Obviously, from watching the recent jogging explosion, the answer is "yes" for many.

Jogging is popular because it requires nothing more than a good pair of shoes, a front door to walk out of, and a willing spirit. It is the most effective way to train the cardiovascular system because it uses the largest muscles in the body, the leg muscles, demanding large quantities of blood and oxygen. This demand is what requires the heart to work harder than usual, and the heart, like any muscle, becomes stronger, more efficient, more resilient when trained correctly.

Slowly, progressively increase your training in small doses (no more than a mile or 10% increase in distance a week) until you are able to achieve your **target-heart-rate** for thirty minutes, four times a week, without excessive fatigue or injury. And not just for a week or two, but week in and week out, for fitness cannot be stored. The benefits you gain from training will be lost in just a few weeks if you stop.

While your cardiovascular system is being trained other parts of your body will also be getting in shape. You'll be burning extra calories (there are 3,500 calories in a pound of fat—100 calories can be burned while covering a mile on foot; over the course of a year a lot of extra calories can be burned), and, surprisingly to the new jogger, jogging will soon become a real pleasure. However, the pleasures of jogging aren't discovered while it's still associated with fatigue, guilt, flab and whipping yourself into shape. Only once the base level is achieved and you are able to cover thirty minutes of low-key regular jogging will the real surprises begin to unfold. In over-enthusiasm the new jogger often tries to rush to this goal—and, tragically, this is when many well-intentioned programs are lost in pain, frustration, and failure.

Before You Begin

Nearly anyone can jog by taking it slowly enough and learning to enjoy it.

In order to guarantee that you're in good shape to begin a new exercise program, we recommend that if you're over 30 you check with your doctor. If you are over 40, a maximal-stress-treadmill test is suggested in order to make sure you aren't one of the 10–15% of the American population with undiagnosed heart disease. If you have a disease which stands in the way of a vigorous program, regular endurance exercise under correct medical supervision can be very beneficial.

Another suggestion that will help you get off to a good start is to go where other joggers gather and watch some experienced men and women put in some miles. You'll notice two types of jogger: the person carrying strain and tension throughout the entire body, and the jogger who just glides along, looking as though jogging's enjoyable. Which type do you want to be? While you're jogging, stay relaxed and look good; freedom of movement you get from this type of motion will contribute tremendously to your feeling of well-being.

Don't try to stop a jogger in midstride to discuss jogging, but if you can walk with a person who's cooling down, or perhaps discuss jogging with someone you know, you'll be able to discover some helpful hints about jogging.

Estimating Your Target Heart Rate

By knowing what your target heart rate is, you can maximize the effectiveness of your jogging. To figure out what your target pulse count should be, use the following formula:

Write down 220.

Subtract your age.

This number represents your maximum heart rate, per minute.

Multiply this number by 0.70 (0.75 if you have been jogging regularly for a good period of time; 0.65 if you smoke more than 4 cigarettes a day, if you are more than 20 pounds over optimum weight—don't include pregnancy gain here—or if you are recovering from surgery or a serious illness).

This number represents the number of times your heart can probably beat safely per minute and still get sufficient aerobic training. This is your target heart rate.

Divide your target heart rate by 6.

This number represents a 10 second pulse count and is your target pulse count. You should monitor your pulse frequently when you begin to jog, and keep it within a couple of beats of this target pulse. Measure your pulse by interrupting your run for a few moments. Some have difficulty checking a wrist pulse; if you do check the pulse in your neck by pressing against your carotid artery. If your pulse beat is consistently way above this, your heart is working too hard. If it is consistently below this, your heart is not working hard enough to get aerobic training effects without additional distance, although your leg muscles and abdominals are getting a good workout.

Beginning

The jogging program outlined here can be performed by most males and females of all ages. Perhaps the most difficult skill to learn in the hobby-sport of jogging is that of pace, discovering exactly how fast to jog and how rapidly to progress. Because individuals are at different levels of fitness, some will be able to progress through an entire 12-week program in a few weeks; others may take months before they can successfully complete our minimum definition of fitness. This is up to you. The important thing is not to hurry. Hurrying and rushing are the building blocks of failure. Don't hold yourself back if you're ready for the next step, but don't feel compelled to move to the next step if you're not thoroughly familiar and comfortable with your current schedule. Knowing when to speed up, when to slow down, and when to stop is the essential art of jogging and physical well-being.

The pace at which you jog should not leave you breathless. This means you should always be able to pass the so-called *Talk Test*. If you are pushing too hard to carry on a conversation while jogging you are not taking full advantage of your training because you are working harder than your muscles can adapt to new stress. Slow down. And remember, sprinting at the end of your jog is not a good idea. Your run is all over at that point and you should finish with ease and consistency. Effective training will come through long-slow-distance, breaking up your jogs with walking as needed. The experienced jogger will finish a workout with 5 to 10 minutes of relaxed walking, refreshed rather than fatigued.

As strange as it may seem, the body adapts to stress during your rest periods, not during jogging itself. Because rest and relaxation are so important to successful jogging we recommend six days of work a week and one full day of rest. The schedule of your six work days should alternate between *hard (long)* and *easy (short)* days, thus allowing plenty of rest between your longer workouts.

As you become a skilled jogger, you may decide you only want to work out 4 days a week, but we recommend the beginner devote some time to his or her new schedule six days a week since it is too familiar for the new jogger to miss a day, then postpone jogging one more day, and then another until the whole program is forgotten.

Including warming up, cooling down, changing clothes, and some stretching an ideal jogging program allows a full hour for exercise six days a week, right from day one—although, certainly, the first few days and weeks will not require much of the hour for jogging.

Get into the habit and schedule of regular, long, endurance exercise. An excellent motivational tool is a jogging diary, available through NJA for $1.50. With it you can plan tentative schedules a week in advance as well as record your actual progress. As you become a successful jogger you will be amused and fascinated by the entries you made during the first few months. Each workout should be preceded by 10–15 minutes of warm-up and slow stretching exercises. Stretching should also be repeated at the end of your workout.

Shoes and Clothes

One of the attractions of jogging is that it requires very little equipment. Good jogging shoes are essential. Do not try to substitute a tennis or gym shoe as they do not offer the support, cushioning, and stability that are found in a good training shoe designed to take the shock of long-distance jogging on paths as well as roadways. Once you get a good pair of jogging shoes, wear them only for jogging and walking, not for court games or everyday recreation. This kind of use causes them to wear down. Imbalances caused by a wornout jogging shoe can lead to foot, knee, even lower-back pain.

Shoes should fit perfectly right from the beginning; a well fitting jogging shoe needs no breaking in. Most joggers like the feel and comfort of a wool or cotton athletic sock. High socks prevent adequate heat loss. When trying on a new shoe, make sure you try on both; lace them up well and wear them around the store for a few minutes. There should be no slip in the heel.

Criteria to use in selecting shoes include the following:

1. Soles with a tough outer layer of rubber and a softer mid-sole that runs the full length of the shoe.
2. Soles should be flexible.
3. Wide, stable heel and a full heel cup in the uppers.
4. The sole area of the shoe under the foot arch should give firm support, but must be flexible.
5. A slight heel lift that is somewhat like the lift given by heels in street shoes.
6. Built in arch supports if needed.
7. Outside uppers that will remain soft with aging, repeated soaking from sweat, wet grass and rain (nylon does this best).
8. The right size.

Remember, good shoes are your best insurance against blisters, sore feet, ankles, knees, and will contribute significantly to getting your program off to a good start.

The most important thing about your jogging outfit is that it must be comfortable. Experimentation will lead you to what's right for you. An expensive jogging suit may be exactly what you need, but for others a T-shirt and a pair of shorts will be fine. Women should avoid support garments or clothing that restrict blood flow in any way. Joan Ullyot, MD, a world-class marathoner, states emphatically that bouncing does not cause damage to breasts or any female organ. A woman may wear a bra for comfort, but it is not necessary physiologically. Men, in the same manner, need not fear "swinging loose." Initially the free movement you feel without traditional support can be discomforting, but will usually be overcome in a few days.

Do not wear rubberized or plastic clothing while jogging to increase sweating as this will not cause any permanent loss of body weight and can be harmful. Rubberized or plastic clothing can cause your temperature to rise to a dangerous level. When sweat cannot evaporate body temperature increases and this causes more sweating which can lead to excessive dehydration and salt loss. This can result in possible heat stroke or heat exhaustion.

During cold weather jogging wear several layers of light clothing so you can add and subtract as you go. One hundred percent wool is the best insulator since it retains nearly all its warming quality even when wet. The synthetics, as nice as they may look, can actually rob you of needed body heat.

When?

Any time, day or night, that you are actually able to get in the habit of doing it, is the best time for you. Many people find that jogging first thing in the morning provides the structure they need. Others have replaced their traditional lunch hour with an hour of jogging and find that thirty or more minutes of new oxygen to the brain is an invigorating way to begin the afternoon. This often has the double advantage of exercise plus reducing caloric intake. Other joggers find jogging at the end of the work day to be a great way to relax and get revitalized for the evening ahead. Experiment with different times to find which time of day suits you best.

It's important to note that even though your friend down the street seems to be able to jog under any condition and in an old pair of bedroom slippers, you probably won't be able to copy him. Most people find that jogging after meals is uncomfortable and therefore not a good idea. Some people report that exercise right before eating helps to cut appetites.

Bad weather and pollution? Try to stay as far as you can from busy roadways, and don't jog when smog alerts are severe. If you develop a headache or nausea while jogging, you know it's a good time to slow down your jogging until the air clears. Perhaps walking during these extreme periods is a good substitute for more vigorous exercise.

It may be difficult to learn to jog in a wide range of temperatures and conditions, but joggers do it from the frozen arctic tundra to equatorial jungles. It takes acclimatization and, like all jogging, a gentle approach that will allow you to adjust slowly.

Jogging in bad weather can heighten satisfaction for many. Of course, prudence is your best adviser, and there are a number of days every year when a wise jogger will take an extra rest day and wait for a break in the weather.

If you like jogging in the rain, go ahead and get wet; it's the cold, not the wet, that may run you into trouble. Change into dry clothes as soon as you complete your run. If jogging in the rain is just too unpleasant, take the day off or find a substitute like an indoor track or jumping rope.

Extreme heat can be a problem. Jog during the coolest part of the day. Search out shade, wear a hat, and most importantly, make sure you drink plenty of water. The old myth about not drinking during exercise has been completely exploded. If you are going to sweat heavily, you should drink right before jogging and then make sure to drink another cup or more of water at least every twenty minutes. Water, water, and more water during hot weather. Dehydration can be very dangerous.

Conclusion: Work, Sweat, Tedium, and Fun *understand overcome*

Jogging is a difficult sport. It requires discipline, time, commitment. Its accomplishment involves occasional discouragement, embarrassment, fatigue, injury, guilt, and failure. These are the barriers which you are up against and which take considerable time to understand and overcome. The rewards of jogging are as numerous: fitness, better looks, adventure, challenge, joy, play, overall well-being. Although jogging requires patience and can seem a harsh taskmaster at times, it would not be as popular as it obviously is if the rewards weren't rather immediate and very satisfying. People wouldn't jog for long unless they soon began to reap some very significant good feelings. This is important to remember, because every single jogging day will not be a joy. It's what the single days add up to that proves the pudding. You may find after 12 weeks that jogging's just not for you. However, far many more people find that they look back upon their first 12 weeks with real satisfaction and look forward to continuing.

Skimming Questions: *Circle the letter of the best answer.*

1. During hot weather, you should:
   a. drink water right before jogging
   b. drink water right after jogging
   c. drink water right before and during jogging
   d. not drink water right before, during, or right after jogging

2. The most important item for jogging is:
   a. a good pair of jogging shoes
   b. a wide-brimmed hat
   c. loose-fitting shorts
   d. a support garment

3. After jogging, you should:
   a. be breathless
   b. sit down right away
   c. be able to talk
   d. sprint

4. The author suggests that you jog:
   a. in the morning
   b. in the evening
   c. during your lunch hour
   d. any time that suits you

5. During cold weather, you should:
   a. not jog
   b. wear many layers of light clothing
   c. wear rubberized clothing
   d. wear a single layer of heavy wool clothing

Scanning Questions

1. ___WHAT___ percent of the American population has undiagnosed heart disease.

2. To become fit, you must exercise for a minimum of ___15___ minutes during each exercise period.

3. A maximum-stress treadmill test is recommended if you are over ___40___ years old.

4. A beginner should jog ___THREE___ days a week.

5. The number ___220___ minus your age represents your maximum heart rate.

Time-Rate Conversion Chart

Min:Sec	WPM	Min:Sec	WPM	Min:Sec	WPM	Min:Sec	WPM	Min:Sec	WPM
1:00	2950	7:00	421	13:00	227	19:00	155	25:00	118
1:10	2529	7:10	412	13:10	224	19:10	154	25:10	117
1:20	2213	7:20	402	13:20	221	19:20	153	25:20	116
1:30	1967	7:30	393	13:30	219	19:30	151	25:30	116
1:40	1770	7:40	385	13:40	216	19:40	150	25:40	115
1:50	1609	7:50	377	13:50	213	19:50	149	25:50	114
2:00	1475	8:00	369	14:00	211	20:00	148	26:00	113
2:10	1362	8:10	361	14:10	208	20:10	146	26:10	113
2:20	1264	8:20	354	14:20	206	20:20	145	26:20	112
2:30	1180	8:30	347	14:30	203	20:30	144	26:30	111
2:40	1106	8:40	340	14:40	201	20:40	143	26:40	111
2:50	1041	8:50	334	14:50	199	20:50	142	26:50	110
3:00	983	9:00	328	15:00	197	21:00	140	27:00	109
3:10	932	9:10	322	15:10	195	21:10	139	27:10	109
3:20	885	9:20	316	15:20	192	21:20	138	27:20	108
3:30	843	9:30	311	15:30	190	21:30	137	27:30	107
3:40	805	9:40	305	15:40	188	21:40	136	27:40	107
3:50	770	9:50	300	15:50	186	21:50	135	27:50	106
4:00	738	10:00	295	16:00	184	22:00	134	28:00	105
4:10	708	10:10	290	16:10	182	22:10	133	28:10	105
4:20	681	10:20	285	16:20	181	22:20	132	28:20	104
4:30	656	10:30	281	16:30	179	22:30	131	28:30	104
4:40	632	10:40	277	16:40	177	22:40	130	28:40	103
4:50	610	10:50	272	16:50	175	22:50	129	28:50	102
5:00	590	11:00	268	17:00	174	23:00	128	29:00	102
5:10	571	11:10	264	17:10	172	23:10	127	29:10	101
5:20	553	11:20	260	17:20	170	23:20	126	29:20	101
5:30	536	11:30	257	17:30	169	23:30	126	29:30	100
5:40	521	11:40	253	17:40	167	23:40	125		
5:50	506	11:50	249	17:50	165	23:50	124		
6:00	492	12:00	246	18:00	164	24:00	123		
6:10	478	12:10	242	18:10	162	24:10	122		
6:20	466	12:20	239	18:20	161	24:20	121		
6:30	454	12:30	236	18:30	159	24:30	120		
6:40	443	12:40	233	18:40	158	24:40	120		
6:50	432	12:50	230	18:50	157	24:50	119		

Unit 4 Answer Key

Exercise 4.0

1. b 2. c 3. a 4. a

Exercise 4.1 (Figure 4.0)

1. amount retained
2. number of elapsed weeks
3. forgetting occurs rapidly
4. forgetting and memory

Figure 4.1

1. numbers, in thousands
2. year
3. 1850–1900
4. There has been a steady growth in professional societies.

Exercise 4.2

1. a 2. a

Exercise 4.3

1. d 2. a

Exercise 4.4

1. history of Aviation
2. Four
3. Gliders; the Wright Brothers; Other pioneers
4. b
5. Probably "Bird Flight", since that is one of the main topics

Exercise 4.5

Education: 7, 14, 21
Religion: 3, 8, 13, 20
Family: 2, 9, 12, 17
Social Control: 1, 4, 5, 6, 10, 11, 15, 16, 18, 19

Exercise 4.6

Meat	Vegetables	Fruit
steak	celery	apples
veal	peas	peaches
pork	carrots	pears
chicken	beans	oranges

Unit Comprehension Check

1. (a) provides a warm-up
   (b) increases overall reading rate
   (c) can help your understanding
2. Main ideas; details
3. flash cards
4. literal; interpretive, applied
5. interpretive
6. reciting the information to be learned aloud
7. Turn them into questions to read for the answer to
8. 7 plus or minus 2, e.g., 5 to 9
9. (a) associating what you want to know with something you already know is a powerful memory aid.
   (b) We remember best what we can visualize.
10. Meaningful

Vocabulary Development

1. biography, life
2. miniature, small
3. biological, live
4. monologue, single
5. polygamist, many
6. minimum, smallest
7. monogamous, one
8. polyclinic, many
9. monotone, one
10. biochemistry, life

Skim/Scan Exercise

Skim
   1. c   2. a   3. c   4. d   5. b

Scan
   1. 10–15   2. 30   3. 40   4. six   5. 220

Unit 5

Reading for Ideas and Details

Unit Five: *Reading for Ideas and Details*

Reading comprehension is a two-way process: The author's task is to communicate with the reader and the reader's task, in turn, is to understand the author. Imagine the writer of a book as a football quarterback, and you, the reader, as the pass receiver. The message the author wants to get to you is the football. The quarterback throws the ball and you try to catch it. Both activities, throwing and catching, are very active processes. On a football team the quarterback and the receiver work together. The same should be true of the relationship between the author of a book and the reader. The author uses certain techniques to get the message as clearly as possible to the reader. The reader should take advantage of these techniques in order to get the message as effectively as possible.

Understanding How Information is Organized

When you are studying written material your understanding is helped along if you know how it is going to be presented. In fact, most types subject areas has its' own unique method for presentation. For example, if you are reading a novel you know that most, if not all, novels are organized around certain key elements. Knowing this should help you keep the facts straight and ultimately help your understanding. Some of the elements that are in most novels include: 1. Setting, time, place, major characters; 2. A beginning event; a problem that starts the story; 3. how the character(s) react to the problem; 4. how the characters try to reach their goal or solve the problem; and, 5. the solution or lack of solution to the problem.

If you read a lot of stories, understanding of the story structure is basically intuitive. However, if you don't read much, your understanding is helped if you know that most, if not all, novels follow this same formula.

When reading textbook material it helps understanding if you are aware that each author follows a more or less standard approach to presenting information. In fact, each subject matter has its own special approach for presenting information.

One way that you can use to understand this structure is to know how the author has organized each chapter. A technique that many students have found useful for this purpose is **Semantic Mapping.**

As you recall from Unit Four, in Semantic Mapping the reader draws in graphic form the organization of the chapter on a sheet of paper prior to a more careful reading. By drawing the organization on a sheet of paper the reader is better able to "see" how the material is being presented and is therefore better able to follow the flow of facts and ideas.

Figure 5.0 is an example of how this has been done for a chapter in a nutrition textbook.

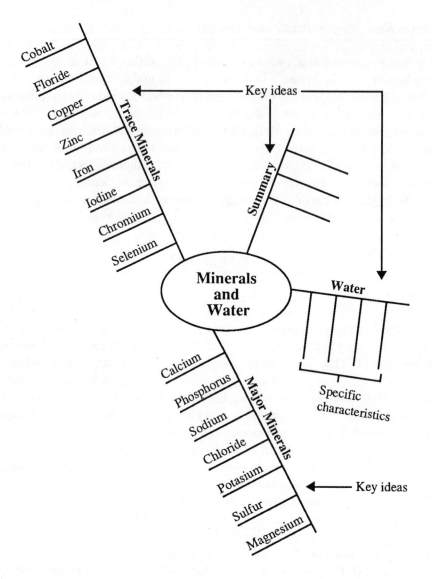

Figure 5.0

You can see from this "map" that the chapter is organized into three main sections with a summary. Since the chapter is about minerals and water you can see that the main topics discussed are minerals and water and that minerals are divided into major and trace elements. With this graphic summary in mind (and on paper) the reader can now read the chapter with a clearer view of how all of the facts that will be presented fit into the goal of the chapter.

This semantic map was developed by using the major and minor headings that are found in most textbook chapters. The chapter title is placed in the center of the page and the major headings are radiated out from the center with the secondary headings drawn onto the major headings.

By developing the map prior to a more careful reading the reader can not only see how the topic is organized but can begin to make some intelligent guesses as to what will be discussed, including the relative importance the author is placing on each of the topics. As you can see from figure 5.0, the author seems to place more emphasis on the minerals than on the water. This knowledge can be helpful for later study since there may be more test questions dealing with minerals than water.

Understanding Main Ideas

Everything we read has a main idea or ideas. Having the ability to identify the main idea is often a process of inference, a higher level thinking skill. Look at the drawing in figure 5.1. Try to "infer" the main idea.

The "main idea" of this picture is, *The Contents of a Woman's Purse*. If you are able to infer this main idea you probably had no problem determining that item number 4 was a lipstick case and that item number 8 was a hair pin. Unless you were able to determine the main idea you may have been stumped regarding these items. Once you determine the main idea, the facts seem to make more sense.

Reading Paragraphs

When you are studying written material, how aware are you of the paragraph divisions? If you aren't paying attention to the way the writer has divided the content, you are missing some useful information. Paragraphs are thought units. Each paragraph usually represents a writer's attempt to develop an idea or part of an idea.

Sentences are the building blocks of paragraphs. You may be able to improve your reading comprehension by learning to tell how each sentence is functioning in a paragraph. There are two main kinds of sentences: main-idea sentences and supporting-detail sentences. Each of these kinds of sentences serves an important role in a paragraph.

Figure 5.1

Main-Idea Statements

Writers usually build each paragraph around a single main idea or, in some cases, a couple of very closely related main ideas. At times the main idea will be stated at or near the beginning of the paragraphs, at or near the end of the paragraph, or both. In some cases, the main-idea statement may be elsewhere in the paragraph or may not appear at all (note figure 5.6). For example, the first sentence in this paragraph (the one you're reading) states the main idea of the paragraph.

Supporting Details

The supporting details in a paragraph are more specific than the main-idea statement or statements. Supporting details elaborate on the main-idea statement in some way. For example, a supporting detail may give an illustration or an example, make a comparison, show a contrast, use an analogy, give a definition, or in some other way clarify the main idea. For instance, the examples given in this paragraph are supporting details.

Paragraph Patterns

Sometimes the main idea is stated early in a paragraph, but this is not always the case. In fact, there are five patterns that are commonly used. If you can analyze paragraphs to determine their patterns, you are well on your way to becoming an active, effective reader.

The five patterns are: 1. **deductive** (main idea early); 2. **inductive** (main idea late); 3. **central** (main idea near the middle); 4. **mixed** (main idea early and repeated near the end) and 5. **descriptive or narrative** (only details—no main idea directly stated). Below are examples of each paragraph pattern with a diagram representing its structure. The main idea sentences are in boldface type.

1. Deductive pattern.

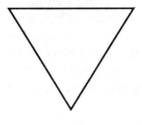

Figure 5.2

Stone (space matter)

You don't have to worry about being hit by a meteorite. Most meteors are about the size of a pea and burn up in the atmosphere. Only rarely does a large one, called a fireball, hit the earth. Ancient Chinese records tell about a fireball killing ten people, but no deaths have been recorded in modern times.

2. Inductive pattern.

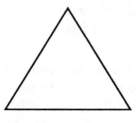

Figure 5.3

They were desert nomads who settled on the eastern edge of the Mediterranean Sea. They lived off the sea, first building small fishing boats, then larger ones. Soon they were sailing up and down the Mediterranean, trading vigorously with other countries. They even sailed their seventy-five foot craft into the Atlantic. **They were the Phoenicians.**

3. Central pattern.

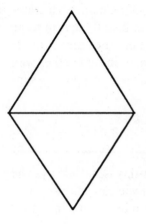

Figure 5.4

This pattern is used when the details in the paragraph are closely related and there is an advantage to having some of the details before and some after the statement of the main idea.

About the middle of the fifteenth century, European scholars began again to study the writings of the ancient Greeks and Romans. Interest gradually spread into many fields, like art, music, science, and exploration. **This period, covering many centuries, is called the Renaissance, meaning "rebirth".** Some of the greatest figures in Western history lived during this time: daVinci, Michelangelo, Copernicus, Columbus, Shakespeare, to name just a few.

4. Mixed pattern.

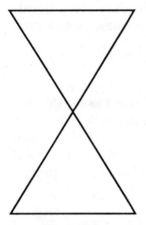

Figure 5.5

With this pattern, the main idea is stated at the beginning of the paragraph and then repeated at the end:

In prehistoric times the types of dinosaurs were as varied as the types of animals are today. There were giant plant eaters like the Brontosaurus and Diplodocus. There were fierce predators like Allosaurus and Tyrannosaurus. There were flyers and swimmers. There was the rhinosaurus-like Triceratops, and there was the Stegosaurus, with giant plates on its back. And there were tiny dinosaurs no larger than a small rodent. **Just like today, there was an animal to fit every space.**

5. Descriptive pattern.

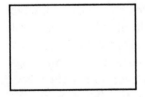

Figure 5.6

This form, where no main idea is directly stated, is used when the author is describing something like a person, scene, or event:

Looking down the runway, the pilot eases the plane's throttle forward and feels the engine respond. At first the small plane moves slowly but then quickly gathers speed. When the airspeed indicator shows 55 miles per hour, the pilot gently pulls backward on the control yoke, lifting the nosewheel off the ground. An instant later the plane is buoyed by solid air.

EXERCISE 5.0 *Distinguishing Paragraph Patterns.*

Reading specialists generally agree that one way to improve reading skills is by learning to distinguish between main ideas and supporting details. Read each of the following six passages of textbook material. Decide which sentence or sentences express the main idea, if, indeed, there is a main-idea sentence. Underline any main-idea sentences you find. Then draw the pattern diagram that shows the form of the paragraph. Check your responses against the answer key at the end of this unit.

Reading specialists generally agree that one way to improve reading skills is by learning to distinguish between main ideas and supporting details. Read each of the following six passages of textbook material. Decide which sentence or sentences express the main idea, if, indeed, there is a main-idea sentence. Underline any main-idea sentences you find. Then draw the pattern diagram that shows the form of the paragraph. Check your responses against the answer key at the end of this unit.

Diagram

1. It has often been said that *informed* people are *free* people . . . are slow to panic, difficult to fool or enslave. So it is good to know that this year Americans are thoughtfully turning the pages of 350,000,000 books drawn from public libraries alone. Each goes out from its little niche in the treasure house . . . leaves its imprint on a free mind . . . and returns to its niche, ready for the next American who wants to *know*.

2. Take a letter, Miss Jones. "To whom it may concern: Thanks for your help. Thanks for spelling better than I do, and for knowing what I don't. Thanks for remembering when a collective noun takes a singular verb, and for wearing a flower on rainy mornings, and for being cheerful when I am not, and for knowing how to work hard and still be human."

3. With a bucket of red paint for gaiety and $300 in cash, Frank Woolworth opened his store. At first there were only a few things on the counters. But each week there were more. For a wonderful thing began to happen. The more people bought with their dimes, the more their dimes were able to buy. Frank Woolworth's little red store had proved a great American truth—that the power of people's nickels and dimes, working together, can accomplish anything.

4. The trumpeter swan came very close to extinction. In 1938, the population had fallen to about 2,000 birds. By 1949 only 500 were left in the U.S. Their numbers continued to drop, and only recently has this beautiful bird started to make a comeback.

5. The job is difficult and the hours long. The training is exacting and the responsibilities heavy. Yet, 300,000 American women have chosen the challenging profession of nursing. They comfort patients, help doctors, and aid in a thousand ways to smooth the operation of hospitals across the nation.

6. Some farms deep in hill country do not have electricity. They lack telephones. Good roads are rare. Sanitary facilities often are very primitive. Homes are poorly heated and dimly lit.

Summary

In most cases a writer will consciously try to organize the material so that it can be well understood. The reader should just as actively work at analyzing the information. One approach is to think of each paragraph in terms of main-idea statements and supporting details. There are five paragraph patterns that are commonly used.

Unit Comprehension Check

If you can answer these questions, you have retained many of the main points of this Unit at the literal level.

1. The quarterback-receiver analogy (opening paragraph) illustrates what main idea?

2. Why are paragraphs important?

3. What are the two main kinds of sentences found in most paragraphs?

4. What are the five main paragraph patterns?

Supplemental Activity

For additional practice, you might analyze the patterns of some paragraphs in your textbooks. You could look to see whether each author has a particular pattern that is used most of the time. You could also try to determine if different subjects seem to have different styles.

EXERCISE 5.1 *Action Plan*

Directions: Determine at least one idea from this Unit that you would like to begin using. Develop an Action Plan to incorporate that idea into your reading.

Goals	Strategies to Complete Goal	Completion Date	Evaluation Procedure

Vocabulary Development

Roots

A root is the main element of a word. Our English words are often built on Latin or Greek root words. To these we can add prefixes (beginnings) or suffixes (endings). For example, you could take the root word *read* and add both a prefix and suffix to get the word *unreadable*.

Sometimes the same word part can serve as a root or prefix, depending on the circumstances. For example, the word part *dict* can be a prefix (*dict*aphone) or a root (e*dict*).

Four Root/Prefix Parts

phot	A Greek word part meaning *light*. E.g.: A *photoflash* bulb provides *light* for taking a picture.
dict	A Latin word part meaning *say, speak,* or *word*. E.g.: A *dictaphone* is used to record words that are transcribed later by a stenographer; an e*dict* is a proclamation issued by an authority.
mit, mis	A Latin word part meaning *send*. E.g.: A *missive* is a letter or message; the president will *transmit* a message sending best wishes.
clud, clus	Versions of the Latin word part meaning to *close* or *shut*. E.g., The visitor was *excluded* from the meeting when the door was closed and locked.

Vocabulary Exercise

Study the word parts presented above. In the sentences below, add the appropriate word part to the italicized word in each sentence. Write the complete word on the line following the sentence. Study the examples before you begin the exercise.

Conclusive evidence in a trial shuts out any doubt the jury may have regarding the defendant. _conclusive_

A *missile* is a projectile sent from one place to another. _missile_

1. A high-intensity electric light called a ~~ELEeTRiTY BoX's~~ *flood* is used to create an illuminated area for the director. _ORCHESTRA_

2. To *con* ~~meetion~~ _e_ a speech is to complete the presentation. _ov PuBLie_

3. A _FREDOM_ *tator's* word is the same as law is in a democratic country. _of SPEECh_

4. The operator used a *trans* _SISTOR_ *ter* to send a message to the stranded travelers. _CEDALIGHl_

5. The *re* _UNIDET_ _e_ shut himself off from family and friends. _____

6. Scientists use a _TRANCESTER_ *detector* that can detect small amounts of light not visible to the naked eye. _____

7. A _UP_ *tum* is a judge's statement of opinion on a legal point of law. _OR DOWN_

Skim/Scan
Exercise 5

1. Record your starting time.
2. Rapidly preview-skim the entire selection.
3. Record your ending time.
4. Answer the skimming questions.
5. Go on to the scanning questions.
6. Determine your skimming and scanning scores and your skimming words-per-minute rate.
7. Enter your skimming score and rate on the progress graph in the appendix at the end of this book.

Suicide

by Elton B. McNeil and Zick Rubin

```
                                    Hour  Min.  Secs.

A. Ending time:          ____  ____  ____

B. Starting time:        ____  ____  ____

C. A − B = Reading time: ____  ____
```

In ancient times suicide was considered a heroic way of dealing with an impossible life situation. The Japanese hero confronted with an intolerable "loss of face" committed Hara-Kiri, just as the Greek or Roman warrior fell on his own sword to save his honor. The social, religious, and legal reactions to suicide have changed over the years. At first it was accepted as a natural event; then it was condemned by the church; next it was defined as a criminal act; and finally it was described as a product of mental derangement. For centuries the suicide of religious martyrs was glorified as an example of dedication to the highest of principles. Later, there was an attempt to design a variety of "punishments." The dead people's property might be confiscated; they might be denied an honorable burial; or they might be hanged for the crime of suicide. In extreme cases, the body of the suicide might be dismembered; the offending hand was buried in one place and the body was buried in another to separate "murderer" from "victim."

The Measure of Suicide

It is difficult to find reliable body counts of suicides, and of course the rate at which people kill themselves differs from place to place and from time to time. Nonetheless, you can get some idea of the size of the problem if you realize that every 30 minutes someone in the United States commits suicide. And for every successful suicide there are probably another ten attempts that fail. Suicide ranks tenth among leading causes of death for adults, and it is third as a cause of death among college students.

Suicide statistics are notoriously unreliable not only because shame is attached to the act but also because people who successfully kill themselves have often tried and failed several times before. One survey of patients at a suicide prevention center showed that 60 percent of those who finally managed to kill themselves had made previous attempts. Also, what looks like an accident may actually be deliberate suicide. We know that more than 55,000 persons die each year in automobile accidents, but no

From pp. 503–507 in THE PSYCHOLOGY OF BEING HUMAN, 2nd Edition by Elton B. McNeil and Zick Rubin. Copyright © 1977 by Marjorie B. McNeil and Zick Rubin. Reprinted by permission of Harper & Row, Publishers, Inc.

one knows how many of these drivers consciously or unconsciously set up the conditions for a fatal crash. When car accidents were carefully examined in one study, up to one-half of the dead drivers had numerous previous driving offenses; over half had also been drinking; and nearly half were suffering from depression. Such self-destructive drivers were characterized as reckless, risk taking, impulsive persons who frequently got behind the wheel after a violent argument.

Box I-2

The Deadliest Attraction

In the Western world, the single most attractive site for suicide is San Francisco's Golden Gate Bridge. Recently it surpassed the Eiffel Tower as a place to end it all. Since 1937 more than 500 people have plunged to their deaths in the water below. In 1971, the average age of persons jumping from the bridge was 29.5 years, and three times as many men as women took the fatal dive. For a long time, San Francisco has had the highest suicide rate in the United States (30 per 100,000 population); 75 percent of those who have jumped have been residents of the San Francisco region.

A survey of known suicides gave this description of the conditions in which self-destruction is most likely to occur: in the spring, in the late afternoon, on a Monday (for males) and at home (in 74 percent of all cases). Suicide is least likely in winter in the early morning. But these details tell only part of the story. The finger on the trigger or the hand fumbling with the bottle of sleeping pills varies according to sex, marital status, and race.

Male Supremacy
Maris studied the cases of more than 2,000 suicides in the Chicago area during a five-year period. His sample showed that men are more likely to commit suicide than are women. However, three times as many women as men attempt suicide. Some think that most of these unsuccessful attempts are probably pleas for help rather than real attempts to take one's own life.

Firearms and explosives accounted for twice as many suicidal deaths among males as among females, whereas five times as many females as males killed themselves with chemical substances, mostly barbiturates.

Wedded Bliss
The suicide rate of married persons is lower than that of single, widowed, or divorced persons. The rate is highest among divorced persons, which suggests the possibility that in marriage the single relationship to the spouse might make all the difference.

A widowed person has lost a relationship to a spouse, but may have the compensation of happy memories or the companionship of sons and daughters. For the divorced person, a relationship that was once meaningful may have left only the pain and resentment of an unhappy affair. Without the help of relationship to others, the likelihood of suicide increases greatly.

For the divorced person, the rate of suicide doesn't level off with age as it does for the single, married, or widowed individual. Instead, the suicide rate increases from early in life and continues to grow even after 75 years of age.

White Death, Black Death

Suicide among blacks is significantly lower than among whites. This lower suicide rate may be related to the generally lower socio-economic status of blacks in our society; if you are already at the bottom of the social class structure, there is less shame attached to not rising in the world. It is often assumed, particularly by black persons, that suicide represents a white solution to white problems. As Dick Gregory once cracked, "You can't kill yourself by jumping out of the basement." And Redd Foxx scoffed, "Only three Negroes have jumped off the Golden Gate Bridge, and two of them were pushed."

Times are changing, though, and recent research suggests that suicide among young, urban black men has soared in the last 15 years. Older blacks are not killing themselves in greater numbers, but the younger blacks seem to be.

Death at an Early Age

"To be or not to be" has long been the question, and "not to be" increasingly has become the answer for some young people. A skyrocketing number of young people no longer believe they "have everything to live for."

The suicide rate among college students is particularly high. It is hard to understand why this relatively privileged group with the advantages of intelligence and educational opportunity would want to close the door on life. Seiden tried to answer this question in a 1966 study of 23 University of California students who committed suicide during the ten-year period from 1952 through 1961. Twice as many older students (over 25) as younger students killed themselves. These students were not in academic trouble (two-thirds of them were above the grade-point average), and they did not kill themselves during those periods when they might have been plagued by the stresses of final exams. The suicides usually occurred early in the semester—in the months of October or February.

This study convinced Seiden that the suicidal act was really a final dramatic gesture summing up a lifetime pattern of inadequate adjustment. To fellow students the suicide seemed to be doing well; but the suicide usually believed that his or her achievements didn't measure up to the expectations of self or others. The fundamental fact is that few of the suicide's fellow students knew the person very well; he or she was typically asocial or withdrawn. "These particular students were uniformly described as terribly shy, virtually friendless individuals, alienated from all but the most minimal social interactions. Frequently they had compensated for their personal solitude by increased study and almost total absorption in schoolwork."

Becoming Suicidal

Some psychiatric theorists insist that about 90 percent of all suicides have serious emotional disturbances. Reconstructing the life of the deceased by studying all available evidence and records and by interviewing those who knew the person best has led most American researchers to agree that suicide is a symptom of depressive emotional illness that produces feelings of helplessness, hopelessness, and worthlessness as well as a loss of interest in food, sex, work, friends, and everything else that normally makes life worth living. These depressions produce distinct physical symptoms: unusual fatigue, disturbed sleep patterns, and an inability or unwillingness to eat. Of all psychiatric conditions, depression is the most likely to be associated with suicide.

Box I-2

Doctor, Heal Thyself

The doctor you expect to preserve your life may be planning to take his or her own. More doctors die of self-inflicted wounds than are killed by automobile accidents, airplane crashes, drownings, and homicides combined. American doctors kill themselves at twice the rate of average American males, and this seems to be the case in other parts of the world as well (Ross, 1971). Surprisingly, of all doctors, psychiatrists are most likely to kill themselves. They are six times more likely to commit suicide than are pediatricians, for example.

Most of us are unhappy some of the time, but it is not easy to understand how suicidal people get so deeply and disastrously depressed. We don't have all the answers yet, but the Los Angeles Suicide Prevention Center has outlined one do-it-yourself method for rearing a suicidally inclined child. They suggest that you begin by giving the child personal experiences that will produce feelings of being inadequate and unloved. The child should also be taught to develop a harsh, punishing conscience filled with powerful feelings of guilt and shame; further, he or she should be instilled with exceptionally high standards and have a compulsion toward intense self-criticism for failure to achieve. Society can help by teaching values that emphasize achievement, the accumulation of wealth, and an unrealistic view of love.

Why are we so concerned about preventing suicide? Why not let individuals decide for themselves when they have had enough of living? One reason we try to prevent suicide is because these people, when prevented, often go on to lead happy, productive lives. In addition, suicide does not involve a single life; it affects the lives of all those connected with the victim. The family suffers not only sorrow, but usually guilt; they blame themselves for not preventing the tragedy. Children, too, suffer from the social stigma attached to the suicide of a parent; frequently, they become fearful that they are destined to follow the parent's example. Considering that ten attempts are made for every successful suicide, we must believe that most people really don't want to die and would not kill themselves if there were any other solution to life's problems.

Another good reason for doing everything we can to prevent suicide is offered by Seligman:

> Suicide usually has its roots in depression, and depression dissipates in time. When a person is depressed, his view of the future is bleak; he sees himself as helpless and hopeless. But in many cases, if he waited a few weeks, this cognitive set would be changed, and by reason of time alone the future would seem less hopeless. . . . One of the most tragic aspects of suicide is that often, if the person could be rendered inactive for a week or two, he would no longer wish to kill himself.

Summary

1. Suicide statistics are notoriously unreliable. Nevertheless, they do seem to indicate that men are more likely to commit suicide than women, although three times as many women as men *attempt* suicide unsuccessfully. Married persons are less likely to commit suicide than single, widowed, or divorced persons, and the suicide rate is lower for blacks than for whites.
2. The suicide rate for college students is particularly high. Those students who take their lives are typically asocial and withdrawn, although they seem to be doing well academically.
3. Suicide and depression go hand in hand. Potential suicides have feelings of helplessness, hopelessness, and worthlessness and have lost all interest in life. Most people who attempt to kill themselves don't really want to die but simply see no other solution to life's problems.

Skimming Questions: *Circle the letter of the best answer.*

1. In ancient times, suicide was considered:
   a. heroic
   b. cowardly
   c. sinful
   d. illegal

2. Suicide statistics are described by the author as:
    a. very precise
    b. fairly accurate
    c. somewhat inaccurate
    d. notoriously unreliable

3. _____ persons have the lowest suicide rate.
    a. single
    b. widowed
    c. divorced
    d. married

4. The suicide rate among college students is described as:
    a. particularly high
    b. about average
    c. somewhat below average
    d. extremely low

5. The suicide rate among young urban black men is:
    a. increasing rapidly
    b. staying about the same
    c. decreasing rapidly
    d. decreasing slowly

Scanning Questions

1. Of all psychiatric conditions, _____ is most likely to be associated with suicide.

2. Of all doctors, _____ are most likely to kill themselves.

3. Since 1937 more than _____ people have jumped off the Golden Gate Bridge.

4. _____ percent of all suicides are commited at home.

5. Someone in the United States commits suicide every _____

    _____ .

Time-Rate Conversion Chart

Min:Sec	WPM	Min:Sec	WPM	Min:Sec	WPM	Min:Sec	WPM	Min:Sec	WPM
1:00	2310	5:20	433	9:40	239	14:10	163	18:40	124
1:10	1980	5:30	420	9:50	235	14:20	161	18:50	123
1:20	1733	5:40	408	10:00	231	14:30	159	19:00	122
1:30	1540	5:50	396	10:10	227	14:40	158	19:10	121
1:40	1386	6:00	385	10:20	224	14:50	156	19:20	119
1:50	1260	6:10	375	10:30	220	15:00	154	19:30	118
2:00	1155	6:20	365	10:40	217	15:10	152	19:40	117
2:10	1066	6:30	355	10:50	213	15:20	151	19:50	116
2:20	990	6:40	347	11:00	210	15:30	149	20:00	116
2:30	924	6:50	338	11:10	207	15:40	147	20:10	115
2:40	866	7:00	330	11:20	204	15:50	146	20:20	114
2:50	815	7:10	322	11:30	201	16:00	144	20:30	113
3:00	770	7:20	315	11:40	198	16:10	143	20:40	112
3:10	729	7:30	308	11:50	195	16:20	141	20:50	111
3:20	693	7:40	301	12:00	193	16:30	140	21:00	110
3:30	660	7:50	295	12:10	190	16:40	139	21:10	109
3:40	630	8:00	289	12:20	187	16:50	137	21:20	108
3:50	603	8:10	283	12:30	185	17:00	136	21:30	107
4:00	578	8:20	277	12:40	182	17:10	135	21:40	107
4:10	554	8:30	272	12:50	180	17:20	133	21:50	106
4:20	533	8:40	267	13:00	178	17:30	132	22:00	105
4:30	513	8:50	262	13:10	175	17:40	131	22:10	104
4:40	495	9:00	257	13:20	173	17:50	130	22:20	103
4:50	478	9:10	252	13:30	171	18:00	128	22:30	103
5:00	462	9:20	248	13:40	169	18:10	127	22:40	102
5:10	447	9:30	243	13:50	167	18:20	126	22:50	101
				14:00	165	18:30	125	23:00	100

Unit 5 Answer Key

Exercise 3.1

1. 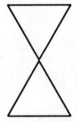 2. 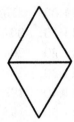 3.

4.   5.   6.

Unit Comprehension Check

1. The writer and reader should work as a team.
2. Because they are logical thought units, the building blocks of larger units of organization.
3. Main-idea statements and supporting details
4. (a) early
   (b) late
   (c) middle
   (D) beginning and end
   (e) no main idea directly stated

Vocabulary Development

1. photoflood
2. conclude
3. dictator's
4. transmitter
5. recluse
6. photodetector
7. dictum

Skim/Scan Exercise

Skimming
1. a. 2. d 3. d 4. a 5. a

Scanning
1. depression
2. psychiatrists
3. 500
4. 74
5. 30 minutes

Unit 6

Applying the PREP System to Textbooks, Works of Literature and Newspapers

Unit 6: *Applying the PREP System to the Mastery of Textbooks, Works of Literature, and Newspapers*

In earlier units the concept of reading flexibility was discussed. The point was made that you should adapt your reading rate and comprehension strategies to fit your purpose. The writer's purpose may also influence how you should read the material. In this unit, the idea of reading flexibility will be applied to three important—and very different—forms of written communication: textbooks, works of literature, and newspapers.

Reading Textbooks

The textbook is the key source of information in almost all school courses. In this unit we will provide you with some additional suggestions for reading this type of book.

There are exceptions, but in most textbooks the writer's purpose is to inform the reader. In some cases (perhaps too few) the writer may have the secondary purpose of entertaining the reader. And, once in a while, the writer may also want to persuade the reader. But, as we said before, the primary purpose of most textbooks is to inform, to instruct, to teach.

A famous design school in Germany once taught that "form follows function." This principle can be applied to textbooks as well. Because most textbooks are intended to inform you, they are designed so as to best accomplish this purpose. Most textbooks contain some or all of the following elements: title, preface, introduction, copyright date, table of contents, chapters divided into subsections, glossary, appendix and index. Each of these parts can provide you useful information.

The Title

Frequently we can tell the purpose of a book just by its title. For example, a textbook entitled **How to Read Scientific Material** will very likely outline and discuss the steps one should follow when reading scientific material. Contrast that title with one like **Contemporary Biology.** This book would probably deal much more with theory than the previous one. A title can give a clue to the book's purpose and the intention of the author, and will help you in choosing the proper approach to follow while reading the book.

The Preface and Introduction

These two sources of information often are overlooked. The preface especially may be the only place where the author speaks to you directly and informally, sharing the reasons for writing the book, his or her purposes, and so forth. The introduction may give you an overview that will help you make sense of the organization.

The Copyright Date

The year the book was first published is very important, especially in the sciences. Research is happening at such a rapid rate in all subjects that the copyright date should be of concern to you. What is true today may be modified or even incorrect tomorrow. Therefore, the copyright date is an important clue as to the accuracy of the information contained within a given book. If the text has a copyright date within three years of the present date, you can be fairly certain the information is current. This is not to say that books with older copyright dates should be avoided. There may be a very good reason to use an older book—especially in the humanities—for historic reasons or because the information may simply not be wrong—maybe just out of vogue!

The Table of Contents

This is another overlooked study aid. The Table of Contents will reveal the general topics covered, perhaps the depth in which a particular topic is discussed, and the organization of the topics. For example, a book might start by discussing its subject in broad terms and then go into specific details. The opposite might also be true, or other organization might be followed.

Textbook Chapters

Just as a paragraph usually focuses on a single main idea, a chapter normally focuses on one main topic of the textbook. The title of the chapter may simply state the topic, like "Motivation in Animals," or may also try to catch your attention, like "The Small World of the Atom." Chapters often are subdivided into sections headed in boldface or italic type. By carefully noting how the subdivisions are arranged, you will likely gain a greater awareness of the organization of the chapter.

The Appendix

An Appendix, located at the back of the book, contains supplementary material that is more easily kept separate from the main part of the book, for example, a table of atomic weights or a statistical table.

The Index and Glossaries

These aids usually are found at the back of a textbook. Arranged alphabetically, an index may list subjects and names separately or may combine them in one listing.

An Index can be used in a number of ways. First, it can help you locate all the places where a particular topic is discussed. Second, it can be used to see what subjects are covered and their relative importance in the book. For instance, here are two entries from a textbook:

> Aristotle, 25
> Bacon, Francis, quoted, 14,
> 22–24; life, 30–42

You can readily see that in this volume Bacon is dealt with in more detail than Aristotle. Third, an index can be a very handy checklist to use when preparing for an exam. If you are expected to have a thorough knowledge of the material in a textbook, check yourself by looking at the index entries. Look up those entries that seem important but that you are uncertain about.

A Glossary is a sort of miniature dictionary. It lists and defines important terms that are used in a book. Not every textbook (or even most) has a glossary, but if one is included, it can be very useful, especially if the text contains many terms that are new to you.

Other Important Features

When previewing or reading a textbook, you should also notice pictures, graphs, and charts; headings and subheadings; and chapter summaries.

While most textbooks have similarities, each one, like a person, is an individual. Therefore, you should also look for features that distinguish a textbook from others you have seen. For example, Book Two of Reading and Study Skills has a placement guide, a feature not found in most textbooks. Your reading probably will be more pleasant and efficient if you first acquaint yourself with the "personality" of the textbook.

Signpost Words

Clues to help you follow the progression of thoughts are useful in any reading situation, but especially when you are reading difficult material like that often found in textbooks. One kind of clue given by an author trying to present ideas clearly is the use of what we call "signpost words". Signpost words function much like road signs and markers to direct you to where you want to go. You should practice becoming alert to such words as you read. Here are a few common examples:

Signpost Words	**Message**
For example . . . For instance . . .	Here is an illustration of what I just said.
Hence . . . Thus . . . Therefore . . .	Here is something that follows from what I just said.
But . . . Yet . . . On the other hand . . . However . . . Conversely . . .	Here is an idea that takes a different direction from what I just said.

EXERCISE 6.0 *Identifying Signpost Words*

As you read the selection below, underline any signpost words you find. Check your work against the answer key at the end of this unit.

There are many reasons why workers join unions. For example, workers are stronger as a group than they are individually. A union has much more leverage in negotiations than would separate individuals. Another reason workers join unions is to feel more important.

On the other hand, arguments can be made against unions too. Some critics suggest that many unions, especially the larger ones, have become corrupt. Therefore, these unions no longer meet the needs of their members as well as they might.

Other Clues

Textbook authors will give you many other clues, too, and if you are sensitive to them, you will become a more efficient reader and will increase your comprehension of the material being presented.

What clues are most frequently used? Common ones are typographic devices such as centered and indented headings, boldface type, which stands out from the text, italicized words, and underlined words. Watch for the use of numbers, as in "four kinds" or "three reasons" or "six principles," followed by sentences or statements marked with letters, numbers, or words: (a), (b), (c); 1., 2., 3., 4.; first, second, third, fourth. These indicate a series of steps you should follow, a list of important facts you should pay close attention to, or a sequential order of reasons, arguments, or justifications or prove a specific point. Other clues to important material include introductory phrases like these: first of all, to begin with, in addition, still another, and in conclusion. And pay particular attention to any charts, diagrams, illustrations, or maps, since authors frequently use these devices to emphasize important ideas.

EXERCISE 6.1 *Signpost Words*

Underline clues to important material in the following selections. Check your work against the answer key.

1. Why is it important to underline or take notes in your book while reading? First, it forces your attention. In the second place, reading is thinking, and thinking is an active process which tends to express itself in language. The book that is underlined and has notations in the margins is usually the book that has been thought through. Finally, these underlinings and notations can be used for later review so that you can remember the thoughts you had, or the thoughts of the author.

2. Of first importance in learning how to deal with test panic is recognizing that a person cannot experience anxiety while completely relaxed. Therefore, the process of desensitization involves three steps: (1) learning how to reach a state of deep relaxation, (2) determining your hierarchy of anxiety, and (3) while relaxed, visualizing the anxiety-producing situations.

With practice, you probably will become more aware of clues in textbook material. Very likely, you will feel much more in tune with the author because you are following the thought process better.

Reading Works of Literature

The range of genres or types of literature is very broad: novels, short stories, plays, essays, poems. Because each type differs in form from the others, you must adjust your reading method to fit what you are reading. The prose fiction types of literature—novels, short stories, and plays—are similar enough so that some characteristics common to them all can be discussed.

The Writer's Purpose

We mentioned that the textbook writer's purpose usually is to inform. On the other hand, prose fiction may wish to inform, entertain, and/or persuade the reader. As with other forms of writing, how you read should depend in part on the writer's purpose.

Techniques for reading fiction can be discussed within the framework of the PREP study system. Naturally, you will use each part of the system somewhat differently than you would for studying a textbook.

Previewing

Should you preview works of fiction? The answer depends on your purpose. If one of your main goals is to be entertained, then you may not wish to lose the enjoyment that comes from surprises in the story. On the other hand, if your main purpose is to gain a deep awareness of every level of meaning in the work, then a preview can be very useful. During the preview, concentrate on learning about the basic plot and character development. Then, as you read the work in more detail, you can focus your attention on deeper levels, such as symbolism and subtle character development.

Active Reading

For a discussion of the active reading process, let us focus on two of the most popular forms of prose fiction, the novel and the short story. Individual works vary greatly in complexity. The simpler ones may use only a few of the possible writing techniques, while more complicated ones may use a variety of techniques that interact in interesting ways. One problem for some students is that they are used to dealing only with plot and very obvious forms of character development. A steady diet of television drama and adventure novels has limited many readers' ability to fully appreciate more complex works of literature.

A novel may include a few or many of the following elements:

1. Setting. Most stories take place in a particular place—a certain locale, certain buildings, and so forth. The setting may be as narrow as a single room or the imagination of a character, or as broad as the entire world or even beyond.
2. Plot. Most stories involve a series of events. The entire sequence and interplay of these events forms the plot of the story.
3. Characterizations. In most stories, the events are determined in part by the characters. The characters are the people (or other beings) whose thoughts and deeds are depicted in the story. In some stories the roles of the characters are very clearly defined: there are protagonists (the "good guys") and antagonists (the "bad guys"). But in other stories these distinctions are not as definite.
4. Narrative point of view. Naive readers of fiction often make the mistake of confusing the author's point of view with the narrative point of view. This confusion is especially easy when the story is written in the first person ("I"). The reader should keep in mind that, unlike writers of nonfiction, writers of fiction frequently establish a persona that is actually doing the talking. The persona may have a personality and point of view very different from that of the author. For example, the persona who speaks in the short story **The Liar** is a self-deceiving young man, not the author.

    Through the years many kinds of points of view have developed in fiction. To even begin to appreciate a fictional story, you should be aware of what point of view is being employed. Some of the most common points of view are:
    (a) First-person-involved, in which the story is told by one of the principal characters. You must always ask yourself whether the first-person narrator's comments should be believed or not. Some first-person narrators are either deceiving themselves or trying to deceive the reader.
    (b) First-person-peripheral, in which the story is told by one of the less important characters. These narrators, because they are less involved with the action, often are ignorant about some of what is happening. An excellent example of the first-person-peripheral point of view are the Sherlock Holmes stories. Dr. Watson, the narrator and friend of Holmes, is often only dimly aware of the true nature of the events he is describing. This approach allows the author to withhold information from the reader for dramatic or other reasons.

(c) Third-person-limited, in which the story is told in the third person ("he," "she," "they"), but the narrative is limited to describing the thoughts and experiences of one character. This point of view also is called "central intelligence."

(d) Third-person-omniscient, in which the narrator has access to the thoughts and actions of all the characters. There may be varied degrees of access as well.

5. Symbolism. At one level, the people, events, objects, and the like in a story can be viewed literally. Within the context of the story, events can be thought of as "really" happening and people "really" existing. At another level, there can be symbolic meaning as well. Something is a symbol when it represents something else—most commonly, something intangible or abstract. Symbols are powerful tools for a writer because they relate to the subjects of our strongest emotions, like life (the valentine), and death (the color black). When we dream, our deepest fears and hopes are often expressed in symbolic form.

Some stories make little use of symbols, while others rely heavily on them. For example, Forester's Hornblower stories and Melville's Billy Budd are all sea-faring adventure stories. In the **Hornblower** stories, the events and characters usually are meant to be taken at the literal level only. On the other hand, **Billy Budd** is packed with symbolism. For example, the main character, Billy Budd, is seen by some as a Christ figure. Thus, if you read every story at the literal level only, you may be missing much of the author's message.

6. Theme. All the elements mentioned so far combine to form the story. This story, in turn, usually reflects an attitude or view of life. The author manipulates plot, character development, symbolism, and the other elements to present the view of life—the theme of the story. In essays and in some fiction, the theme may be presented directly, as with the statement, "We are controlled by events." But in most fiction, especially recent fiction, the theme is not directly stated. Instead, you must infer the theme from the events in the story.

Examining

As with textbooks and other kinds of reading, you can read fiction at many levels. These levels were discussed in Unit Four and elsewhere. Here are some questions you might ask about a fictional work at each of these levels of understanding:

1. Literal level
   a. What is the setting?
   b. What is the plot?
   c. Who are the characters?

2. Interpretive level
   a. Why was the setting chosen?
   b. What traits do the characters have?
   c. What narrative point of view is used?
   d. Are any symbols used? What message do they convey?
   e. What is the theme? *CENTROL OF THE STORY*
   f. How imaginative is the author?
   g. How well does the author control the elements of plot, character, setting, etc., to produce the overall effect?
   h. How valid is the author's theme? *SHOWS*
   i. How accurately does the author depict life?
4. Applied level
   a. What can I learn about *Made up* fiction writing techniques from this book?
   b. What can I learn about life, human nature, etc., from this book?

Of course, you can also ask more specific questions of a particular work, such as "What do the flowers symbolize in Steinbeck's, **The Chrysanthemums**?"

If you have been used to reading fiction mostly at the literal level, you will have to adjust your reading methods to read fiction assigned in courses. Usually an instructor will expect you to read at the inferential level and perhaps at the applied level.

EXERCISE 6.2 *Level of Question*

Identify the level of each of the questions below as literal (L), interpretive (I), or aplied (A).

_____ 1. Fitzgerald's The Great Gatsby is written from what narrative point of view?

_____ 2. How well developed is the main character in Hemingway's A Farewell to Arms?

_____ 3. How realistic are Hemingway's male protagonists?

_____ 4. Maria's actions tell you what about her personality?

_____ 5. How effective is the use of a limited-third-person point of view in The Valiant Woman?

_____ 6. What is the sequence of events in Gogol's The Overcoat?

_____ 7. After reading this story, do you have a better understanding of people different from yourself?

Prompting

To do well on exams in literature courses, you may need a good memory of the works that you have been assigned. Some of the prompting techniques that were discussed earlier might help. For example, when studying a work of fiction, you might use the six elements mentioned earlier (setting, theme, etc.) as anchor points upon which to cluster information about the story. And, of course, use recitation to drill yourself on the information you need to learn.

Reading Newspapers

At times you will have to read newspapers for preparing reports, reviewing current events, or writing term papers. Because of the special nature of newspapers, you need to adjust your reading methods.

Functions of the Newspaper

A newspaper combines all the main purposes that we have discussed: to inform, to persuade, and to entertain. Some sections of the paper emphasize one purpose more than another. For example, the news sections primarily inform, the editorial page includes attempts to persuade, and the comics and some columns are intended mainly to entertain. Therefore, you should try to determine the writer's purpose as you read and adjust your reading accordingly.

Newspapers can be discussed in terms of the PREP study system, just as textbooks and works of literature can. Of course, you will use the PREP system differently for newspapers than for other forms of written communication.

Previewing
Previewing is an important time-saving step when reading newspapers. A preview will tell you whether you need to read the article more carefully; in many cases it will give you enough information to make a more detailed reading unnecessary.

Because most newspapers follow a similar format, previewing them is easy. Here are some features of newspapers that aid previewing:

1. Headlines. Headlines function much like titles and subtitles in a textbook. They tell you very briefly what the article is about. You can use headlines to decide whether you want to read an article.
2. Article structure. Newspaper articles are organized to make reading as easy as possible. The most important facts are usually given in the first few paragraphs; the less important facts follow; and, finally, the least important information appears at the end of the article. Thus, if you preview the first few paragraphs, you

are assured of receiving most of the important information. Then you can decide, based on your purpose, whether to read the more detailed information in the rest of the article.

3. Layout. Each newspaper, like each textbook, is organized in a particular way. Most newspapers will have a table of contents on the first or second page of section one. And somewhere on or near the first page, many newspapers have a summary of important news items. This summary may be divided into international, national, and local events. A preview of this summary will help you decide which article should be read in more detail.

Even the layout of the first page may provide useful aids. For example, a particular newspaper may always have the most important news item in the same place every day. **The New York Times** uses the extreme right-hand column for this purpose. Some papers use the extreme left-hand column. You should become familiar with the layout of papers you read regularly.

Reading

How you read a newspaper article will naturally depend on your purpose. In many cases a preview may be enough. In other cases you may want to read in more detail. If you are reading an article to use in a report, you may wish to highlight useful information or take notes.

Examining

Examining was described earlier in this book as the "art of active questioning." Newspaper articles help the questioning process because they usually try to answer the questions Who? What? Why? How? When? and Where? So, as you read an article, you might try to answer these questions for yourself. You may also have other more specific questions, depending on your purpose.

In many cases you will want to question newspaper articles at various levels. In addition to the literal level, you might ask interpretive questions (Why did this event occur?, How believable are the facts, quotations, etc.?), and applied questions (What lesson can I learn from this event?).

Prompting

You are likely to remember news information better if you relate it to what you already know about the subject or similar subjects. Most news stories develop out of events that are already known. For example, if you read that a small country has been overthrown, you might relate this event to what you already knew about the economic and social problems in the country. Remember that news events do not occur in a vacuum.

Summary

In school courses, textbooks often are a major source of information. But you sometimes are required to read other sources, such as newspapers and works of literature. In each case, you should adapt your reading methods to fit the material as well as to fit your purposes. Knowing the special characteristics of each written form helps you to deal with that material better.

Unit Comprehension Check

If you can answer these questions, you have retained many of the main points at the literal level.

1. Where in a textbook would you look to find:
    a. the pages on which a particular individual is mentioned?

    b. the author's explanation of why he wrote the book?

    c. an overview of how the book is divided into chapters?

    d. the definition of a special term used in the text?

    d. a supplementary table not included in the main part of the textbook?

2. What should you concentrate on when previewing a work of fiction?

3. In fiction you should not confuse the narrative point of view with the
    _____'s point of view.

4. Define the word symbol.

5. In much modern fiction, is the theme directly stated?

6. What are the three functions of a newspaper?

7. What six questions do most news articles try to answer?

Study Questions

1. Examine the textbooks you are using this term. How useful is each of the parts of the textbooks? For example, do the prefaces give you added insight about the textbooks?

2. At what levels are you used to reading fiction? Do you often try to make inferences or evaluations?

EXERCISE 6.3. *Action Plan*

Directions: Choose one or more ideas from this Unit to incorporate into your reading. Develop an Action Plan for these ideas.

Goals	Strategies to Complete Goal	Completion Date	Evaluation Procedure

Vocabulary Development

Three Roots

scrib, *script*	A Latin root meaning to *write*. The author *inscribed* the book with a written message and signature.
rupt	A Latin root meaning to *break*. The phone call was *interrupted* by an operator who broke into the conversation.
prim	A Latin root meaning *first*. *Prime* beef is the number one, first quality meat sold at the market.

Vocabulary Exercise

Study the three roots presented above. In the following sentences, locate the word that includes the root and underline it. In the blank space in each sentence fill in the best root meaning. Study the examples before you begin the exercise:

A <u>ruptured</u> blood vessel is _broken_ .

A <u>primary</u> election is the _first_ election before the general election.

1. To describe a flower you might <u>write</u> down its important feature.

2. The primary grades in elementary school are the _first_ three grades.

3. Corruption occurs when people _BRook_ the law without penalty.

4. After a medical examination, the doctor _PRESCRIBED_ the patient a prescription.

5. The meeting was disrupted when several people _BREKING_ into the hall

and caused a violent scene.

6. The reading primer is the _first_ textbook used to help children learn

how to read.

7. The student _WROTE_ his essay in a neat script.

8. John _____ into the discussion and interrupted the panel of speakers.

9. The law of primogeniture gives the _____ born son the sole right of

inheritance of his father's estate.

Common Word Parts

Word Part	Meaning	Examples
1. *auto*	self	automatic, automation
2. *audio*	hear	audiovisual, audience
3. *bene*	good	beneficiary, benevolent
4. *cede, ceed, cess*	go, move, yield	recede, proceed, access
5. *chron*	time	chronology, synchronize
6. *corp*	body	corpse, corpuscle
7. *cred*	believe	credence, credit
8. *cur, cour*	run	current, courier
9. *dem, demo*	people	demagogue, demographer
10. *dict*	say, speak, tell	dictator, dictaphone
11. *doc, doct*	teach	doctrine, indoctrinate
12. *dox*	belief, teaching, opinion	doxology, orthodox
13. *duc, duct,*	lead	conduct
14. *dyna*	power	dynasty, dynamite
15. *ego*	self	egotist, egocentric
16. *fac, fact*	do, make	facile, manufacture
17. *flex, flect*	bends, twist	flexible, genuflect
18. *frag, fract*	break	fragile, fracture
19. *frater*	brother	fraternity, fraternal
20. *gen*	birth, race	congenital, genealogy

Word Part	Meaning	Examples
21. *grad, gress*	step, go	degrade, digress
22. *hydr*	water	hydroponics, hydroplane
23. *jac, ject*	throw, hurl	ejaculation, reject
24. *loc*	place	location, local
25. *log, logy*	speech, study of collection of	monologue, zoology
26. *mal—mal*	bad	malady, malevolent
27. *mit, miss*	send	transmit, remission
28. *micro*	small	microbe, micrometer
29. *mort*	death	mortal, mortuary
30. *omni*	all	omnibus, omnipotent
31. *pater*	father	paternal, paternity
32. *path*	feeling, suffering	sympathy, apathy
33. *ped, pod*	foot	pedestrian, tripod
34. *pos*	place	position, impose
35. *poly*	many	polygamy, polysyllabic
36. *proto*	first, fundamental	protocol, protoplasm
37. *psych*	soul, mind	psychic, psychology
38. *scrib, script*	write	ascribe, subscription
39. *scop*	see	horoscope, telescope
40. *sent, sens*	feel	sentiment, sensuous
41. *sol*	alone	solitude, solo
42. *soph*	wise	philosophy, sophomore
43. *spec, spic*	look, see	aspect, conspicuous
44. *tele*	far	telegraph, telepathy
45. *ten, tain*	hold	tenacious, retain
46. *tort*	twist	contortion, tortuous
47. *tract*	draw, pull	distract, traction
48. *vert, vers*	turn	invert, conversion
49. *vid, vis*	see	video, supervise
50. *voc, vok*	call	vocal, invoke

Skim-Scan
Exercise 6

1. Record your starting time.
2. Rapidly preview-skim the entire selection.
3. Record your ending time.
4. Answer the skimming questions.
5. Go on to the scanning questions.
6. Determine your skimming and scanning scores and your skimming words-per-minute rate.
7. Enter your skimming score and rate on the progress graph in the appendix at the end of this book.

Population Economics

by Roger LeRoy Miller

	Hour	Min.	Secs.
A. Ending time:	——	——	——
B. Starting time:	——	——	——
C. A – B = Reading time:	——	——	

Just about everybody has heard that there is a population explosion. Many books and articles tell us that the world will come to an end if we don't cut back the growth of population. The arithmetic of population economics is not hard to figure out, but it is deceiving, as we will see when we talk about the economic and social consequences of zero population growth. First, however, we'll see how demographers—those who study population—measure trends in population growth. We'll also look at the economic variables that determine fertility and mortality. By doing this, then perhaps we will be better equipped to analyze the arguments presented by those who advocate zero population growth.

The Arithmetic of Population Growth

Demographers like to look at the difference between birth rates and death rates. They calculate for a given country and a given year what is called the **crude birth rate**—the number of babies born per 1000 people in the population. Then they look at the **crude death rate,** which is the number of deaths per 1000 people in the population. When we subtract the crude death rate from the crude birth rate, we come up with the change in population per 1000 people in that year. If we divide that by 10 we get the result as a percentage, and we have the annual **population rate of growth.** Let's look at a few examples. In Table 1, we listed the crude death rate and the crude birth rate for several countries. When the difference is divided by 10, we find that the rate of increase of population in these countries varies from 3.48 percent per year to a low of −0.02 percent per year in East Germany.

The rate of growth of population is not, therefore, just a function of the birth rate, but also a function of the death rate. We would expect that any improvement in death control, as it were, would lead to an increase in population growth.

From p. 349–352 in ECONOMICS TODAY: THE MICRO VIEW, 2nd Ed. by Roger LeRoy Miller. Copyright © 1973, 1976 by Roger LeRoy Miller. Courtesy of Harper & Row, Publishers, Inc.

Table 1. Birth and Death Rates and Rate of Increase of Population for Selected Countries

Column 2 shows the crude birth rate per 1000 people per year in each of these countries. Column 3 shows the crude death rate per year. Column 4 is the difference between the crude birth rate and the crude death rate divided by 10. It represents the percentage annual rate of change per year of population.

Country	Crude Birth Rate	Crude Death Rate	Rate of Increase
United States	15.6	9.4	0.62
France	16.9	10.8	0.61
Germany—East	11.8	13.8	−0.02
Israel	27.8	7.2	2.06
Japan	19.3	6.6	1.27
Mexico	43.2	8.9	3.43
Sweden	13.8	10.4	0.34
U.S.S.R.	18.0	8.5	0.95

Source: Statistical Office of the United Nations

Doubling Time

Population experts like to translate rates of population growth per annum into what is called the **doubling time.** in other words, if the population of Luxembourg is growing at 0.4 percent a year, how many years will it take for the populaton to double? In the case of Luxembourg, this would take almost 175 years!

In Table 2 we see the doubling time for the populations of the countries in Table 1. A good rule to use to figure out the doubling time is the *rule of 72.* If you divide the percentage rate of increase in population into 72, you get an approximate doubling time. In our example of Luxembourg, the growth rate of population is 0.4 percent a year. Thus, 72 divided by 0.4 equals 180 years, just about the figure we got before.

Doubling times are fascinating numbers because if we extend them indefinitely into the future, we find that the population of very small Latin American countries will increase until there are so many people there will no longer be a place to walk. The countries literally will be covered with people. Even if the doubling time is 175 years, as in Luxembourg, if you extend that rate of growth far enough into the future, the result is one horrendously large number. That's one reason Zero Population Growth people are so adamant about the necessity of limiting the number of births not only in countries where the populations are unbelievably dense, as in Hong Kong, but also in countries where populations is much less dense.

Table 2. The Doubling Time for Selected Countries Populations

Here we show how many years it takes for each country's population to double. The range is immense, from Mexico's 21 years to Sweden's 212 years.

Country	Doubling Time
United States	116
France	118
Israel	35
Japan	57
Mexico	21
Sweden	212
U.S.S.R.	76

Source: Statistical Office of the United States

Net Reproduction Rate

Demographers also like to talk in terms of net reproduction rate. This rate is calculated on the basis of the total number of female children born to every 1000 mothers. If every mother has exactly one daughter in her lifetime, then the net reproduction rate will be exactly 1. What do you think will happen to the population? It will eventually stabilize (assuming life expectancy doesn't change). If mothers tend to have more than one daughter throughout their child-bearing years, then the net reproduction rate will be in excess of 1 and the population will grow.

The net reproduction rate is probably the most important statistic to look at when you want to find what the future holds for a particular country. Japan is a good example. There, the crude birth rate is about 19 per 1000, and the crude death rate is about 6.6 per 1000. The rate of growth in population is therefore in excess of 1 percent per annum. Even a 1 percent annual growth rate in population leads to a doubling every 72 years. But Japan really isn't worried about that. In fact, Japan's worries are in the opposite direction. The net reproduction rate is now less than 1 in Japan. The Japanese have legalized abortion, and there is widespread birth control. Given that the net reproduction rate is less than 1, after a few more years of growth, the Japanese population will begin a long steady decline. In fact, by extending net reproduction rates into the future forever without any change, you would find that the population of Japan will eventually disappear. Some time ago, Japanese businesspersons were publicized as complaining that their profits were going to fall in the future because of a diminishing labor supply. They would have to start paying higher wages to have a sufficient number of workers.

Where the People Are

It is interesting to note that even though population seems to be exploding all around us, the centers of population are really the only places where this is the case. Historically, we find that people moved where jobs were. Jobs were usually in ports or places with many natural resources. After transportation became relatively cheap, people started to live where they wanted to, and jobs then followed people. And people are going to the cities. Indeed, the percentage of people in urban centers has increased from 5 to 74 percent in the last 185 years. Additionally, in the United States, population has shifted out of the central areas to the south and to the west. The south and the west happen to have more agreeable climates.

If people did not find benefits from living in large cities, there would probably be a much more even population distribution throughout our entire land area. Presumably, if this were the case, there would be less concern over population explosion. Indeed, one need only take a drive or a plane trip across the United States to realize how sparsely populated these United States really are. This is not to say that we should or should not do something about population growth. Rather, the paucity of people in certain areas may merely serve to demonstrate that overpopulation is really only a problem in overcrowded urban environments.

The Population Curve

If we were to examine population growth in other animal species, we would find that there are natural limits to the total population a particular species can obtain. An experiment can be run with a pair of willing fruit flies in a small enclosure. At first, the population grows by leaps and bounds. It increases at a geometric rate: first 2, then 4, then 8, then 16, and so on. If this geometric progression of the fruit fly population were extended way into the future, we would find that their mass would eventually overcome the earth. However, this geometric growth rate does not continue for very long. Eventually it peters out because there just aren't enough resources for the flies to continue growing.

In our particular example, one resource that holds the fruit flies back is the size of the container. For other populations, it might be the food supply. In any event, reproduction slows down, and at some point, a ceiling is reached. The ceiling is called the *natural population limit*. It is determined by the supply of the resources that are needed for survival.

However, the growth line of population has for some reason just kept going up and up. This is what seems to have happened with the world population. Instead of slowing down, the growth rate has actually increased. Doubling time has fallen from 2000 years to 1000 years to 500 years, down to its present 35 years. However, we know that there has to be a ceiling somewhere. As one famous economist characterized the earth, it is a spaceship; it can only hold so many people because it has a fixed amount of space and a fixed number of resources. (And we can live under- and above-ground, too). Population obviously cannot continue to grow forever.

Skimming Questions: *Circle the letter of the best answer.*

1. _____ like to look at the difference between birth and death rates.
   a. population economists
   b. geographers
   c. actuaries
   d. demographers

2. This selection is mainly about:
   a. birth control
   b. changes in the death rate
   c. how a large population affects the economy
   d. the population explosion

3. Population experts like to translate population growth into what is called:
   a. the death ratio
   b. the birth ratio
   c. doubling time
   d. decline per annum

4. Demographers like to talk in terms of the "net _____."
   a. birth ratio
   b. reproduction rate
   c. death rate
   d. decline per annum

5. We can see natural limits to the size of the total population if we examine population growth in:
   a. small towns
   b. rural areas
   c. other animal species
   d. underdeveloped nations

Scanning Questions

1. Doubling time of the world population is now at _____ years.

2. The crude death rate for East Germany is listed as _____ .

3. Overpopulation is really only a problem in overcrowded _____ environments.

4. The percentage of people in urban centers has increased from 5 to 74 percent in

   the last _____ years.

5. According to Table 2 the doubling time for the U.S.S.R. is now _____

   years.

Time-Rate Conversion Chart

Min:Sec	WPM	Min:Sec	WPM	Min:Sec	WPM	Min:Sec	WPM	Min:Sec	WPM
1:00	2575	6:00	429	11:00	234	16:00	161	21:00	123
1:10	2207	6:10	418	11:10	231	16:10	159	21:10	122
1:20	1931	6:20	407	11:20	227	16:20	158	21:20	121
1:30	1717	6:30	396	11:30	224	16:30	156	21:30	120
1:40	1545	6:40	386	11:40	221	16:40	155	21:40	119
1:50	1405	6:50	377	11:50	218	16:50	153	21:50	118
2:00	1288	7:00	368	12:00	215	17:00	151	22:00	117
2:10	1188	7:10	359	12:10	212	17:10	150	22:10	116
2:20	1104	7:20	351	12:20	209	17:20	149	22:20	115
2:30	1030	7:30	343	12:30	206	17:30	147	22:30	114
2:40	966	7:40	336	12:40	203	17:40	146	22:40	114
2:50	909	7:50	329	12:50	201	17:50	144	22:50	113
3:00	858	8:00	322	13:00	198	18:00	143	23:00	112
3:10	813	8:10	315	13:10	196	18:10	142	23:10	111
3:20	773	8:20	309	13:20	193	18:20	140	23:20	110
3:30	736	8:30	303	13:30	191	18:30	139	23:30	110
3:40	702	8:40	297	13:40	188	18:40	138	23:40	109
3:50	672	8:50	292	13:50	186	18:50	137	23:50	108
4:00	644	9:00	286	14:00	184	19:00	136	24:00	107
4:10	618	9:10	281	14:10	182	19:10	134	24:10	107
4:20	594	9:20	276	14:20	180	19:20	133	24:20	106
4:30	572	9:30	271	14:30	178	19:30	132	24:30	105
4:40	552	9:40	266	14:40	176	19:40	131	24:40	104
4:50	533	9:50	262	14:50	174	19:50	130	24:50	104
5:00	515	10:00	258	15:00	172	20:00	129	25:00	103
5:10	498	10:10	253	15:10	170	20:10	128	25:10	102
5:20	483	10:20	249	15:20	168	20:20	127	25:20	102
5:30	468	10:30	245	15:30	166	20:30	126	25:30	101
5:40	454	10:40	241	15:40	164	20:40	125	25:40	100
5:50	441	10:50	238	15:50	163	20:50	124		

Unit 6 Answer Key

Exercise 6.0

For example . . . Another reason . . . on the other hand . . . therefore

Exercise 6.1

1. First . . . In the second place . . . thinking. . . . finally
2. of first importance . . . therefore . . . (1) . . . (2) . . . (3). . . .

Exercise 6.2

1. I You would infer the point of view from the story
2. I You would make this evaluation as you read the story
3. I
4. I You would infer her personality from her actions
5. A
6. L Sequence can be found directly in the material
7. A This question asks whether you can apply what you have read to a different situation.

Unit Comprehension Check

1. (a) Index
   (b) Preface
   (c) Table of Contents
   (d) Glossary
   (e) Appendix
2. The basic plot and character development
3. Author's
4. A symbol is something that represents something else, often something intangible.
5. No. The theme is often implied by the events
6. To inform, persuade, and to entertain
7. Who? What? Why? How? When? Where?

Vocabulary Development

1. Describe, write
2. primary, first
3. corruption, break
4. prescription, wrote
5. disrupted, broke
6. primer, first
7. wrote, script
8. broke, interrupted
9. primogeniture, first

Skim/Scan Exercise

Skim
1. d   2. d   3. c   4. b   5. c

Scan
1. 35   2. −0.02   3. urban   4. 185   5. 76

PART 3

Output Skills

Unit 7

Preparing to Take Examinations

Examinations are part of a student's "facts of life". It is natural for us to try to avoid doing things that we dislike. Therefore, if you hate taking tests, you are likely to put off thinking about them for as long as possible. Then, at the last minute you end up cramming for the test. A more realistic attitude is to think of exams as an evaluation. An evaluation of how much and how well you have learned, as well as an evaluation of how well your instructor has done in teaching the material.

Most exams are fair. If you make a serious effort to prepare for them it is very likely that your instructor will be able to honestly evaluate your knowledge, and too, you will get a good idea of how well you are mastering the course content. In this unit we will outline a system you can use to prepare for exams.

How To Prepare For Examinations

Whatever method you use to prepare for exams, you should try to start your preparation as early as possible. In fact, it is best to start preparing for tests from the first day of classes. You should take lecture notes and study textbooks with the idea that you are going to be tested on the information. If you do not take this attitude you may not take adequate lecture notes or strive hard enough to understand the textbook. Then, when the reality of test time hits you, you may be overwhelmed with all of the learning that must take place in so short a time.

Steps To Follow When Preparing For Exams

Step One: Decide How to Divide Your Energies and Time. This step is based on the idea that you should not study the same way for every class. Different types of learning require different types of study methods. Also, instructors differ in what they want you to learn in their class. So you must adapt your study habits to meet the orientation of the instructor.

According to a persistent myth, you are supposed to study about two hours for every hour of class. This is, however, not supported by studies that have looked into this issue. Based on our experience the study-time you may need to spend might be based, at least in part, on how well you have scored on either SAT total scores or ACT composites.

According to this study framework, a person who has a SAT total of 1260 or ACT composite of 27 should study for about 1 hour every hour in class (excluding papers), take no more than 16 credit hours and feel free to engage in outside activities, such as involvement in various campus organizations. Contrast this with a person who has an ACT composite of 15.

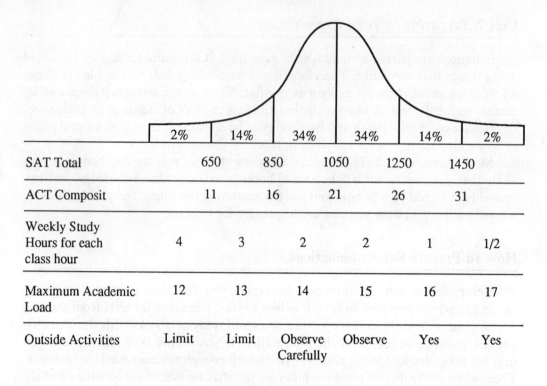

	2%	14%	34%	34%	14%	2%
SAT Total		650	850	1050	1250	1450	
ACT Composit		11	16	21	26	31	
Weekly Study Hours for each class hour		4	3	2	2	1	1/2
Maximum Academic Load		12	13	14	15	16	17
Outside Activities		Limit	Limit	Observe Carefully	Observe	Yes	Yes

Figure 7.0

These recommendations are useful for a typical student who is just beginning his or her college career. However, we want to emphasize that you need to be flexible in your study. Also, as you learn good study habits you will find that less study time is needed to learn your course material.

When trying to determine how much time you should spend studying you should consider your grade goals for the course and how difficult the material is for you. Some factors that affect this decision include:

1. What overall grade average do you want? You may need a certain minimum grade average to enter a special program or to transfer to another school. In that case, you will want to do well enough in all your courses to maintain that average.
2. Why you are taking a specific course? If the course is related to your career objectives, you will probably have a higher grade goal than if the course is being used to fulfill general education requirements.
3. How interested in the course are you? You may wish to spend more time and energy on some courses because they interest you more.

Remember, then, that you do not necessarily have to strive for the highest possible grades in all the courses you are taking during a term. For some courses, a "C" or similar grade may be satisfactory. Then, you can devote extra time to more important courses.

Step Two: Learn as Much as Possible about What to Expect on the Tests. From time to time scandals hit our schools because some students carry this advice too far and cheat. Actually, you can learn a lot about upcoming tests in honest ways, without having to resort to cheating or thievery. For example, the instructor usually is an excellent source of information and often will give information directly or by implication. A class syllabus or the instructor's comments in class may give you direct information. Indirect information comes from what the instructor stresses during lectures—for example, if an anthropology instructor were to frequently compare different cultures, test questions requiring comparisons would be likely. And you should not hesitate to ask the instructor for guidance. Of course, you would not say, "Tell me what's on the test!" But you might remark, "I notice that the textbook gives a lot of details. Should I spend time memorizing those?"

There are other valuable sources of information about what to expect on tests. You might talk to someone who has taken the course from the same instructor. Also, you might find out whether the school library or the individual department keeps a file of past exams and makes them available to students. By spending a little time determining what to expect on an exam, you may save yourself many hours of studying the wrong information. Although this advice is important for everybody, it is probably even more important for those people who have been out of school for some years.

Here is a checklist of questions to ask yourself about an upcoming exam:

1. What form(s) will the test questions take? True-false? Multiple-choice? Short-answer? Or some combinations? This is an important question if you feel more comfortable with one kind of test than another. The special features of different test formats are discussed in unit 8.
2. What is the scope (range of items) of the test? Scope can be thought of in a couple of ways. First, how detailed is your knowledge expected to be? Should you memorize names, dates, or formulas? Second, will the test cover information assigned since the previous test only, or will it be cumulative?
3. What proportion of items will come from each possible source? In most courses the two main sources of information are the lectures and the assigned readings. Often, but not always, you can expect a roughly equal number of questions from each source. You should learn whether one source will be stressed more than another. Also, if there are reserved readings assigned at the library, how important are they?

4. What level(s) of understanding are expected? This question is similar to the one about scope. You may recall earlier that three levels of understanding have been discussed. Exam questions could be written to test your knowledge at any or all of these levels. For example:
   a. Who invented the steam engine? (literal understanding of details)
   b. What are the characteristics of a nomadic society? (literal understanding of main ideas or interpretive)
   c. Based on the characters that he developed, what do you believe was Hemingway's view of the male role? (interpretive)
   d. Evaluate Thompson's racial theory. (interpretive)
   e. Give an example, not covered in the course, of Archimedes' principle. (applied)

Step Three: Decide on a Study Strategy to Fit Your Goals and the Kind of Test Expected.

When you are deciding on a study strategy for each course, there are a number of study aids to choose from. Figure 7.1 shows the strengths and weaknesses of the study aids that have been discussed so far.

	Under-lining	Marginal notes	Summary sheets	Semantic mapping	Concept mapping	Flash cards
Input time	These take less time		These take more time			
Allows recitation	No	Yes	Yes	Yes	Yes	Yes
Shows relationship between ideas	No	No	Yes	Yes	Yes	No

Figure 7.1 Some study aids.

Course	Grade Goal	Expected Test	Study Strategy
Psych.	A or B	Mult. Choice, very detailed literal & some applied questions	Flash cards for important facts; semantic mapping for each chapter
Algebra	B	All are problem-solving	work all assigned problems. Also some supplementary problems. Re-do the hard ones before the test.
Biology	C or B	Mult. choice, General concepts & terms (literal)	Just underline the textbook. Use marginal notes. Review with some recitation. (Not as much as for Psych.)
English Lit.	C	Essay questions (Memory of plots & evaluation)	Semantic mapping of major plots. Develop and answer the most likely essay questions.

Figure 7.2 Sample Analysis of Courses for Erika Williams (listed in priority order).

Applying the Three-Step Method

To illustrate how you might follow the three-step method, let us consider the case of Erika Williams. She is taking four courses: psychology (she needs this course for her major requirement); algebra (for her major requirement); biology (to fulfill general requirements); and English literature (also for general requirements). Because Erika works twenty hours a week at a job, she cannot hope to receive A's and B's in all of these courses. So she first makes up the analysis sheet shown in Figure 7.2.

You can see from Figure 7.2 that Erika is going to study these courses in different ways. For example, even though the psychology and biology courses have similar kinds of tests, she plans to be more thorough in the more important psychology course. Since the test in algebra involves problem solving, she will concentrate on working exercise problems in that course. In English, her lowest priority class, she will not try to learn everything in great detail. Instead, she will concentrate on the material that is most likely to be on the test.

By spending a little time developing a study strategy for each course, you may find yourself feeling better about your studies.

EXERCISE 7.0. *Course Analysis*

For the courses you are taking this term, make a course analysis similar to the sample shown in Figure 7.3.

Course	Grade Goal	Expected Test	Study Strategy

Figure 7.3 Sample Analysis of Courses (listed in priority order).

Developing a "Universe of Knowledge"

For a course you want to do well in, you might want to develop a "universe of knowledge"—a summary of all of the main points you must remember for a test. This summary is developed by collecting all of your lecture, textbook and special reading notes. If you used summary sheets with a recall column when taking notes, developing the universe of knowledge would be quite easy.

First, you should divide your notes into the major course topics. Second, organize your notes under these topics—(this may involve cutting and pasting some of your notes to fit under the topics). Third, review the sub-topics to determine if any of them can be placed under any other topic (in order to keep their number to a minimum). Finally, set your books aside and study just your notes.

There are three essential features to this method. They are:

1. Making sure that all major topics that were covered in the course are in your "universe".
2. Carefully organizing your notes to insure that all related subtopics are under the correct major topic.
3. Using all relevant sources of information in developing the universe.

An added benefit to this method is that once completed you can use it to predict test questions. With all of the course information neatly laid out you can determine the emphasis placed on each section (you can be sure there will be more test questions over the sections that received the most emphasis) as well as pointing out areas of conflicting points of view (another prime area for test questions). Therefore, this will allow you to have a pretty good idea beforehand of the make-up of the test.

Studying for Final Exams

Final exams have some special features that should be considered as you develop your study strategy. They often are cumulative, covering the entire term. Therefore, you have a great deal of information to review, some of it from a long time back. Final exams often are scheduled close together. Therefore, you may not be able to study sequentially, preparing for and taking one exam before you start studying for the next. Scheduling your time becomes very important. Final exams also come at the end of a term. Therefore, you have to guard against getting "burned out". If you try to review every part of every course, you may run out of steam and have little energy left for actually taking the exams.

Course	Work	Estimated Time
Psych:	- Read ch. [22pp.] develop sementic maps	2 hrs.
	- Read ch. 15 [18 pp.] semantic map	2 hrs.
	- Flash cards on chs. 14 & 15	2 hrs.
	- Review chs. 1, 2, 5, 7, 8, 10, & 12	5 hrs.
	- Review lecture notes	6 hrs.
	- Review all flash cards	4 hrs.
Algebra:	- Work problem-set 8	3 hrs.
	- Re-work key problems	6 hrs.
Biology:	- Read & underline ch. 6 [15 pp.]	1 1/2 hrs.
	- Review underlineed parts of previous chapters	4 hrs.
	- Review lecture notes	3 hrs.
English Literature:	- Read last 3 assigned short stories	5 hrs.
	- Review lecture notes	3 hrs.

Figure 7.4 Sample work list for Erika Williams.

Develop a "battle plan". Because final exams are very demanding, careful planning is important. Students often become so concerned about how much work is involved that they spend more time worrying than studying, fretting over where to begin or how much time to spend on each part. A couple of hours of planning can save much wasted time and energy. Here is an explanation of how you might prepare a final-exam "battle plan":

1. The three steps described earlier would be continued when you are preparing for final exams: You would rank your courses by importance, try to determine the kinds of tests likely to be given, and decide on your study strategies.
2. Next, about two weeks before the first final exam is to be taken, make a list of the work to be done in each course. As Figure 7.4 shows, this list should include both assignments yet to be completed and material to review.
3. Then, make an extended time schedule for the last two weeks before your final exams begin. This time schedule would be similar to the one shown in Figure 7.4 but would cover two weeks rather than one. During the final two weeks of the term you may have to schedule more study time than usual because of the extra workload. On the time schedule you would distribute the hours estimated on your work list.

Not all of your work-time estimates will be correct, but at least they will give you a starting point for planning your time. If possible, reserve on your time schedule some open spaces of time right before exams. These time blocks can be used for last-minute studying if necessary.

Getting Down to It

Once you have analyzed your courses and decided on a study strategy, the next step is to start the hard work. Beware of letting the preliminaries become an excuse to avoid the actual studying!

Exam Panic

Most of us become somewhat nervous when we are going to be evaluated. This nervousness is natural and, in fact, can even help performance. Someone who is totally relaxed might not work at top efficiency on a test. On the other hand, too much worry and anxiety can severely hinder performance.

Studies have shown that the ability to concentrate and remember is adversely affected by too much tension. Even simple, familiar information can be "forgotten". Often people who have been away from school for some time suffer more from exam panic than other students. Also, people who are less assertive or who lack a good vocabulary suffer more from debilitating anxiety than others.

Exam panic is becoming so nervous when taking a test that you lose your ability to concentrate and think clearly.

Basic Mechanism of Exam Panic

Imagine that you are sitting in a classroom and your teacher hands back a test you took last week. If you are normal, grades are important to you and failure is unpleasant. When your test is handed to you, you see that you received an "F". What happens? If we observe you carefully, we see that your muscles tense, your pupils dilate, your pulse and blood pressure increases and, you begin to perspire—especially on your palms. This set of physical responses, taken together, characterize panic or anxiety.

Imagine again that your instructor announces a surprise quiz immediately after handing back the test on which you received the "F". What might happen? We would probably observe all of the physiological indicators of panic—increased pulse rate, sweaty palms, and so forth. We may also discover that your ability to concentrate and remember is reduced. If we asked how you felt you might say something like, "I can see where the answer is in my book, but I just can't read it.", or "Last night I knew this stuff, but now it escapes me". These two phenomena, the physiological signs of panic and temporary forgetting and remembering the information after the test, are what we mean by test panic.

Dealing with the Problem

There are a number of ways of dealing with exam panic. Probably the best way is by preparing well for the test in the first place. At a midwestern university it was discovered that exam panic, in the vast majority of people, was caused by not knowing how to adequately prepare for their exams. Once they learned how to prepare, their panic disappeared.

If you suffer from exam panic, by all means, try to deal with the problem before an exam, not during it. In addition to preparing well for the exam you should avoid sitting next to someone in an exam who is also anxious. Anxiety seems to be contagious. You might also take a course in assertiveness training because studies show that assertive people tend to suffer less from exam panic. If you still panic on exams after trying the above suggestions, you might see whether relaxation techniques would help.

Relaxation Training

There are two facts about human nature that make relaxation training work: (1) It is impossible to be anxious while you are completely relaxed, and (2) your subconscious mind cannot distinguish between something that you experience and something that you vividly imagine. Therefore, you can reduce some kinds of anxiety by first learning how to become completely relaxed and then, while in a state of relaxation, visualizing yourself in the anxiety-producing situation. By repeating this process many times, you may find that eventually you can also remain relaxed in the real situation you have been visualizing.

The first step of relaxation training is to practice some techniques that help you reach a state of very deep relaxation. Here is an example of such a technique:

1. Sit in a comfortable chair in a quiet room. Tense each of the following muscle groups, one after the other, for a count of ten. In each case, notice how much better you feel when relaxed than when tense.
2. Tighten your hands into fists: then relax them.
3. Straighten your arms, and tense the muscles along your arms.
4. Bend your arms to tense the shoulder muscles.
5. Pull your shoulders back to tense the shoulder muscles.
6. Lean your head back to tighten your neck muscles.
7. Clench your jaw.
8. Wrinkle your brow.
9. Tighten your chest muscles.

10. Push out with your abdomen muscles.
11. Fill your lungs with air. As you exhale, try to release any remaining tension. Repeat this step two or three times.
12. Push your heels against the floor and tighten your thigh and leg muscles.
13. Raise your heels to tense your calf muscles.
14. Repeat the process for any area where tension remains.

By the time you finish these exercises, you probably will be very relaxed. If not, repeat the process later, maybe the next day. Some people take longer than others to learn how to relax. You may want to tape record the instructions, with pauses for doing the exercises, so you do not have to think about which exercise to do next.

After you have succeeded in becoming completely relaxed, you can work at reducing the specific exam anxiety. Begin by vividly visualizing an only mildly threatening aspect of the topic, such as imagining yourself walking to the testing room. Imagine a pleasant, peaceful scene for a while, thinking the word "relax" over and over. Periodically, imagine the test-related scene again. Gradually deal with more and more difficult aspects of the situation, until you can imagine the most stressful parts of taking tests. You may find that these practices, combined with good study techniques, will help reduce your tension.

Relaxation exercises are useful in many situations. For example, you can use them if you have trouble going to sleep or if you are anxious when speaking to a group. After you have practiced the exercises a few times, you probably will be able to relax almost at will.

Cramming

Imagine yourself sitting in your room listening to the radio. A friend drops by and reminds you of the test you have tomorrow. One you had forgotten all about. It's an important course and one in which you want to do well. Your reaction may be similar to the one you might have if you are speeding and see a police car in your rear view mirror. A panic reaction! What can you do? If you haven't kept up with the course very well cramming may be your only recourse to survival.

How to Cram: A 3 Step Method

In order to cram effectively you must approach the task realistically. You must recognize that if you haven't studied up to this point there is no way that you will be able to learn everything. The best you can expect is to survive to the next test. If you follow the steps outlined here you can put some order into what could turn into a very frustrating experience.

Step 1: Set Limits on What You Are Going to Study.

Find out as much as you can about the test. Will it cover the whole term or just a portion of the term? Once this is determined you can focus your energies on studying the appropriate material. Don't worry if the test is essay or multiple choice—study as if it were an essay test. Research shows that if you approach your study as if it were an essay your grade will likely be higher than if you studied as if it was a multiple choice or true-false test.

Step 2: Gather Together Your Study Materials

Bring together your lecture notes, your textbook and any other available materials, e.g., handouts, notes from outside readings, old quizzes, etc. that you can use to study.

Step 3: Study Selectively

In Unit Four we mentoned that our short term memory is limited. When cramming you cannot expect to remember everything. You must select very carefully the most pertinent information to study. You can do this by following this procedure:

a. Determine what your instructors emphasis has been in the course. Look through your lecture notes and find what topics he/she has spent the most time on. Ask yourself if there have been any facts that have been especially stressed. If so, note these topics on paper.

b. Skim each chapter in your textbook carefully. Pick out the main ideas and relevant supporting detail. Do the same with your lecture and outside reading notes.

c. Place all of this information on note paper using the summary sheet method. In the recall column record the headings that are to be used as cues to recitation. In the right hand column record all supporting information. Write on only one side of the page.

d. Once all of the main points and supporting evidence has been put on paper (limit yourself to no more than 15 pages) put your books and lecture notes aside. Now direct your attention to these 5–15 pages of new notes and recite them over and over to yourself. By limiting yourself to only certain key items you take the risk of learning the wrong material, but a least you will have learned something well. Contrast this with trying to learn everything. A frustrating task at best and at worst a complete failure.

Although cramming is only a stop gap measure it does work. However, there are certain cautions to be aware of. Try not to become overly anxious. We have seen that anxiety can have a severely negative effect on your memory. Also try to avoid spending all night studying. Loss of sleep must be weighted against the cost of loss of alertness when actually confronted with the test.

It is obviously better to avoid situations where cramming is necessary. But if it is unavoidable, cram as we suggest. The right procedure will maximize your chances of passing the test.

Summary

By preparing for exams in a systematic way, you may be able to improve your performance and reduce your anxiety. A suggested sequence is: (1) Decide how to divide your study energies and time; (2) try to determine roughly what to expect on the tests; and (3) at least partly on the basis of the result of steps 1 and 2, decide on your study strategy for each course. Final exams have some special characteristics that require a somewhat different approach. It is recommended that you develop a final-exam "battle plan" covering the last two weeks or so before your final exams begin. Always be sure to use your study strategies. If exam panic is a big problem for you, relaxation training is a possible remedy. Cramming successfully involves a 3 step process, limiting the amount you study, gathering together the appropriate material and studying selectively.

Unit Comprehension Check

If you can answer these questions, you have retained many of the main points of this unit at the literal level.

1. What attitude about taking exams is recommended?

2. When should you start to prepare for exams?

3. What are the three recommended steps for preparing for tests?

4. Name at least three (ethical) sources from which you can learn what to expect on a test.

5. List at least three questions to ask yourself about an exam you will be taking.

6. Should you study the same way for all your tests?

7. What is a "universe of knowledge"?

8. What are the two main kinds of tasks that should be included on a list of work to be done before final exams?

9. What are two facts about human nature that make relaxation training work as a remedy for exam panic?

10. List the 3 steps to successful cramming.

Study Questions

1. Compare the way you now prepare for exams with the method suggested in this unit.

2. What do you see as the strong and weak points about the suggested preparation methods?

Supplemental Activity

Make it a point to see each instructor at least once during the term to discuss how to prepare for the exam.

EXERCISE 7.1. *Action Plan*

Directions: Identify one or more ideas from this Unit that you believe that you can successfully incorporate into your study. Develop an Action Plan to help yourself become more effective.

Goals	Strategies to Complete Goal	Completion Date	Evaluation Procedure

Vocabulary Development

Suffixes

A suffix is a word part added to the end of a word. Usually this addition does not change the basic meaning of the word, only its part of speech. The ending will tell you if the word is a noun, verb, adverb, or adjective. For example, the word *soft* (adjective) becomes an adverb by adding *ly* to form *softly*. An example of each usage follows:

noun: king + dom = kingdom
verb: class + ify = classify
adverb: quick + ly = quickly
adjective: thought + less = thoughtless

In the following exercises you will become familiar with various suffixes that can help you expand your vocabulary.

Four Noun Suffixes

hood   An Old English suffix. The noun *man* remains a noun when it becomes *manhood*.

ness   An Old English suffix. The adjective *sweet* changes to a noun when it becomes *sweetness*.

ism   A Greek suffix. The noun *republic* remains a noun when it becomes republicanism.

ive   A Latin suffix. The verb *detect* changes to a noun when it becomes *detective*.

Vocabulary Exercise 1

Study the four noun suffixes presented above. In the following sentences, change the italicized word by using one of the suffixes. Write the new word on the line following each sentence.

1. The other workers find her *happy* contagious. _____

2. The early *child* stage is an interesting phase of development to study. _____

3. *Social* has been advocated by people throughout the ages. _____

4. Often *cap* people become very depressed. _____

5. There is a *like* that the race may be cancelled because of heavy rains.

   _____

6. Throughout the late 1800s *industry* flourished. _____

7. There was great *sad* over the death of the president. _____

8. A *direct* was sent to all department heads concerning overtime pay.

   _____

Vocabulary Exercise 2

Match the noun suffixes in column B to the words in Column A by writing the identifying letter in column B on the line in column A. Then write the new word in Column C. Study the example before you begin.

A		B	C
c	foolish	a. ive	foolishness
a	invent	b. hood	inventive
b	father	c. ness	fatherhood

A	B	C
1. _____ pay	a. ee	_____
2. _____ boy	b. age	_____
3. _____ friend	c. ster	_____
4. _____ waste	d. ment	_____
5. _____ refer	e. hood	_____
6. _____ gang	f. ship	_____
7. _____ detect	g. ist	_____
8. _____ private	h. ness	_____
9. _____ pretty	i. ive	_____
10. _____ noble	j. dom	_____
11. _____ science	k. ity	_____
12. _____ king	l. cy	_____

Skim/Scan
Exercise 7

1. Record your starting time.
2. Rapidly preview-skim the entire selection.
3. Record your ending time.
4. Answer the skimming questions.
5. Go on to the scanning questions.
6. Determine your skimming and scanning scores and your skimming words-per-minute rate.
7. Enter your skimming score and rate on the progress graph in the appendix at the end of this book.

Computerizing Supermarket Checkout

by Irene Malbin

	Hour	Min.	Secs.
A. Ending time:	____	____	____
B. Starting time:	____	____	____
C. A − B = Reading time:		____	____

UPC. These letters do not stand for a new government agency, a new chemical, or a new football league. They are shorthand for "Universal Product Code." Supermarket shoppers across the Nation are seeing the UPC symbol on the packages of all kinds of products, from food to paper towels to detergents to over-the-counter (non-prescription) drugs. The symbol consists of many closely spaced lines, bars, and numbers and will be popping up on more and more items as time goes by.

The lines and bars in the code symbol are unique to that product and can be read by a computer.

When the customer reaches the checkout stand, the clerk slides the product, UPC side down, over a scanning device which uses a laser beam. As the product is passed over the scanner, a message is sent to the store's computer, which identifies the item, "rings" it up on the computer terminal at the checkout counter, and prints a description of the item and the price on the customer's receipt. In addition to identifying the product, the UPC, when used in conjunction with a computer, also can function as an automated inventory system. The computer can tell management how much of a specific item is on hand, how fast it is being sold, when and how much to order, and community buying patterns.

The UPC symbol itself does not contain the price, only information about the name, manufacturer, and size of the product. The computer is programmed to reflect the current price. For chain stores, price information can be stored in a central computer serving an entire city or similar geographic area. The central computer will feed data to smaller computers located in each of the chain's stores.

This means that a supermarket firm can keep an exact, up-to-the-minute inventory of all UPC items in each store using the system, and an overall inventory for all the outlets served by the central computer. The manager of an individual outlet, by using the small computer in the store, can tell exactly how much money should be in cash registers at any given time, the dollar amount of sales handled by each clerk, and which products are moving fastest off the shelves.

Reprinted from the November, 1975, *FDA Consumer*.

Under the UPC system, each item is rung up separately. The computer can be programmed, however, to permit volume discounts, such as an item that is priced at "3 for 29 cents." In this instance, the computer would charge 10 cents for the first and second items, but 9 cents for the third. The computer also can be programmed to permit the use of food stamps and special promotional campaigns such as "cents-off" coupons that are acceptable as partial payment for certain products.

The kind of cash register receipt the customer gets at the checkout counter will vary somewhat, depending on the type of computer-assisted system used. In one system installed in the Washington, D.C., area, the customer sees the brand name and price of each item flashed on an electronic screen as it is rung up at the checkout counter and the brand name and price also is printed on the receipt. Not all systems show the name of the product on the receipt, however.

All this new technology and equipment does not come cheap. The supermarket industry estimates that it costs about $100,000 per store to set up the computerized UPC checkout system, but maintains that the equipment ultimately will more than pay for itself through increased operating efficiency and that the savings could be passed on to the consumer in the form of lower food prices.

The major supermarkets and the food manufacturers, processors, and distributors have agreed on the design of the UPC symbol and on the technology needed to make it work. But the system is not being implemented without controversy. Consumer and labor groups have raised a number of questions and issues. Among them:

• Checkout speed: Industry contends that the checkout process will be much faster and that each checker will be able to handle more customers. Consumer and labor groups see a potential for increased checkout speed, but say the supermarket may use the faster-moving lines as a justification for reducing the number of checkout stands. If this happens, the result would be faster-moving but longer lines—with little or no time saved by the customer.

• Checkout errors: Industry says that because most of the prices will be "rung up" on the register automatically by the computer, there will be fewer errors caused by the clerk ringing up the wrong price. Those opposed to the system agree that fewer errors of this type will occur, but say that the information fed into the computer could be wrong, or the computer could malfunction. They also argue that price increases may be coded into the computer before the price posted on the shelf or stamped on the product is changed. Thus, consumers would pay more than the posted price and may not be aware of the difference.

• Sales receipts: Some computer assisted checkout systems produce receipts that show the price, size, type, and brand name of each product purchased. With this system the consumer can save the receipts and check back on past prices and also check prices among stores. If the system does not have this feature, then the customer is no better off than with the familiar cash register receipts that show prices and sometimes the type of product, such as meat or produce, but not the brand or size.

• Check cashing: Because the computer can store information on regular customers, a check can be approved immediately. Consumer advocates agree that this would save time but are concerned that this information might be sold to credit bureaus or direct mail houses.

• Item Pricing: This is the most controversial part of the system. Industry maintains that to make the most efficient use of and achieve the maximum savings from the UPC computer checkout system prices no longer should be stamped or otherwise marked on individual items. The industry wants to continue the practice of placing the price on the shelf under the product to which it applies, but eliminate the price on each item. Industry points out that in addition to being posted on the shelf, the price of each item appears on the cash register receipt and, in some UPC systems, is flashed on the electronic monitor at the checkout counter. This should provide the consumer with sufficient price information, industry says.

The Consumer Federation of America (CFA) calls the proposed elimination of item pricing "a new supermarket ripoff" and charges that package price information is second only to supermarket cleanliness as a consumer desire. If prices are not placed on individual items, the Federation says, shoppers will have difficulty comparing the price of various products—such as canned vs. frozen vs. fresh—since these are in separate parts of the store and the customer would have to remember a shelf tag price instead of being able to look at the package. Also, the rapid checkout and bagging could make it difficult for the purchaser to keep up with the price information being flashed on the monitor at the checkout counter.

Other consumer objections are that prices placed on very high or very low shelves will be hard to read, and that unless the shelves are kept neat the customer may not know which posted price refers to which product.

Some consumers also complain that if the price is not stamped on each item, they will not be able to compare the current price of a product with what it cost the last time they purchased it unless they save their register receipts. Even these receipts will not make price comparisons possible unless they include information on the brand and size of the products purchased.

The result, CFA feels will be reduced price consciousness by consumers, a tendency that can lead to wasteful buying practices.

Supermarket firms estimate that use of the UPC system would result in monthly savings to the company of $10,000 per store or $120,000 per year. The supermarkets say that if they eliminate marking prices on individual items food prices may not go up as quickly and, in some cases, may be stabilized. CFA estimates savings to the industry at considerably less than $10,000 per store, per month. It says that if item pricing is eliminated a supermarket with annual sales of $3 million would save $34,700 per year by using the UPC system. The same store would save $23,000 if it continued to mark the price on each item, CRA contends. The weekly difference in savings— $225—is worth it to the store to satisfy consumer desire for price information, CFA believes.

One chain, Giant Food, is conducting an experiment in two stores in Maryland that are equipped with the UPC system. One store is continuing to use item pricing; the other is not. The stores are similar in size. At the end of the year, the company will evaluate consumer reaction to both systems and compare costs benefits to the company.

Four states, California, Connecticut, Massachusetts, and Rhode Island, and the city of Chicago have adopted laws requiring the posting of prices on each item. Several other states and cities are considering such laws. The supermarket industry says it should be given a chance to try out a system without prices on packages. Consumer advocates fear that if item pricing is once eliminated it will never be brought back.

As the agency with primary authority over food labeling, FDA has no objection to use of the UPC on the labels of regulated products so long as its location does not interfere with the placement or clarity of certain required information. Information required by FDA on the label of a food prduct includes a list of ingredients (except on some standardized foods), the name and address of the manufacturer, the name of the product, net contents, and nuitrition information if nutrients are added or a nutritional claim is made for the product.

Because it has regulatory responsibility for certain products that emit electronic rays, including lasers, FDA had to be sure that the laser beam used in the electronic checkout system was safe. FDA has approved the laser beam system as safe both for store employees and customers.

Although it is most often associated with food and related products, the UPC system also can be used on drugs. Under its National Drug Code (NDC), FDA is assigning an identification number to every drug, prescription as well as over-the-counter. This will help FDA to identify all drugs commercially marketed in this country, and to track more effectively drug products that are recalled from the market.

A company may voluntarily list this NDC number on the label of the drug. Since the NDC number can be read by the scanners used in the UPC system, the NDC number on a nonprescription drug sold in a computerized supermarket also will be used as the UPC for that product.

Prescription drugs bearing the NDC/UPC number on the label and packaged in the most commonly prescribed sizes could be processed through the computer checkout systems of supermarkets that offer pharmacy services or at drug stores which may adopt computer checkout.

Many medical products, such as crutches, bandages, and similar items, also are sold in supermarkets. Since the National Health Related Items Code established by FDA for these products is compatible with the UPC, they too can be incorporated into computerized checkout systems.

One other use of the compatible NDC/UPC number is in health insurance reimbursement for drug expenses. The pharmacist, instead of filling out the name, quantity, and description of a drug, would only need to put down the NDC/UPC number on insurance forms to provide the insurance company with a complete identification of the drug ordered.

Skimming Questions: *Circle the letter of the best answer.*

1. The UPC symbol does *not* contain the:
   a. product name
   b. product size
   c. manufacturer
   d. price

2. Consumer groups predict that UPC may cause:
   a. more checkout errors
   b. longer checkout lines
   c. slower checkout lines
   d. higher operation costs

3. The most controversial part of the UPC system involves:
   a. item pricing
   b. checkout errors
   c. sales receipts
   d. check cashing

4. In addition to food and related products, UPC will be used on:
   a. hardware items
   b. drugs
   c. books
   d. automobile parts

5. Some states and cities have passed laws that:
   a. prohibit use of UPC
   b. regulate the beam used in the system
   c. require posting of prices on individual items
   d. limit use of UPC to food items

Scanning Questions

1. It costs about $ _____ per store to set up a UPC system.

2. Supermarket firms estimate a savings of $ _____ per year for each

   store.

3. The letters "UPC" stand for the words _____ _____

   _____ .

4. The scanning device in a UPC system uses a _____ beam.

5. The _____ supermarket chain is conducting an experiment to determine the cost savings from UPC.

Time-Rate Conversion Chart

Min:Sec	WPM	Min:Sec	WPM	Min:Sec	WPM	Min:Sec	WPM	Min:Sec	WPM
1:00	1985	4:50	411	8:40	229	12:30	159	16:20	122
1:10	1701	5:00	397	8:50	225	12:40	157	16:30	120
1:20	1489	5:10	384	9:00	221	12:50	155	16:40	119
1:30	1323	5:20	372	9:10	217	13:00	153	16:50	118
1:40	1191	5:30	361	9:20	213	13:10	151	17:00	117
1:50	1083	5:40	350	9:30	209	13:20	149	17:10	116
2:00	993	5:50	340	9:40	205	13:30	147	17:20	115
2:10	916	6:00	331	9:50	202	13:40	145	17:30	113
2:20	851	6:10	322	10:00	199	13:50	143	17:40	112
2:30	794	6:20	313	10:10	195	14:00	142	17:50	111
2:40	744	6:30	305	10:20	192	14:10	140	18:00	110
2:50	701	6:40	298	10:30	189	14:20	138	18:10	109
3:00	662	6:50	290	10:40	186	14:30	137	18:20	108
3:10	627	7:00	284	10:50	183	14:40	135	18:30	107
3:20	596	7:10	277	11:00	180	14:50	134	18:40	106
3:30	567	7:20	271	11:10	178	15:00	132	18:50	105
3:40	541	7:30	265	11:20	175	15:10	131	19:00	104
3:50	518	7:40	259	11:30	173	15:20	129	19:10	104
4:00	496	7:50	253	11:40	170	15:30	128	19:20	103
4:10	476	8:00	248	11:50	168	15:40	127	19:30	102
4:20	458	8:10	243	12:00	165	15:50	125	19:40	101
4:30	441	8:20	238	12:10	163	16:00	124	19:50	100
4:40	425	8:30	234	12:20	161	16:10	123		

Unit 7 Answer Key

Unit Comprehension Check

1. Think of exams as evaluations instead of as punishments.
2. The first day of classes, or as soon as possible
3. (a) decide how to divide your time and energy (b) learn what to expect on the tests (c) decide on your study strategy
4. For example: From the syllabus, from what the instructor tells you directly in class, from what the instructor stresses in lectures, from talking with the instructor, from a student who has taken the course, or from a file of past exams.
5. For example: What form(s) will be used for the questions? How detailed must your knowledge be? How much of the material will be covered? What proportion of items will come from each source? What levels of understanding are required?
6. No. Your study strategies should vary depending on the nature of the test and your own goals.
7. A summary of all the important information in the course
8. (a) assigning work yet to be done (b) material to be reviewed.
9. (a) you can not be anxious while relaxed (b)If you visualize something vividly, your subconscious mind cannot distinguish it from an actual experience.
10. (a) set limits on what you are going to study (b) gather together your study materials (c) study selectively.

Vocabulary Development

Exercise 1
1. happiness
2. childhood
3. socialism
4. captive
5. likelihood
6. industrialism
7. sadness
8. directive

Exercise 2
1. d, payment
2. e, boyhood
3. f, friendship
4. b, wastage
5. a, refer
6. c, gangster

7. i, detective
8. l, privacy
9. h, prettiness
10. k, nobility
11. g, scientist
12. j, kingdom

Skim/Scan Exercise

Skim
1. d 2. b 3. a 4. b 5. c

Scan
1. $100,000
2. $120,000
3. Universal Product Code
4. laser
5. Giant Food

Unit 8

How to Take Examinations

Students vary in their ability to handle tests. Some students seem to be able to do well on them without putting in a lot of study. Others work hard, putting in a lot of extra study time only to do poorly. There are many reasons for these differences in ability to do well on an exam. One important reason that we will discuss in this unit is that some students are simply better test takers; they are more "test-wise". The skills involved in test-wiseness have very little to do with your knowledge of the material; they are related to how well you can squeeze every possible point out of the test. Naturally, the more information you know, the higher your test score should be. But a skillful test taker also knows how to make the best of a bad situation.

Your attitude is important. To be an effective test taker you need a positive, "I-can-do-it" attitude. You might look upon a test as an interesting challenge instead of dreadful ordeal. On the other hand, you should probably not be overly confident. You should know that your confidence is based on being properly prepared. Some nervousness can help your performance on tests. However, too much nervousness probably will have a negative effect.

Some General Suggestions

As mentioned in Unit Seven, there are different types of test questions. There are also different types of exams in general. They fall into two main categories: objective (Multiple-choice, true–false, matching) and essay exams.

Special techniques for dealing with each of these kinds of tests are discussed later. But there are a few suggestions that apply to all test-taking situations, regardless of the kind of test.

Read Directions Carefully

"Oh, my gosh! My time's up and I just realized that it says to answer only TWO of the three questions, I wasted all that time on that third question!" Many students have horror stories like this to report. Being rushed and nervous, they launch into the test without closely reading the instructions. Or they misread an essay question and write an answer with the wrong emphasis.

Keep in mind the danger of misreading. To reduce the danger, underline key words as you read. Take a few extra seconds, if necessary, to make sure you understand the instructions. Typical student errors when reading test directions include:

1. Failing to find out how much time is allowed. Sometimes tests take more than the usual class period and sometimes you are allowed less than the class period. Understanding how much time you have is important because tests are graded

on the number of points you are able to accrue in the allotted time. The better you understand the time limit, the greater the chance you will use the test period productively.

2. Failure to know if special study aids are allowed. How often do you hear "I didn't know that we could use _____ on the test. If only I would have known I'd done a lot better (fill in the blank with calculator, a list of formulas, scratch paper, etc.)." If you haven't heard that statement you either haven't been in school very long or you associate with some exceptionally good test direction readers or listeners. Make sure you understand what you can or cannot use during a test to make the test taking easier on yourself.

3. Failure to know the number of questions that are to be answered, if only several are to be answered from a list. Students lose a great many points if they fail to understand this part of the directions. They either waste their time answering questions they don't need to—thereby losing points by not answering a fewer number of questions more completely—or losing points because they answered a question they were not supposed to answer—thereby wasting time they could have spent answering the right questions.

4. Failure to understand the scoring system. Tests are graded based on the number of correct responses and the number of points you make. Some tests differ in the point value given to certain questions—some questions are worth more points than others. Your task is to decide where you should spend your time to get the most points. For example, if you have a choice of 50 True/False questions worth 2 points each and 2 essay questions worth 10 points each, you would be foolish to spend a major portion of your time on the essay questions.

If you are in doubt about the directions make certain you get clarification from the examiner. Research done at the University of Chicago has shown that poor test takers tend to misread directions and questions. Do not join their ranks.

Budget Your Time

Two of your goals when taking a test should be: (a) to complete all the items you are expected to, and (b) to have a little time for review at the end. If you do not complete all the items you will unnecessarily lose points. In almost every case it is better to finish the test, even though you may have to spend a little less time than you would like on some items. Since this problem is especially critical for essay exams, it is discussed in more detail in that section. Review time is important because it gives you a chance to catch errors made through haste. For instance, you might see that you left out a critical "not" that changes the whole meaning of your statement.

If the testing room does not have a clock, beg, borrow, or buy a watch if you don't have one. Without some way to keep track of the time, you will not be able to pace yourself. When taking a test, you do not need the extra worry of wondering how much time you have left.

Answer the Easiest Questions First

This procedure has at least three advantages. First, by starting with questions that you can more easily answer, you are likely to build up your confidence and become more relaxed. Second, you will get credit for all the questions you are sure of. And third, you may find clues in the easy questions (especially on multiple-choice tests) that will help you answer other questions.

Answer Every Item, Usually

If there is no penalty for guessing, you definitely should attempt every question. You probably know more than you are giving yourself credit for. Your "I-can-do-it" attitude would tell you to try your best on every item. But what if there is a penalty for guessing, as is sometimes the case on true-false and multiple-choice tests? Try to find out exactly what kind of "penalty" system is being used by the instructor. Most "penalty-for-guessing" systems do not actually penalize. Since they only correct for chance, you are better off trying every item. You probably will do better than chance on the ones you are not sure of because you usually can narrow down the possibilities by eliminating some incorrect choices in an item.

Control Anxiety

There are ways to prevent or control excessive anxiety. For example, it is recommended that you do not come to the testing room too early. If you arrive early, your anticipation may increase your anxiety. Also, don't get involved in discussions about the material right before the test. Someone is likely to ask a question you cannot answer, raising your anxiety an extra notch. If during the test a difficult item makes you nervous, keep in mind that on most tests, especially objective ones, you are not expected to know the answer to every question. Switch to another question and return to the stumper later. Or take a deep breath and let it out slowly before tackling the item. Also, remember that it is normal to have an initial feeling sometimes that you don't know the answer to a question. The answer may begin to reveal itself once you've actually begun to work on the problem.

Taking Objective Exams

Multiple-choice, true–false, matching and similar exams are called objective tests because there is only one correct answer for each item. No matter who scores the test, the results should be the same unless a scoring error is made. Therefore, your main goal is to match the question to your knowledge and decide on the most reasonable answer.

Don't Overinterpret a Question

A very common problem among students who do poorly on objective tests is reading too much into the questions. Perhaps this habit comes from expecting trick questions. For example, suppose a question reads:

The tendency to avoid remembering something fearful is called:

a. rejection
b. avoidance
c. repression (correct answer)
d. withdrawal

The distrustful student might think, "I believe 'C' is the answer, but that seems almost too easy. Maybe the instructor expects me to grab at the obvious. Could it be "rejection" instead?" Thus, the student manages to eliminate the correct answer. In fact, few instructors try to write "trick" questions. Your best policy is to select the answer that seems most reasonable.

Don't Be Afraid to Change Answers

Do not be afraid to change your mind after you have selected an answer if you have a good reason. A myth still survives that you should stick with your original choice. But numerous research studies indicate the opposite. These studies indicate that most students are at least likely to change an incorrect answer to a correct one than the other way around. For some students the odds are closer to four to one in their favor. But since individuals vary, you should check your own record by examining some old tests. Total the number of changes from right to wrong and the number from wrong to right.

Have a System for Rechecking Items You Are Uncertain About

When you are somewhat unsure about an answer you have chosen, you might put a small dot next to the item. Then, after completing the test, you can recheck the uncertain items if there is time. By that time the answer may be more clear to you.

Make An Attempt at Every Question

When you come up against a difficult question, think it through, be aggressive in trying to answer it. If necessary, try to reword the question. For example, the question "What economic changes took place between the years 1940 to 1945," might more easily be understood by re-wording it this way: "What economic changes took place just prior to and during World War II." Try to make the questions as concrete as possible. After answering the questions, evaluate your answer to make sure it makes sense.

Test-Wiseness Clues

Instructor-made tests seldom are perfect. Unless an instructor uses the same test a number of times and weeds out poor items, the test is likely to contain clues to correct answers. These "test-wiseness" clues may allow you to answer correctly a few more questions than you would be able to otherwise. But before you decide to sell your textbooks and stop attending lectures, you should be aware of some cautions about test-wiseness clues:

1. Test-wiseness clues do not make studying obsolete. Sorry. These clues only slightly raise your chances of correctly answering a question. If you don't know the material, using the clues will simply mean that you will still do poorly, but with a slightly higher score. Therefore, you should only use clues for items that cannot be answered in any other way.
2. If the instructor knows about test-wiseness clues, beware. It's fair game to make questions that you would answer incorrectly if you responded on the basis of an apparent clue.
3. Test-wiseness clues tend not to help on carefully constructed standardized tests, such as the SAT. In these tests, questions with such clues usually have been detected and revised or eliminated.

With these limitations in mind, let's consider some of the most useful clues.

Clues Outside the Test

Two of your most valuable aids are your common sense and background knowledge. If you cannot choose an answer on the basis of what you have learned in class, you may be able to make a choice, or at least narrow your choices, on the basis of common sense and general knowledge. For example:

Homo erectus is mainly distinguished from Homo sapiens by Homo erectus' less highly evolved:

a. head and brain
b. pelvis
c. feet
d. hands

Suppose you know general background knowledge that Homo sapiens is modern man and that none of his ancestors matched man's intelligence (brain). Then your common sense may tell you to choose "head and brain," which is the correct answer.

Clues in Other Test Items

It is very difficult for an instructor to make up a long objective test without writing some test items that give clues to other items. This is one reason why you should answer the easiest items first. Then, when you work on the more difficult items, you may recall a clue from the other items. For example:

Homo sapiens' orthograde skeletal structure is most similar to:

a. beavers
b. apes
c. bears
c. deer

An animal with an orthograde skeletal structure is said to:

a. live in the water
b. walk on two legs
c. walk on four legs
d. have no foramen magnum

The first item tells you that Homo sapiens has an orthograde skeleton. Thus, you can conclude that "walk on two legs" must be the correct answer to the second item.

Clues Between the Stem and Alternatives

The "stem" is the first part of the multiple-choice item. There are two main clues between the stem and alternatives:

1. Grammatical agreement. You usually can eliminate a choice if it does not grammatically agree with the stem. You must read an item very carefully to spot these errors. However, the error may be a typographical mistake, so if you believe the choice is the correct one use it anyway.

   An ancient Greek coin is a:

   a. icon
   b. drashma
   c. escudo
   d. eulalia

In this item, all the choices except "b" can be eliminated because they would require "an" instead of "a" to be grammatically correct.

2. Word association. Sometimes a word or phrase in the stem may give a clue to the incorrect choice. For example:

Charles Dickens' Hard Times deals with:

a. the limits of growth
b. the court of King Stephen of Russia
c. the difficult life of a factory worker
d. the politics of the French countryside

The title Hard Times points to "c" as the correct answer.

On the other hand, sometimes an instructor will purposely use a similar word in the stem and in an incorrect choice to mislead students who do not know the correct answer. For instance, in the first example in the section, about avoiding remembering something fearful, there appears to be a word-association clue between the word "avoid" and the incorrect choice, "avoidance". In this case, the apparent clue is a false lead.

Clues Where the Multiple Choices Are Compared

In some cases you can make or narrow your choices by comparing the alternatives. Two of the most effective comparison clues are mentioned here:

1. Middle values. When the choices give a range of numerical values, the correct answer may be one of the middle values. There is a strong tendency for most instructors to want the correct answer to be within a range of values instead of at either extreme. For example:

The most effective temporal relationship between the US and CS is:

a. simultaneous presentation
b. a three-second interval
c. a .05-second interval
d. a half-second interval

The middle-value clue would indicate that the correct answer is either "c" or "d". In fact, the correct answer is "d".

2. Opposites. If two choices are opposite or nearly opposite in meaning, one of them may be the correct choice. This tendency exists because when an instructor is trying to think of some effective distractors (incorrect choices), the opposite of the correct choice comes to mind. For example:

The planarian has:

a. an anterior brain
b. a posterior brain
c. six legs
d. an undeveloped rotus cepter

The "opposites" clue would point to "a" or "b" as the correct answer. (The correct answer is "a".)

3. The Specific-Determiner Clue. This clue can be used in multiple-choice and true–false tests. The basic idea is that in the real world there are exceptions to many statements. For example, you could not say "All books are composed of paper" because somewhere there may be one book made of some other material. Therefore, certain absolute words are clues that an item or choice may be false. Some of these words are always, never, totally, completely, and forever. For example:

T-F: Cressey feels that the legal definition of embezzlement is thoroughly adequate for scientific purposes.

The phrase "thoroughly adequate" would indicate that this statement is false.

But, as with all clues, you must use your common sense with specific determiners. In some disciplines, such as the sciences, it is possible to make absolute statements that are true. For example:

T-F: Insects always have six legs.

Since having six legs is part of the definition of an insect, this item is correct even though the absolute word "always" is included. Can you think of some other scientific absolutes?

Of course, test-wiseness clues are not always as clear-cut as these examples indicate. Sometimes there may be two or more apparent clues in an item, each clue leading to a different answer. And, above all, remember that these clues should be used only as a last resort.

EXERCISE 8.0: *Test Wiseness Clues*

Answer these questions on the basis of apparent test-wiseness clues. Check your responses against the answer key at the end of this unit.

1. Aesthetic distance generally is connected with:
   a. intellect
   b. emotion
   c. culture
   d. viewing space
   Clue: _____

   Choice: _____

2. The percentage of conventional offenders in a typical adult prison is approximately:
   a. 10 percent
   b. 50 percent
   c. 75 percent
   d. 90 percent
   Clue: _____

   Choice: _____

3. The Strong-Campbell Vocational Interest Inventory is used for:
   a. reading skills
   b. investment decisions
   c. career decisions
   d. math placement
   Clue: _____

   Choice: _____

4. T-F: Anxiety is always a sign of neuroticism.
   Clue: _____

   Choice: _____

5. The variable that affect depth of field are:
    a. shutter speed
    b. subject distance
    c. focal length and aperture setting
    d. light level
    Clue: _____

    Choice: _____

6. T-F: Rewards are always more effective than punishments to change behavior.
    Clue: _____

    Choice: _____

Multiple Options

Some students become confused when given a question that has multiple options, such as:

You can improve your memory by:

a. clustering information into approximately seven groups
b. studying for prolonged periods
c. associating new information with what you know
d. a and b
e. a and c
f. b and c
g. all of the above
h. none of the above

To handle this kind of question, deal with each of the original choices (in this case, a, b, and c) as a true-false item. If possible, lightly write a "T" or "F" next to each item. In the example, "a" and "c" are true and "b" is false. Next, simply inspect your choices until you find the one that fits. Since two choices are true in the example, you can rule out "g" and "h". You know the correct answer is either "d", "e" or "f". Since "a" and "c" are the true ones, the correct choice must be "e".

Taking Essay Exams

For some students, learning that they will be taking an essay exam feels roughly like learning that they will have to swim across a lake with their hands tied. These students are usually the ones who do not write well. They realize that they will be penalized because of their lack of writing skills—and they are right. Essay-exam scores are based on more than just how much you know. They also are based on how well you can organize and express your ideas. Because of this, some testing experts question whether essay exams are fair for courses in which writing skills are not part of the course contest.

Fair or not, essay exams are a fact of life for many students. Whether or not you are a good writer, you may be able to improve your performance on essay exams by developing an effective system.

How Essay Exams Are Scored

Looking at essay tests from the scorer's point of view may help you perform better on them. First of all, you should realize that you can receive a low score on a response even though everything you write is correct. You usually are being compared with the other students on how detailed your answer is as well as how accurate it is. One scoring method involves sorting responses into piles according to their quality. If you were the scorer and had two responses, both accurate, but one with 20 words and another with 150 words, would you put them both in the same pile?

The importance of completeness should affect how you prepare for an essay exam. Put aside the notion that you only need to learn general concepts. Instead, think of yourself as a lawyer who will have to defend a case with evidence: examples, explanations, and so forth. You will usually need both main ideas and supporting details.

Neatness Counts

We are not talking about a job interview, but the situations are very similar. You know how important first impressions can be. Also, you are not helping your case if the scorer gets a headache from trying to read your writing. In one research study, scorers were given piles of papers to correct. Unknown to the scorers, the content was the same on some papers, but the penmanship varied. Poor penmanship costs some responses as much as one letter grade compared with the neater versions. So use a proper writing instrument. Print if necessary. In other words, be as neat as you can without unduly sacrificing speed. Also, be aware of the color of the ink you use. Some instructors may unconsciously be biased toward a student who uses a color or ink other than blue or black. Certainly don't use red ink when writing your essay exam!

Always Write Something

If you don't write anything, you leave the scorer no choice but to give you zero points. On the other hand, if you write anything at all you may receive partial credit, or possibly even full credit. With essay exams you should always assume that you can say something of value about the topic.

A Systematic Approach

During a fire drill everyone follows certain prescribed steps. After enough drills, each person can accomplish these steps automatically despite the anxiety caused by the situation. Do you have a fire-drill routine for taking an essay exam? Some students only think about essay exams while taking them. They waste time and lose points trying to figure out how to get organized. A little preplanning might help. Here are some steps to consider. Some have already been mentioned in the "general suggestions" section earlier, but they are repeated and expanded on here because they are especially useful in dealing with essay exams.

1. Preview the questions. Read all the questions first. Underline any key words. Jot down brief notes for any ideas that come to mind on your first reading. If you don't write down a thought, you might forget it by the time you are ready to start writing.
2. Budget your time. This is a very important step. In most cases you are not expected to have the time to write everything you know about a topic. Yet some students spend so much time on one question that they have little or no time left for another one. Consider the following case in which there are two questions, each worth twenty-five points, to be answered during fifty minutes:

> Student A received only a few more points than Student B on question 1, and lost many points on question 2. Spending extra time and effort on a few final details may earn you few or no extra points and take valuable time away from other questions. Therefore, be sure to budget your time according to the value of each question. If point weights are not given, base your time budgeting on the estimated time needed to write each response.

EXERCISE 8.1: *Time Management in Tests*

If you had sixty minutes, how would you divide your time for these essay questions, assuming you knew enough information on each question? Check your responses against the answer key.

3. Select your first question. Begin with an easy one. Starting with an easy question will help you relax and develop confidence. But be sure to stop when your budgeted time is up, even if you could write more!

Before beginning to write, reread the directions to be certain you understand them. Essay-exam "questions" usually are not really in the form of questions, but rather in the form of·instructions. And these instructions usually contain certain key words that must be understood if the directions are to be followed correctly. If you misunderstand, you may spend your time writing an excellent essay emphasizing the wrong thing. For example, you might describe something when you have been asked to evaluate it. Or you might compare two things when the instructions say to contrast them. Below is a list of some key instruction words that you should be aware of:

Compare. (e.g., Compare the Greek and Roman forms of government.) You should examine qualities or characteristics. Usually similarities are stressed, but differences can also be discussed.

Contrast. (e.g., Contrast the conservative and liberal views of the role of the federal government.) You should concentrate on differences between the things you are asked to contrast.

Criticize. (e.g., Criticize one of the assigned plays.) In everyday usage the word "criticize" usually means emphasizing the negative. But when used in essay-exam instructions, the word means to judge both the merits and faults of the thing being considered. A critic, in the case, should try to give a balanced evaluation.

Define. (e.g., Define the term "metaphor".) A definition should be a short, clear explanation of the meaning of the word. Details are not required, but limitations of the meaning should be stated. You should state how the particular object differs from others of the same class.

Describe. (e.g., Describe the architecture of ancient Greece.) When describing, you tell about something in detail. Usually you try to be objective. You are not making judgments about value or worth.

Diagram. (e.g., Make a diagram of our solar system.) Present a properly labeled drawing, chart, or plan.

Discuss. (e.g., Discuss the events that led to the First World War.) This instruction calls for a detailed analysis that can include description, comparison, contrast, and evaluation. The term "discuss" is broader than most of the others mentioned on this list.

Enumerate. (e.g., Enumerate the reasons why the Roman Empire fell.) "Enumeration" contains the root word "numeral". So this instruction asks you to list and briefly discuss the points asked for.

Evaluate. (e.g., Evaluate the architecture of ancient Greece.) Notice that, except for changing the key instruction word, the example used here is exactly the same as the one used for the term "describe". However, changing the word "describe" to "evaluate" drastically changes the meaning of the instructions. When evaluating, you should give your opinion, supported by examples. Discuss both the advantages and disadvantages.

Explain. (e.g., Explain the common ways that mountains are formed.) When explaining something, clarify and interpret the material you are dealing with. You should state the "how" or "why" and discuss any differences of opinion among experts or differences in experimental results.

Illustrate.	The exact meaning of this term will depend on the context. "Illustrate the forgetting curve" probably means to draw a graph of the curve. But "illustrate" on an essay exam will likely mean to give a clear example. For instance, "Illustrate the law of effect with an example".
Interpret.	(e.g., Interpret the poem "The Solitary Reaper.") Interpreting and explaining are similar. You should translate, give examples, solve, or discuss the subject. Also include your judgment or feelings about the problem.
Justify.	(e.g., Predict the kind of government you expect the United States to have in fifty years. Justify your prediction.) When justifying give evidence to support your conclusions.
List.	(e.g., List the steps in the problem-solving system discussed in class.) Listing is like enumerating. You are expected to present an itemized series.
Outline.	(e.g., Outline the major events in the Battle of Gettysburg.) An outline is an organized description that concentrates on the most important points and omits minor details.
Prove.	(e.g., Describe an experiment you could use to prove that light travels at 186,000 miles per second.) Proof demands that you confirm or verify. You should make your point with certainty by logical reasoning or by stating and evaluating evidence.
Relate.	"Relate" can have two meanings. "Relate the start of the Second World War to the events following the First World War" means to show a relationship. Your answer should show connections or associations in a descriptive manner. "Relate" could also mean simply to tell, as, for example, "Relate the events leading to the Great Depression."
Review.	(e.g., Review the strengths and weaknesses of the "Big Bang" theory.) A review requires a critical examination. You should systematically analyze the major points of the problem.
State.	(e.g., State the theory of relativity.) When stating, you are being asked to briefly express the main points. Details usually are omitted.
Summarize.	(e.g., Summarize the evidence that led Darwin to develop this evolutionary theory.) A summary is a condensed discussion of the main points or facts. For example, each unit in this book contains a summary at the end.
Trace.	(e.g., Trace the development of the automobile.) You should describe a series of events in chronological or other logical order.

EXERCISE 8.2: *Test Vocabulary*

Read each of the explanations below. In the blank space, write a term that the instructor might use when composing the question. Choose the term from the above list. Check your responses against the answer key.

1. In a management course the professor wants the students to show differences between the functions and responsibilities of a president and executive vice-president. Which term should he use in his question?

   _____

2. A professor of economics has discussed a particular economic policy held by the government. He suggests how this policy could be used to overcome a particular situation. If he wants the students to express their judgments on the merits of the plan, which term should he use in his question? (There are two possibilities.)

   _____

3. Which term would he use if a professor wanted a concrete example of a principle in management?

   _____

4. When and where did psychoanalysis have its beginning? What has been the general history of its development? The professor wants the students to follow the course of its progress. What term should he use?

   _____

5. In an economics class the professor has discussed the effects of import taxes on consumer costs. On an examination she wants the students to think over the topic and consider it from different points of view. She wants to present all of the problem. Which term should she use?

   _____

6. In a geography class the professor wants the students to make clear the nature of the last ice age, when it occurred and what effect it had on the North American landscape. Which term would she use in her question?

_____

7. In a political science course the professor has discussed the political philosophies of Marx, Engels, and Castro. On a written examination he wants the students to pick out the main points of the discussion and bring them together in a concise overall statement. What term should he use in his question?

_____

8. In a reading class the professor has told the students how to preview a textbook chapter. On a quiz she wants the students to give the steps, one after the other. What term should she use?

_____

9. In a speech class the professor has explained the term "extemporaneous". On a quiz she wants to be sure that the students know the meaning of the term. What term should she use in her question?

_____

10. In a marketing class the professor wants her students to consider the ways in which the marketing programs of Exxon and Sears are alike and the ways in which they are different. What term should she use in her question?

_____

4. Develop a Semantic Map of Your Answer

Once you have selected the first question to work on, your next job is to organize your thoughts. Unless your response will be very brief, you should make a semantic map before you begin your essay. A semantic map is a hierarchial arrangement of concepts related to the topic which goes from a high level of abstraction down to the concrete details. This technique is an extremely useful one because it is built on memory associations. For example, suppose the instructions say: "Describe the composition of the Federal Government," your semantic map would look something like this:

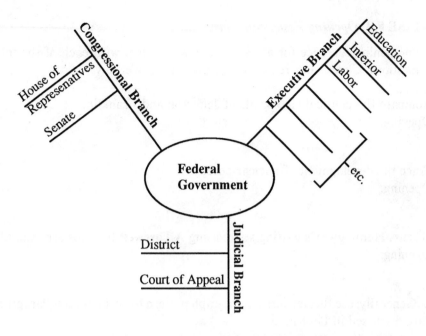

Figure 8.0

Notice that as you move down through each sub-part of the map it becomes more and more concrete and that each part cues you into the next part. A map such as this has a number of advantages. First, you simplify your total task. If your ideas are organized in advance you can concentrate on how to word your thoughts when you write. Second, the map serves as a help in remembering all important concepts and principles in order to answer the question well. Under the pressure of an exam, you might forget an important idea if you don't jot it down. Third, if you are unable to complete your essay, the instructor at least can see that you knew the information and may give you some credit for what is in your map.

5. Write your essay. There are certain steps you can follow when writing your essay. If you have these steps clearly in mind, you may be able to save writing time and make your response more effective.

a. Begin your response by rephrasing the essay question in sentence form. This gives you an easy way to start. Also, by rephrasing the question, you are forcing yourself to read the question one more time, another check against misunderstanding the instructions. For instance, suppose the directions say, "Contrast the economic situation in the South before versus after the War Between the States." You might begin your essay this way: "The South had a different economy after the War between the States than it did before." (Since the term "contrast" means to stress differences, you can safely include the expression "different".)

EXERCISE 8.3 *Opening Essay Summary*

Write an opening sentence for an essay that would deal with each of the following essay questions. Check your responses against the answer key.

1. Compare the political viewpoints of Jefferson and Franklin.
   Opening:

2. Trace the development of nuclear energy.
   Opening:

3. Discuss Hemingway's writing style, using **A Farewell to Arms** for examples.
   Opening:

   b. Generally, use the deductive paragraph pattern for your essays. Paragraph patterns are discussed in Unit Five.

   In the deductive pattern, the main idea is stated, and then supporting details are given. Remember that you always should support your general assertions with some kind of evidence. The kind of examples or other evidence you use will indicate the depth of your knowledge.

   c. Write a brief summary at the end of your essay, if you have time. This step is not essential, but it provides a nice stylistic touch.

   Here is a portion of an essay response that follows these three steps:

   Instructions: Briefly discuss three principles of memory that are helpful for studying.

   Response:

   > Three principles of memory that are helpful for studying are: (1) selectivity, (2) recitation, and (3) consolidation.
   > You must be selective; otherwise you will overload your memory. Then you won't be able to remember the important information when you need it. Since the average adult can hold only about seven pieces of information at a time, you need to decide what is important.
   > Recitation is one of the most powerful aids to . . .

   > In summary, you can improve your memory by using methods like selectivity, recitation, and consolidation.

When you have completed a response, leave some extra space below it. You may think of another important point to add later. Then choose your next question and repeat the process.

6. Proofread your answer. Be certain you have not left out any details. Many times we think faster than we can write and we skip writing down some essentials.

Practicing to Improve

If you feel uncomfortable about essay exams, practicing the methods mentioned above may help. But the worst time to practice is during an actual test. Instead, use the concept of simulation. Simulation is used to practice many pressure situations because more learning takes place when the student is relaxed. For example, flight simulators are used to teach basic flying techniques on the ground.

To use simulation for improving your essay exams, make up some likely essay-exam questions from your course material. Try using instruction words like those listed in this unit. Then, set a reasonable time limit for writing your essay. Next, write your response, using the suggested method. Finally, evaluate your essay to see where it could be improved.

Summary

Your test-taking skills can make a difference in your performance on exams. First, work on developing a positive attitude about tests. Then, follow some basic principles about taking tests. In general, read directions, carefully, learn to budget your time, answer the easiest questions first, usually answer every item, and control any excess anxiety. On objective exams, don't overinterpret questions and don't be afraid to change answers. Also, use test-wiseness clues when all else fails. On essay exams, support your general remarks with solid evidence. Be neat, and always write something on every item you are supposed to answer. Develop a system for dealing with essay exams, such as: (1) preview the test, (2) budget your time, (3) select an easy question first, (4) make a semantic map except for very brief essays, (5) write your response in an organized, logical fashion, and (6) proofread your answer.

Unit Comprehension Check

If you can answer these questions, you have retained many of the main points of this unit at the literal level.

1. You can reduce the danger of misreading test instructions and essay questions by _____ing key words.

2. You should try to answer the _____est questions first.

3. A penalty for guessing usually corrects for _____ .

4. It is recommended that you come to the testing room early to trade questions with other students. (True or false?)

5. Research studies indicate that most students are more likely to change a wrong answer to a right one than the other way around. (True or false?)

6. Test-wiseness clues will (a) slightly (b) greatly increase your score on some instructor-made tests.

7. Test-wiseness clues are not likely to help on a standardized reading test. (True or false?)

8. What are two test-wiseness clues between an item stem and choices?

9. When the choices on a multiple-choice test are numerical values, the correct choice may be a _____ value.

10. Words like absolutely, always, and never may be clue that an item is: (a) true (b) false.

11. If you have a multiple-option item, with choices like "a and b" and "all of the above," treat each original choice as a _____ _____ _____ .

12. Essay exams test more than your knowledge of the course content. (True or false?)

13. Neatness has little effect on an essay-exam score. (True or false?)

14. If you feel that you don't know anything about an essay-exam topic, should you write something anyway?

15. List the five steps recommended for dealing with essay exams.

Exercise 8.4 *Action Plan*

Directions: Choose one or more ideas from this Unit to incorporate into your test taking. Develop an Action Plan for that idea.

Goals	Strategies to Complete Goal	Completion Date	Evaluation Procedure

Vocabulary Development

Three Noun Suffixes

tion   A Latin suffix. The verb *act* changes to a noun when it becomes *action*.

ist   A Greek suffix. E.g.: *humor—humorist; piano—pianist; tour—tourist.*

ment   A Latin suffix. Verbs such as *refresh, encourage*, and *establish* can be changed to the nouns *refreshment, encouragement*, and *establishment*.

Four Adjective Suffixes

able   A Latin suffix meaning "capable." The noun *read* changes to an adjective when it becomes *readable*.

less   An Old English suffix meaning "lack of." The noun *hope* changes to an adjective when it becomes *hopeless*.

ic   A Greek suffix meaning "of," "pertaining to" or "characteristic of." The noun *poet* changes to an adjective when it becomes *poetic*.

ful   An Old English suffix meaning "fullness," "tendency," or "having the characteristics." The noun *cheer* changes to an adjective when it becomes *cheerful*.

Vocabulary Exercise

Study the three noun suffixes presented above. In the following sentences, change the italicized word by using one of the suffixes. Write the new word on the line following each sentence.

1. The *science* reached a conclusion after completing the experiment. _____

2. Through his *create* the sculptor expressed his personal identity. _____

3. Travel agencies attempt to help the *tour* traveling to foreign countries. _____

4. The *Social* Party became very active in the community. _____

5. The *refresh* stand was closed. _____

6. Often we heed a *suggest* from a friend. _____

7. To offer *encourage* to a new employee is essential for his or her success. _____

8. This painting is from Picasso's *cube* period. _____

Study the four adjective suffixes presented above. In the following sentences, change the italicized word by using one of the suffixes. Write the new word on the line following each sentence.

9. How *comfort* is the new desk chair you purchased? _____

10. The Star of David is *symbol* of Judaism. _____

11. Joan spent some *sleep* nights worrying. _____

12. The firemen were *mind* of the danger as they entered the flaming building.

_____

13. The desert was coated with *volcano* dust, giving it the appearance of the surface

of the moon. _____

14. *Favor* weather conditions prevailed for the gold tournament. _____

15. John is a *graph* arts major. _____

16. The *delight* host kept the party alive. _____

17. The ship steamed forward so smoothly it felt *motion* to the passengers.

_____

Common Suffixes

Noun Suffixes

Suffix	Examples
1. *age*	postage, coverage
2. *ance*	reliance, circumstance
3. *ence*	dependence, credence
4. *cy*	privacy, decency
5. *dom*	freedom, boredom
6. *ee*	employee, nominee
7. *er*	singer, painter
8. *hood*	neighborhood, manhood
9. *ism*	communism, patriotism
10. *ist*	chemist, biologist
11. *ity*	nobility, sanity
12. *ment*	judgment, fulfillment
13. *ness*	goodness, forgiveness
14. *ship*	friendship, companionship
15. *ster*	gangster, pollster

Adjective Suffixes

16. *able*	readable, agreeable
17. *ar*	lunar, circular
18. *ary*	customary, contrary
19. *ed*	aged, beloved
20. *en*	golden, woolen

Adjective Suffixes (cont.)

	Examples
21. *ent*	diffident, intelligent
22. *ful*	cheerful, delightful
23. *ic*	comic, symphonic
24. *ing*	interesting, rewarding
25. *ive*	massive, cooperative
26. less	reckless, motionless
27. *ous*	fabulous, pious

Verb Suffixes

28. *ate*	create, navigate
29. *en*	lighten, straighten
30. *ify*	classify, clarify
31. *ize*	sterilize, agonize

Adverb Suffixes

32. *ward*	backward, eastward
33. *where*	somewhere, elsewhere
34. *wise*	likewise, clockwise

Skim/Scan
Exercise 8

1. Record your starting time.
2. Rapidly preview-skim the entire selection.
3. Record your ending time.
4. Answer the skimming questions.
5. Go on to the scanning questions.
6. Determine your skimming and scanning scores and your skimming words-per-minute rate.
7. Enter your skimming score and rate on the progress graph in the appendix at the end of this book.

Are Americans Careful Food Shoppers?

by Joseph R. Pearce

	Hour	Min.	Secs.
A. Ending time:	⎯⎯	⎯⎯	⎯⎯
B. Starting time:	⎯⎯	⎯⎯	⎯⎯
C. A − B = Reading time:		⎯⎯	⎯⎯

What are some of the aids American shoppers use to make informed food purchases? Do most food shoppers make a list of items to be bought before going to the market? Do they read ads for specials? Do they check the list of ingredients on food packages, use open dating, unit pricing, and nutrition labels? In short, are Americans careful food shoppers in these respects?

To answer these and other questions, FDA contracted with Response Analysis Corporation to conduct nationwide surveys of American food shoppers in 1973 and 1975.

The 1975 findings—based on interviews with 1,664 shoppers—showed that the shopping aid used by the largest number of consumers was open dating, which tells the customer the date by which the product should be sold. About 75 percent of shoppers said they looked for open dating the last time they did the main food shopping, an 18 percent increase over 1973. Over the two-year period, open dating replaced reading ads for specials as the shopping aid used by the largest percentage of consumers.

Sixty-eight percent of the shoppers interviewed in 1975 said they read ads for specials, an 8 percent increase over 1973. Only about 40 percent of the shoppers in both years said they looked for unit pricing the last time they were in the store. Although most shoppers keep a close eye out for specials, a majority have yet to use unit pricing. Unit pricing is a system used by some stores to help consumers compare prices of different sized packages of the same type of product. Shelf tags state the cost of an item per ounce or pound, thus making it easier for a consumer to make a price comparison between a 16-ounce can of peas and a 24-ounce can of peas.

The proportion of shoppers who made a shopping list before leaving for the market—approximately 62 percent—remained about the same in 1975 as it was in 1973.

Only 46 percent of those interviewed in 1975 indicated that they checked the list of ingredients on cans or packaged foods (up a few percentage points from 1973) and only 33 percent said they have used nutrition labels for the purpose of making choices between different foods.

FDA Consumer.

TABLE 1 Careful Shopper Score

	Low	Medium	High
All Food Shoppers	22%	50%	28%
Sex			
Female	20	50	30
Male	32	48	20
Education			
Less than High School	45	44	11
High School	20	51	30
College	14	52	34
Age			
18–34	20	50	31
35–49	19	52	29
50-over	26	48	26
Race			
Non-black	20	51	29
Black	35	42	23
Socioeconomic Status			
Low	34	46	19
Medium	16	53	31
High	14	50	36
Nutrition Knowledge			
Low	32	48	20
Medium	21	49	30
High	12	53	35

Note: Total percentages may not add to 100 due to rounding of decimals.

Based on the 1975 research, a "careful shopper" score was constructed by giving each shopper interviewed a point for every one of the shopping aids used: making a shopping list, reading for specials, checking lists of ingredients, using unit pricing, looking for open dates, and using nutrition labels. A score of zero to two points was considered "low," three or four points "medium," five or six "high." On the basis of this scoring system, 22 percent of the shoppers interviewed scored low, 50 percent medium, and 28 percent high. (See Table 1.)

The survey showed that women tend to be more careful shoppers than men. Three out of ten men scored low on careful shopping comparing to two out of ten women, while two out of ten men and three out of ten women scored high.

There is a slight tendency for younger shoppers to be "more careful" than older shoppers. Shoppers with more education, higher socioeconomic status, and greater nutrition knowledge were more likely to rate as careful shoppers than those who had less education, lower socioeconomic status, and less nutrition knowledge.

Table 2 Use of Nutrition Labeling

	Have Used	Have not Used	Not sure/ No Answer
All Food Shoppers	33%	66%	1%
Sex			
Female	35	65	0
Male	22	76	2
Education			
Less than High School	17	83	0
High School	32	67	1
College	42	57	1
Age			
18–34	43	57	0
35–49	32	67	1
50-over	25	74	1
Socioeconomic Status			
Low	24	75	1
Medium	35	64	1
High	41	58	1
Nutrition Knowledge			
Low	22	77	1
Medium	33	66	1
High	45	54	1

The information developed in the 1975 survey on nutrition labeling is of special interest and importance to FDA and the food industry. (There was no data on this issue in the 1973 survey since FDA's nutrition labeling program was not officially underway until later.) About 60 percent of the shoppers interviewed said they had seen nutrition labeling and about one-third said they had actually used it. The data showed that a greater percentage of persons in the younger age ranges made use of the labels than did older persons.

Education had a significant influence on whether a person used nutrition labels. (See Table 2.) Only 17 percent of those with less than a high school education used the labels, compared to 32 percent for high school graduates and 42 percent for college-educated shoppers. Shoppers with high socioeconomic status were more likely to use the labels than those with lower status. Non-blacks had more of a tendency to use nutrition labels than blacks. Among the people surveyed, those who scored high on nutrition knowledge and who were rated as careful shoppers were more likely to use nutrition labeling than those who did not score high on these factors.

These survey findings provide feedback to FDA's Bureau of Foods from consumers on trends in general shopping practices and on the extent to which nutrition labeling has become a useful aid to food shoppers.

Skimming Questions: *Circle the letter of the best answer.*

1. The survey in this selection was conducted by:
   a. Response Analysis Corporation
   b. The Rand Corporation
   c. The Gallup Poll
   d. The Brookings Institute

2. What percent of the shoppers interviewed in 1975 said they read ads for specials?
   a. 90 percent
   b. 68 percent
   c. 50 percent
   d. 38 percent

3. The survey found a slight tendency for _____ shoppers to be more careful.
   a. younger
   b. poorer
   c. older
   d. middle class

4. _____ had a significant influence on whether a person used nutrition labels.
   a. Age
   b. Sex
   c. Education
   d. Weight

5. The survey showed that women tend to be more _____ shoppers than men.
   a. careful
   b. wasteful
   c. careless
   d. impulsive

Scanning Questions

1. According to the Table 2 _____ percent of 18- to 34-year olds have used nutrition labeling.

2. In both years of the survey about 40 percent of the shoppers said they looked for _____ the last time they were in the store.

3. According to Table 1 _____ percent of college educated shoppers scored low on the careful shopper score.

4. In 1975 _____ percent of the shoppers said they checked the list of ingredients on cans.

5. The surveys in this selection were conducted in _____ and _____ .

Time-Rate Conversion Chart

Min:Sec	WPM	Min:Sec	WPM	Min:Sec	WPM	Min:Sec	WPM	Min:Sec	WPM
1:00	775	2:30	310	4:00	194	5:20	145	6:40	116
1:10	664	2:40	291	4:10	186	5:30	141	6:50	113
1:20	581	2:50	274	4:20	179	5:40	137	7:00	111
1:30	517	3:00	258	4:30	172	5:50	133	7:10	108
1:40	465	3:10	245	4:40	166	6:00	129	7:20	106
1:50	423	3:20	233	4:50	160	6:10	126	7:30	103
2:00	388	3:30	221	5:00	155	6:20	122	7:40	101
2:10	358	3:40	211	5:10	150	6:30	119	7:50	99
2:20	332	3:50	202						

Unit 8 Answer Key

Exercise 8.0

1. Clue: opposites (intellect vs. emotion; Choice: a
2. Clue: middle value; Choice: b
3. Clue: word association: Choice: c
4. Clue: specific determiner ("always" is an absolute word); Choice: f
5. Clue: grammatical agreement (the choice that agrees with the plural "variables . . . are" in the stem is "c"; Choice c

Exercise 8.1

The time might have been divided this way: Question 1–20 mins; Question 2–20 mins; Question 3–10 mins; Question 4–10 mins. Or a couple of minutes could have been shaved off each of these times to allow a few minutes at the end to check for errors and omissions.

Exercise 8.2

1. contrast;
2. criticize or evaluate;
3. illustrate;
4. trace;
5. discuss;
6. explain;
7. summarize;
8. enumerate;
9. define;
10. compare

Exercise 8.3

(These are examples. Your sentences may differ and be just as correct)

1. Jefferson and Franklin shared some political viewpoints and differed on others.
2. Nuclear energy developed in a series of steps.
3. A **Farewell to Arms** shows some important aspects of Hemingway's writing style.

Unit Comprehension Check

1. Underlining
2. easiest
3. chance
4. False. Coming early may raise your anxiety level.
5. True

6. (a) slightly. They are not a substitute for studying and should be used only as a last resort.
7. True. Usually clues have been weeded out of such tests.
8. (a) Word association; (b) grammatical agreement.
9. middle
10. (b) false
11. true-false item
12. True. They also test your writing and organizing abilities.
13. False. Hard-to-read writing can cost you points.
14. Definitely. You may receive at least partial credit.
15. (a) Preview all the questions;
    (b) budget your time;
    (c) select your first question, preferably an easy one;
    (d) make a quick outline unless your response will be very brief;
    (e) write your response.

Vocabulary Development

1. scientist
2. creation
3. tourist
4. socialist
5. refreshment
6. suggestion
7. encouragement
8. cubist
9. comfortable
10. symbolic
11. sleepless
12. mindful
13. volcanic
14. favorable
15. graphic
16. delightful
17. motionless

Skim/Scan Exercise

Skim
1. a 2. b 3. a 4. c 5. a

Scan
1. 43 2. Unit Pricing 3. 14 4. 48 5. 1973–1975

Unit 9

Reading Rate Boosters

Introduction to Reading Rate Improvement

Did you know that if you hold a book twice as far away you can read twice as fast because you see more print? Did you know that a reader with double vision remembers more because he or she sees each word twice? Ridiculous? Of course. These statements are slightly exaggerated examples of Baloney Science, a very refined form of B.S. Because Baloney Science and true science live side by side, it often is difficult to tell them apart. If someone can make an explanation sound reasonable and scientific, even if it isn's true, many people will accept it. Baloney Science sometimes is used in advertising. One example is that device that is supposed to save your car gasoline because of some very reasonable sounding "scientific" principle.

Unfortunately, Baloney Science has found its way into the reading field as well. Some programs base their high cost on the presumption that they will teach you a special, scientifically based way to read at astounding speeds. We wish these claims were true because then all of us could become supersonic readers. But wishing, as the old saying goes, doesn't make it so.

Careful research conducted by reputable scientists in the reading field gives us a more conservative picture of the reading process. Here is a summary of that research.

Your Eye Span Is Limited

Research indicates that at the usual reading distances, we have approximately 30 percent clearness of vision one-half inch to either side of the point the eye is fixed on. This fact implies that there is a definite limit to the number of words we can see at one time.

Since the late 1800s various recording devices have been developed to study reader's eye movements. The research indicates how limited our eye spans are. For example, it has been found that a college student of average reading ability sees about 1.1 words with each pause of the eyes. A very good college reader sometimes can see as many as 2.7 words at a time.

There are two important conclusions from the research just mentioned: First, you should not expect to read whole lines or even large phrases at a glance. Second, one way to increase your reading rate is by slightly increasing your eye span, if you are seeing less than your potential now. If you are seeing one word at a time, with practice you may be able to double this span.

Skip, Skip, Not Flow, Flow

There are some rather poetic descriptions of what is called "visual" reading. The eyes, we are told, swirl down the page like leaves spiraling in the wind. Like a camera or radar beam, the "visual" reader's eyes scan the page, taking in whole gulps of information at a time. Not only is this description bad poetry, it's not supported by the evidence. Try this experiment: Have someone read a book while holding it at eye level, facing you. Look over the top edge of the book so you can see the person's eyes while he or she is reading. You will notice that instead of moving in a smooth, flowing pattern, the eyes dark or jump from point to point, sometimes jerking forward, sometimes backtracking slightly.

The pauses that the eyes make, called *fixations,* are essential, for you cannot see words clearly when your eyes are moving. Edmund Huey, a pioneer of eye-movement research, suggests this informal experiment. Look at your reflection in a mirror. Notice that when you move your eyes back and forth, you cannot clearly see their movement in the mirror. Only when your eyes are stopped can you see their reflection.*

Eye-movement research provides some enlightening information. College students of average reading ability make about four fixations, or pauses, per second. Very good readers do slightly better, making about five fixations per second. While the differences are not great, a slight improvement in reading speed apparently is possible by increasing the fixation rate.

Some Figures

The numbers we have mentioned suggest what might be an upper reading limit with good comprehension:

	College Readers	
	Average Readers	*Very Good Readers*
1. Words per pause	1.1	2.7
2. Pauses per second	4.0	5.0
3. No. 1 × No. 2	4.4 wds. per sec.	13.5 wds. per sec.
4. No. 3 × 60 seconds	264 wds. per min.	810 wds. per min.

According to these figures, even very good readers seem to have an upper limit of about 800 words per minute when they are reading for good comprehension and seeing every word. (Later we will discuss the point that you needn't see every word in many reading situations.)

The performance of college students on standardized reading tests gives us some more information about how fast people generally can read with good comprehension. Norm-group scores on two tests, the Nelson-Denny Reading Test and the McGraw-Hill Reading Test, tell us the following about rates on easy material: College freshmen at the middle level on both tests read at about 260 words per minute. Students who read faster than three-fourths of those tested read 325 words per minute or better. Very good readers, those in the top 5 percent of the students tested, read 400 words per minute or better on one test and 500 words per minute on the other. Only about

*Edmund Huey, *The Psychology and Pedagogy of Reading* (Cambridge, Mass.: M.I.T. Press, 1968), p. 37.

the top 1 percent of the college freshmen in both groups read faster than 630–650 words per minute. College seniors tested on one of these tests performed only slightly better than their freshmen counterparts.

In conclusion, there is evidence that very few readers read faster than 600 words per minute on easy material that they want to understand well. The average reader reads at about 250 words per minute under these conditions.

What You See Is What You Get

According to a story, Cary Grant once received a telegram from an associate who needed to know his age and wanted to save money by eliminating every word possible. The telegram read, "HOW OLD CARY GRANT?" Mr. Grant promptly telegraphed back, "OLD CARY GRANT FINE. HOW YOU?" Of course, Cary Grant understood the intent of the telegram, but the story raises a couple of points. First, you can eliminate or skip some words in a message and still understand it. Second, if too many words are left out, meaning may begin to suffer. We have seen that our visual system limits us to about 800 words per minute when seeing every word; the actual upper limit for most of us probably is less. A study done by C. B. Bassin suggests that a 30 percent loss of unimportant words does not seriously affect comprehension, but 50 percent does.* In later units the concept of flexible reading is discussed. As a flexible reader, you speed up or slow down depending on your purpose. But keep in mind that you cannot speed up without losing some understanding of the material. Your purpose determines how much comprehension you can afford to lose.

Backtracking Slows You Down

You can read more efficiently by reducing the number of times you backtrack to read a word or phrase a second or third time. All readers backtrack (regress) to some extent. Eye-movement studies suggest that the average number of regressions for college students is about fifteen per one hundred words. Rapid readers are bound to regress occasionally because they are willing to risk missing some words. On the other hand, readers who seldom regress may be reading too slowly because they are afraid to skip any words.

Many of us have developed the habit of unnecessary backtracking. Like most bad habits, this one is easy to slip into and harder to break. With regular practice, however, it often can be changed. A more extreme form of backtracking occurs when someone has lapses of concentration and must reread large sections of material. Slow readers sometimes have this habit because they become bored by the laborious process of reading. Many readers claim that when they begin to read faster, their concentration improves.

*C. B. Bassin, "Telegraphic prose: The effects of three deletion schemes on comprehension and reading rate of three types of literature" (Ph.D. diss., Texas A & M University, 1975).

You should be skeptical of anyone who says they can teach you to read difficult material at super speeds with good comprehension. Such a claim is not supported by what we know about the reading process. Rapid reading is useful in many reading situations, such as when the material is very easy or when you do not need a detailed understanding. But do not feel that you should be able to read your study material at very high speeds.

How to Keep Improving Your Rate

Old habits are hard to break. Many people who are trying to improve their reading rate stay at about the same speed on one exercise after another. They have trouble letting go of their slow-reading habit. There are four steps that may help you to steadily increase your speed on the rate-boost exercises:

1. Remember that you should let your comprehension drop.
2. On each exercise, set a definite rate goal for yourself before beginning.
3. Have some way of knowing that you are moving fast enough to reach your goal.
4. If on an exercise you take very much longer than your goal rate, repeat the *same* selection until you reach your goal.

Setting a Rate Goal

A good rule of thumb is to set your first rate goal about 50 words per minute above your "normal" reading rate on similar material. You can determine your normal rate either from results of a rate section on a reading test or by timing yourself on easy material. As you work through the selections, raise your goal each time you begin to feel comfortable at a certain rate. By raising your goal this way, you will assure yourself of steady progress.

Monitoring Your Rate

You may reach your goal for a selection more easily if you have some way to keep track of your rate as you read. If your instructor has provided you with a pacing device, you always know whether you are maintaining your goal rate. If you are not using such a device, here is a suggested method:

1. Divide the selections into four equal parts, and place a mark in the margin at the first quarter point (that is, one-fourth of the way from the beginning of the material.
2. Decide on your rate goal and use the time-rate conversion table that follows each selection to determine the total time needed to reach that goal.

3. Divide that total time by four. The resulting figure is the time needed to finish one-fourth of the material at your desired rate.
4. Start the rate-boost exercise. When you reach the one-quarter mark on the selection, glance at your timing device to see whether you are close to the one-quarter time you calculated in step 3. Adjust your rate if necessary. For example, if you used a little extra time to reach that one-quarter point, then quicken your pace over the rest of the selection.

Using Your Hand as a Pacer

Keeping track of your rate as you read may help you reach your rate goal. Another aid is to use your hand as a built-in pacer. Many people find that they can read faster when they establish a regular rhythm with their hand. One advantage of using hand pacing is that, unlike mechanical pacing devices, your hand is always with you.

Some people confuse hand pacing with finger pointing. It is an important distinction. When hand pacing, you are using your hand as a *pacer,* not a pointer. Instead of following your hand, your eyes are moving independently and are concentrating on the material. But because your hand is moving with a steady rhythm, you are motivated to try to keep pace with it.

Some reading programs describe numerous different hand motions. We will mention two that will serve most purposes. The first method simply involves moving your hand from left to right under one line of type at a time. Your pace is determined by how quickly you move your hand. An illustration of this method is shown in Figure 9.0. For most reading purposes, this pacing method works very well.

For narrow columns or for rapid skimming, skipping some words, a "Z" pacing pattern can be used. With this pattern, your hand covers more material at one sweep, so you are forced to read faster than with the one-line-at-a-time method. You can regulate your pace by varying the number of lines you drop down during each return sweep; the more lines, the faster your eyes must move to keep up. This method is shown in Figure 9.1.

Because hand pacing is such a radical change for most readers, the method takes some getting used to. At first, your hand may distract you from the words. This is normal and usually improves as you become more accustomed to the method. Also, you may feel self-conscious about using the hand-pacing technique in public. Again, this feeling usually passes with experience.

Using the Rate-boost Exercises to Improve Your Reading Rate

If you work on these rate-boost exercises regularly, consistently, and, yes, religiously, you are likely to gradually eliminate lazy reading habits and approach or reach your rate potential. If you only practice for a while, or do so irregularly, the rewards probably will not be as great.

Line-by-Line Hand Pacing

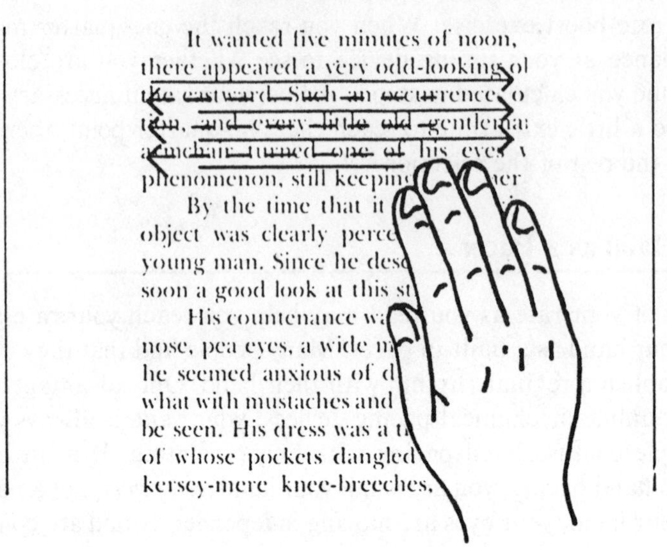

It wanted five minutes of noon,
there appeared a very odd-looking ol
~~the eastward. Such an occurrence o~~
~~ton, and every little old gentlen a~~
~~a chair turned one of his eyes~~
phenomenon, still keepin... er

By the time that it ...
object was clearly perce...
young man. Since he des...
soon a good look at this st...

His countenance wa...
nose, pea eyes, a wide n...
he seemed anxious of d...
what with mustaches and...
be seen. His dress was a t...
of whose pockets dangled...
kersey-mere knee-breeches,...

"Z" Pattern Hand Pacing

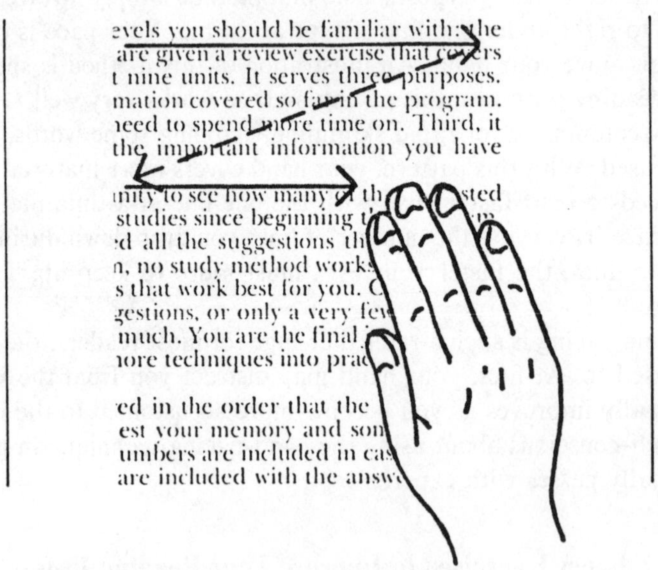

evels you should be familiar with: the
are given a review exercise that covers
t nine units. It serves three purposes.
mation covered so far in the program.
need to spend more time on. Third, it
the important information you have

nity to see how many of th...sted
studies since beginning t... ...m
ed all the suggestions th...
n, no study method work...
s that work best for you. C...
gestions, or only a very fev...
much. You are the final ...
nore techniques into prac...

ed in the order that the...
est your memory and son...
umbers are included in cas...
are included with the answ...

Figure 9.0

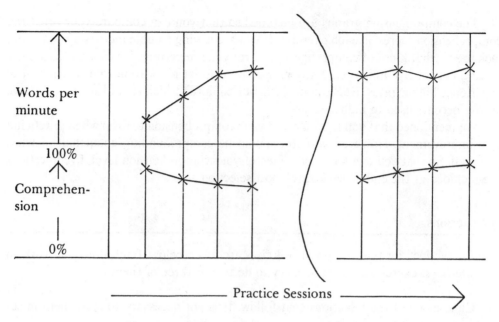

Figure 9.1 Effect of Rate on Comprehension.

One point cannot be stressed enough: Rate-boost exercises are not, repeat, *not*, the same as regular reading. In regular reading you adjust your rate to achieve your desired comprehension. When doing rate-boost exercises, you set a rate goal in advance and let your comprehension drop. Yes—let it drop. Letting go of comprehension is a key to success with rate-boost exercises. Doing so means going against all your habits, all the years of emphasis on comprehension.

Have faith that your comprehension will begin to rise as your mind adapts to the higher speeds. Figure 9.1 shows what usually happens. You can see on the chart that as the rate increases in the beginning, comprehension falls. But later—the exact time needed varies with individuals—the comprehension climbs back up.

Instructions for Using the Progress Graphs

You can plot your reading and skimming rates on the progress graphs. These graphs let you see how you are progressing on the exercises. The top part of each graph is for your words-per-minute rates and the bottom part is for your comprehension scores. After you have worked an exercise, mark your rate on the top graph. On the sample graph, the student's first rate was 275 words per minute. Also, make your comprehension score on the bottom graph. On the sample graph, the student's first comprehension score was four out of a possible four correct.

The comprehension graphs are included so that you can compare your rates and comprehension scores on each exercise. If you are having trouble increasing your rate, look to see what kinds of comprehension scores you are getting. If you are consistently getting four or five items correct, you may need to let go of some comprehension to experience higher rates. Remember that your comprehension should start to improve as you become used to higher rates.

We mentioned that you should allow your comprehension to drop when practicing rate improvement. However, you still should be comprehending about half of what you read. So that you can have some idea of your comprehension level, five questions are included at the end of each rate-boost selection.

Instructions

The instructions for the rate-boost exercises are given below. Each time you work on the rate-boost exercises, you should try to do two or three of them.

1. Choose one of the selections that follow. It is not necessary to read them in sequential order.
2. Record your starting time in the space provided at the beginning of the selection.
3. Push yourself through the selection at a rate that still allows you to understand about half the content. Try to see as many words as you can at this high rate. That is, do not consciously skip large groups of words in order to maintain your rate. You want to force your eyes and mind to register as many words as possible.
4. When you have completed the selection, record your ending time in the space provided at the beginning of the selection.
5. Answer the three comprehension questions that follow the selection. In addition, your instructor may ask you to complete the essay question. Then use the answer key at the end of this section to score yourself.
6. Subtract your starting time from your ending time, and record the answer (your reading time) in the space provided.
7. Determine your comprehension score and your words-per-minute rate.
8. Enter your score and rate on the progress graph in the appendix.
9. If your rate is very far (fifty words per minute or more) below your goal, it is recommended that you reattempt the *same* selection until you reach your goal.
10. Choose another selection and repeat steps 2–9.

SAMPLE

Rate Boost Progress Report

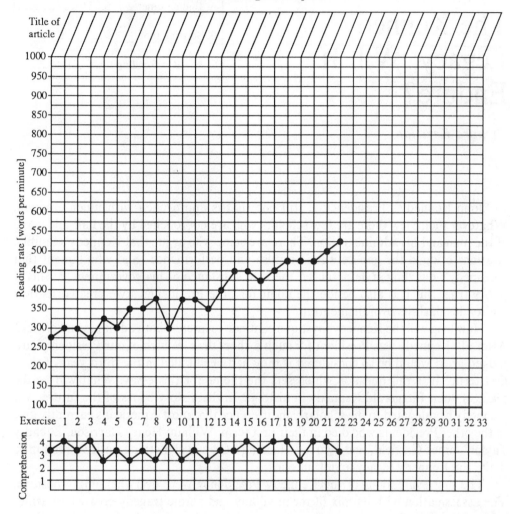

The Kennedy Legacy: Will It Endure?

	Hour	Min.	Secs.
A. Ending time:	____	____	____
B. Starting time:	____	____	____
C. A − B = Reading time:		____	____

Richard Kezirian

John Kennedy's Presidency is still one that is approached with much emotion. Whatever their view there are few scholars who are not touched by the flair and verve of the man and his administration. There are some who argue that Kennedy's "public relations bridged the gap between promise and performance" and who lament that "Kennedy's dazzling style obscured the thin substance of his government."[1] This is partly true. But it is also beside the point for "the President's style created its own reality, his dash its own momentum."[2]

How long will the Kennedy mystique continue to interest both admirers and critics? After all, Kennedy was President for such a short time. Which of our Presidents now judged great would be so considered if they had been killed in the third year of their first term? It is this question which sets the theme for this essay. What will be the place of John Fitzgerald Kennedy in history? In the history books of the future, will Kennedy be relegated to the scholarly indifference that most Americans currently give to the other Presidents who died in their first term: William Henry Harrison, Zachary Taylor, James Garfield, and Warren Harding? Or will something positive remain to make the Kennedy legacy a vibrant one?

The first evaluations of the Kennedy Presidency were overwhelmingly positive. The assassination with its mix of mean villany and heroic tragedy created an atmosphere where the first heart-rending accounts from Administration insiders sealed the "Camelot" image as the dominant one in the popular mind. The dramatic contrast between the grass-roots and folksy Lyndon Johnson and the urbane and sophisticated John Kennedy added to this first inclination. The Camelot image of Kennedy implied a leader who was progressive and creative, who was endowed with an abundance of

1. William O'Neill, *Coming Apart: An Informal History of America in the 1960's* (New York: Quadrangle Books, 1971).
2. O'Neill.

personal attractiveness and charisma. As Camelot, Kennedy exhibited a keen analytical intellect which was skeptical, objective, cool and candid. Like a robust, popular prince he radiated youthful energy, zest for life, articulate and moving rhetoric, and a saving sense of humor.

The knights of Kennedy's Round Table came in for their fair share of praise, too. Indeed, they were evaluated as the most competent, dedicated and brilliant of Presidential "Brain Trusts" in American history. In choosing these men, it was said, Kennedy paid little attention to party qualifications; rather ability, drive and imagination were the requisites for selection.

As far as specific programs and accomplishments, admirers saw Kennedy leading the nation in new directions in three key areas of American policy. First, in the field of economics, Kennedy aimed to instruct the American public about various economic myths which characterized their thinking. For Kennedy the persistence of economic "mythology" was the main obstacle impeding implementation of the sophisticated solutions mandatory for economic success in the 1960s. His most important effort in this regard was a Commencement Speech given at Yale University on June 11, 1962. The political scientist Bruce Miroff succinctly summarized the focal points of Kennedy's discussion in that speech:

> First was the myth of oversized government. Kennedy contended that the growth of the federal government had to be understood in relative terms; he pointed out that, leaving aside defense and space expenditures, the federal government since the Second World War had expanded less rapidly than any other sector of the economy. A second myth concerned fiscal policy and budget. The record of the postwar years, Kennedy remarked, demolished the notion that budget surpluses kept prices stable while budget deficits produced inflation. The same record also undermined the popular myth of a skyrocketing federal debt; the federal debt was, in fact, climbing far more slowly than either private debt or the debts of state and local governments. Finally, Kennedy assaulted the claim that each and every setback to the economy derived from business's lack of conidence in the national administration.[3]

At the end of the speech Kennedy returned to the key economic themes of his administration: that a business-government alliance was needed to solve modern problems, and that specific economic "ideologies" had to be abandoned in favor of improved managerial expertise.

> What is at stake is not some grand warfare of rival ideologies which will sweep the country with passion, but the practical management of a modern economy. What we need is not labels and clichés but more basic discussion of the sophisticated and technical questions involved in keeping a great economic machinery moving ahead.

3. Bruce Miroff, *Pragmatic Illusions* (New York: David McKay Company, 1976).

Secondly, admirers saw Kennedy broaching an equally new era in international relations as exemplified in yet another speech, this time at American University on June 10, 1963. In this speech, Kennedy rose above the third old clichés of the Cold War and put forward a new basis for peace and compromise in a nuclear age. He specifically sought to break the logjam that had developed in the negotiations with the Soviets on atmospheric nuclear testing. Hence, Kennedy announced his decision to send a high-level negotiating team to Moscow to bargain with Nikita Khrushchev. He also urged Americans to reexamine their atttitudes toward Russia. "For in the final analysis, our most common link is that we all inhabit this small planet. We all breathe the same air. We all cherish our children's future. And we are all mortal." Khrushchev called this speech "the greatest speech by an American President since Roosevelt." It was reprinted in it entirely in the Soviet newspaper *Pravda*. Such was its impact that, by July 25, a treaty prohibiting nuclear testing in the atmosphere, in space, and under water was initiated by Moscow by the U.S., Great Britain and the U.S.S.R. The limited test ban treaty has often been called "Kennedy's finest legacy to the world."

Lastly, Kennedy's Civil Rights speech of June 11, 1963 marked a new beginning in domestic affairs. An American President finally and unequivocally placed the federal government against the studied intrasigence of an anachronistic system of Southern segregation policies. Kennedy had foreshadowed such a speech when he sent federal troops and deputies to the University of Mississippi in 1962 to enforce the court-ordered enrollment of James Meredith. He followed this speech with a forceful message to Congress eight days later, and a legislative package which finally became known as the Civil Rights Act of 1964.

In sum, early admirers saw Kennedy as a President whose keen intelligence in an age of political mediocrity, whose inspiration of hope in an age of uncertainty, and whose appeal to social ethics in an age of materialism, made especially tragic the promise which the assassination shattered. Lately, however, the Kennedy historical literature has been characterized more by criticism than by praise. Critics concur with admirers that Kennedy brought a sense of movement to the Presidency, but they disagree that this sense of movement was always positive.

In foreign affairs, for instance, critics argue that Kennedy's impatience, his proclivity for action, and his lack of caution did much to make the early 1960s dangerous years. Due to Kennedy's tendency to view politics in dramatic terms, characterized by tests of personal will, he too easily convinced himself that his Presidency would mark a watershed in the face of a massive Soviet world offensive. With this attitude, it is no wonder, critics remark, that Kennedy's Presidency was distinguished by crisis: the Bay of Pigs, the Cuban Missile Confrontation, the Berlin Scares, and the Fallout Shelter hysteria.

Regarding relations with the Third World, critics find Kennedy as obtuse and uncomprehending as John Foster Dulles, Eisenhower's Secretary of State, often was. Kennedy exhibited a typically American, narrow-minded morality, exemplified by alternating beliefs in the efficacy of overt or covert military threats to insure American supremacy in Third World affairs. The most notorious example here was CIA involvement in the Ngo Dinh Diem coup of November 1963. When Diem became expendable (i.e. not in the U.S. interest consistent with its containment policy) the Kennedy Administration did not really reexamine old attitudes and myths, but instead sought another leader whose regime could be used to contain Ho Chi Minh by counter-insurgency. To summarize, critics see Kennedy as basically a "Cold Warrior" in foreign policy, whose actions, possibly more than Soviet intentions, were responsible for heating up the Cold War.

On domestic matters, critics argue that Kennedy had nothing new to offer; indeed, that he was the prisoner of the most fundamental of American biases. Some historians see Kennedy as an enlightened conservative, at best. For example, Kennedy consistently dashed liberal hopes and expectations by being excessively cautious in his approach to Congress and catering too extensively to Southern conservatives in his program planning. The narrowness of Kennedy's defeat on Medicare, on Aid to Education and on his original tax reform program, critics believe, demonstrated how successful he might have been if he had been more aggressive and more principled. Further, for critics, the fact that Kennedy acquiesced so easily in a tax cut without tax reform attested to the conventionality of his economic beliefs.

Regarding Civil Rights, critics argue that Kennedy was too deeply rooted in elite political values and assumptions to fully come to terms with the black political concern for more democratic representation. They point to Kennedy's attempts to blunt or to channel much of the black protest into areas which he deemed appropriate, rather than encouraging or accepting a black politics of mass participation.

Critics, then, basically evaluate Kennedy as "a relatively conventional American politician longing to be an unconventional hero."[4] As for Kennedy's "knights," though there was no denying their overall brilliance, there was still little guarantee that even the "best and the brightest" would deliver wise or successful policy. As it turned out, a goodly portion of the brain-trust of advisers recruited by the Kennedy Adminstration brought with them intellectual baggage that contained a set of policy assumptions that was distinctly "cold-war" in character and questionable in value.

With this historiographical debate as a background, how then might we assess the Kennedy legacy? One key factor which both critics and admirers tend to minimize is the great continuity which characterized the Kennedy and Johnson Presidencies. Kennedy laid the foundation for Johnson's legislative successes. Kennedy cultivated and stimulated a proper political mood and moral concern without which social legislation cannot be passed. More specifically, Kennedy's tax cut program and his Civil Rights package were well on their way toward enactment. Medicare and Aid to Education were formulated and appropriate strategies plotted. All in all, the embryo of Johnson's great "War on Poverty" was in place. In fact, both Johnson and Kennedy fit into the post-World War II New Deal Tradition. When Johnson took over the essentials of Kennedy's stalled domestic program, there was a culmination taking place of not only the New Frontier but of the New and Fair Deals.

4. Miroff.

In conclusion, the Kennedy Presidency will always be difficult to assess because of the unique problems which are associated with it: its brevity, the gap between expectations and performance, and the fact that the assassination evokes sympathy and pathos. Nonetheless, unlike America's other Presidents who failed to finish their first term, Kennedy was a man who had begun a reshaping of American society. He sensed a shift in the public mood and touched a responsive chord. Above all else, behind the promises Kennedy held a vision, a political prescience, and an ability to move people. He injected idealism into American politics. These factors will not warrant Kennedy a place among America's great Presidents, but they will insure him a special niche more inspired and hallowed than that occupied by William Henry Harrison, Zachary Taylor, James Garfield, and Warren Harding.

The Kennedy Legacy: Will It Endure?

1. According to the author, the Camelot image of Kennedy implied that he was a leader who was:
   a. unrealistic
   b. progressive
   c. creative
   d. b and c

2. In terms of Civil Rights, critics argue that Kennedy:
   a. was too rooted in "elite political values and assumptions"
   b. was strongly influenced by Franklin Roosevelt's New Deal policy
   c. cared little for Civil Rights
   d. was pressured into a positive Civil Rights stance by Dr. Martin Luther King

3. Critics see Kennedy as a _____ in foreign policy.
   a. hot head
   b. cold warrior
   c. compromiser
   d. weakling

Essay Question

Write a brief answer to the following question.

1. Why does the author believe it will be difficult to judge the Kennedy Presidency?

Time-Rate Conversion Chart

Min:Sec	WPM	Min:Sec	WPM	Min:Sec	WPM	Min:Sec	WPM	Min:Sec	WPM
1:00	1926	4:30	428	8:00	241	11:30	167	15:00	128
1:10	1651	4:40	413	8:10	236	11:40	165	15:10	127
1:20	1445	4:50	398	8:20	231	11:50	163	15:20	126
1:30	1284	5:00	385	8:30	227	12:00	161	15:30	124
1:40	1156	5:10	373	8:40	222	12:10	158	15:40	123
1:50	1051	5:20	361	8:50	218	12:20	156	15:50	122
2:00	963	5:30	350	9:00	214	12:30	154		
2:10	889	5:40	340	9:10	210	12:40	152		
2:20	825	5:50	330	9:20	206	12:50	150		
2:30	770	6:00	321	9:30	203	13:00	148		
2:40	722	6:10	312	9:40	199	13:10	146		
2:50	680	6:20	304	9:50	196	13:20	144		
3:00	642	6:30	296	10:00	193	13:30	143		
3:10	608	6:40	289	10:10	189	13:40	141		
3:20	578	6:50	282	10:20	186	13:50	139		
3:30	550	7:00	275	10:30	183	14:00	138		
3:40	525	7:10	269	10:40	181	14:10	136		
3:50	502	7:20	263	10:50	178	14:20	134		
4:00	482	7:30	257	11:00	175	14:30	133		
4:10	462	7:40	251	11:10	172	14:40	131		
4:20	444	7:50	246	11:20	170	14:50	130		

The Mississippi River and 1542

by Mark Twain

	Hour	Min.	Secs.
A. Ending time:	___	___	___
B. Starting time:	___	___	___
C. A – B = Reading time:		___	___

The world and the books are so accustomed to use, and overuse, the word "new" in connection with our country that we early get and permanently retain the impression that there is nothing old about it. We do of course know that there are several comparatively old dates in American history, but the mere figures convey to our minds no just idea, no distinct realizatson, of the stretch of time which they represent. To say that De Soto, the first white man who ever saw the Mississippi River, saw it in 1542, is a remark which states a fact without interpreting it; it is something like giving the dimensions of the sunset by astronomical measurements and cataloguing the colors by their scientific names—as a result, you get the bald fact of the sunset, but you don't see the sunset. It would have been better to paint a picture of it.

The 1542, standing by itself, means little or nothing to us; but when one groups a few neighboring dates and facts around it, he adds perspective and color and then realizes that this is an American date which is quite respectable for age.

For instance, when the Mississippi was first seen by a white man, less than a quarter of a century had elapsed since the death of the renowned artist Raphael, the driving out of the Knights-Hospitallers (Crusaders) from the island of Rhodes by the Turks, and the hammering up of the Ninety-Five Propositions on the church door by Martin Luther—the act which began the Protestant Reformation.

When De Sota took his glimpse of the river, Ignatius Loyala was an obscure name, and the order of the Jesuits, which he founded, was not yet a year old; Michelangelo's paint was not yet dry on the Last Judgment in the Sistine Chapel; Mary, Queen of Scots, was not yet born—but would be before the year was out—and her cousin Elizabeth of England was not yet in her teens.

John Calvin, a famous leader of the Protestant Reformation; Benvenuto Cellini, Italian goldsmith, sculptor, and author; and Charles V, Emperor of the Holy Roman Empire, were at the top of their fame, and each was manufacturing history after his own peculiar fashion. Margaret of Navarre was writing the *Heptameron* and also some religious books—the first survives, but the others are forgotten, wit and indelicacy being sometimes better literature-preservers than holiness. Lax court morals

Adapted from *Life on the Mississippi* by Mark Twain (Samuel L. Clemens).

and the absurd chivalry business were in full feather, and the joust and the tournament were the frequent pasttime of titled fine gentlemen who could fight better than they could spell, while religion was the passion of their ladies.

In fact, all around, religion was in a peculiarly blooming condition: the Council of Trent was being called; the Spanish Inquisition was roasting and racking and burning with a free hand; and elsewhere on the continent the nations were being persuaded to holy living by the sword and fire. In England, Henry VIII had suppressed the monasteries, burned Bishop John Fisher and another bishop or two, and was getting both his English reformation and his harem effectively started.

When De Soto stood on the banks of the Mississippi, it was still two years before Luther's death; *Don Quixote* was not yet written, Shakespeare was not yet born, and a hundred long years must still elapse before Englishmen would hear the name of Oliver Cromwell.

Unquestionably the discovery of the Mississippi is a datable fact which considerably mellows and modifies the shiny newness of our country and gives her a most respectable outside-aspect of rustiness and antiquity.

De Soto merely glimpsed the river, then died and was buried in it by his priests and soldiers. One would expect these explorers to have multiplied the river's dimensions by ten—the Spanish custom of the day—and thus cause other adventurers to go at once and explore it. On the contrary, however, their narrratives when they reached home did not excite that amount of curiosity, and so the Mississippi was left unvisited by whites during a term of years which seems incredible in our energetic days. One may obtain a sense of the length of that period of time by dividing it up this way: After De Soto glmipsed the river, a fraction short of a quarter of a century elapsed before Shakespeare was born; he lived a trifle more than half a century and then died, and when he had been in his grave considerably more than half a century, the *second* white man saw the Mississippi.

In our day we don't allow a hundred and thirty years to elapse between glimpses of a marvel. If somebody should discover a creek in the county next to the one that the North Pole is in, Europe and America would start fifteen costly expeditons thither— one to explore the creek and the other fourteen to hunt for each other.

For more than a hundred and fifty years there had been white settlements on our Atlantic coast. These people were in intimate communication with the Indians: In the south the Spaniards were robbing, slaughtering, enslaving, and converting them; higher up, the English were trading beads and blankets to them for a consideration and throwing in civilization and whiskeys as bonuses; and in Canada the French were schooling them in a simple way, missionarying among them, and drawing whole populations of them at a time to Quebec and later Montreal to buy furs of them. Necessarily, then, these various clusters of whites must have heard of the great river of the far west; and, indeed, they did hear of it vaguely—so vaguely and indefinitely that its course, proportions, and locality were hardly even guessable.

The mere mysteriousness of the matter ought to have fired curiosity and compelled exploration, but this did not occur. Apparently nobody happened to want such a river, nobody needed it, nobody was curious about it; so, for a century and a half the Mississippi remained out of the market and undisturbed. When De Sota found it, he was not hunting for a river and have to present occasion for one; consequently, he did not value it or even take any particular notice of it.

But at last La Salle, a Frenchman, conceived the idea of seeking out that river and exploring it. It always happens that when a man seizes upon a neglected and important idea, people inflamed with the same notion suddenly crop up all around, and it happened so in this instance.

Naturally the question suggests itself: Why did these people want the river now when nobody had wanted it in the five preceding generations? Apparently it was because at this late day they thought they had discovered a way to make it useful, for it had come to be believed that the Mississippi emptied into the Gulf of California and, therefore, afforded a short cut from Canada to China. Previously, of course, the supposition had been that it emptied into the Atlantic, or Sea of Virginia.

Comprehension Questions: *Circle the letter of the best answer.*

1. According to Twain, the sentence *De Sota saw the Mississippi in 1542* would be best described as:
    a. historical
    b. descriptive
    c. misleading
    d. factual

2. In terms of historical events, De Soto's arrival at the Mississippi occurred:
    a. during Cromwell's time
    b. the year Elizabeth I became Queen of England
    c. before Shakespeare was born
    d. before the Indians arrived

3. Twain accuses the Spanish explorers of De Soto's time of:
    a. exaggeration
    b. unreasonable curiosity
    c. ignorance
    d. suppressing information

Essay Question

Write a brief answer to the following question.

1. What attitude does Mark Twain seem to have toward organized Religion. Cite two examples to support your claim.

Time-Rate Conversion Chart

Min:Sec	WPM	Min:Sec	WPM	Min:Sec	WPM	Min:Sec	WPM	Min:Sec	WPM
1:00	1085	3:00	362	5:00	217	7:00	155	9:00	121
1:10	930	3:10	343	5:10	210	7:10	151	9:10	118
1:20	814	3:20	326	5:20	203	7:20	148	9:20	116
1:30	723	3:30	310	5:30	197	7:30	145	9:30	114
1:40	651	3:40	296	5:40	191	7:40	142	9:40	112
1:50	592	3:50	283	5:50	186	7:50	139	9:50	110
2:00	543	4:00	271	6:00	181	8:00	136	10:00	109
2:10	501	4:10	260	6:10	176	8:10	133	10:10	107
2:20	465	4:20	250	6:20	171	8:20	130	10:20	105
2:30	434	4:30	241	6:30	167	8:30	128	10:30	103
2:40	407	4:40	233	6:40	163	8:40	125	10:40	102
2:50	383	4:50	224	6:50	159	8:50	123	10:50	100

Was the U.S.'s Involvement in Vietnam a Success or a Failure?

Richard Kezirian

	Hour	Min.	Secs.
A. Ending time:	____	____	____
B. Starting time:	____	____	____
C. A – B = Reading time:		____	____

Not so very long ago American academicians were fairly unified in their opinion that the Vietnam War was a tragic mistake. The only serious debate among them dealt with the reasons for that error. Essentially there were two broad positions on this matter: for convenience, let us call them the Incrementalist and the Structuralist.

The Incrementalists argued that the Vietnam War and the growing American involvement were the result of a series of seemingly small miscalculations, miscalculations that imperceptibly pulled the U.S. toward an entangling situation. There was no major master plan for intervention, no devious intrigue on the part of the American presidents involved. Rather, they acted incorrectly because of misinformation, or of lack of information, and because of their over-reaction, and the U.S. public's over-reaction, to the hysteria of the Joe McCarthy period. Arthur Schlesinger, Jr., summed up the Incrementalist position in 1967 when he arugued that:

> Vietnam is a triumph of the politics of inadvertence. We have achieved our present entanglement, not after due and deliberate consideration, but through a series of small decisions. . . .Each step in the deepening of the American commitment was reasonably regarded as the last that would be necessary. Yet, in retrospect, each step led only to the next, until we find ourselves entrapped today in that nightmare of American strategists, a land war in Asia—a war which no President, including President Johnson, desired or intended. The Vietnam story is a tragedy without villains.[1]

The Incrementalists concluded with the observation that the U.S. learned valuable lessons from the Vietnam experience, and therefore, another mistake like this was highly unlikely.

From Richard Kezirian: *AMERICAN HISTORY: Major Controversies Reviewed.* Copyright 1987 by Kendall/Hunt Publishing Company. Reprinted by permission.

1. Gabriel Kolko, *Anatomy of a War: Vietnam, the United States, and the Modern Historical Experience* (New York: Pantheon Books, 1985).

The Structuralists disagreed. They saw the cause for American intervention rooted in our aggressive capitalistic system. Structuralists believed that America was truly dominated by a military-industrial complex—an association of imperialistic and counter-revolutionary businessmen in alliance with a warrior caste of high-ranking military officers. Structuralists believed that this highly-placed elite promoted the image of danger abroad so that big corporations' technological and planning needs could be securely, and profitably, decided here at home. Therefore, until this business-military elite was dramatically rooted out of its predominent position, there would be the likelihood of more "Vietnams."

Only the weather, and fashions, change more rapidly than historical interpretations, however. The release of new documents and the opening of new archives have stimulated a major reinterpretation of the Vietnam War, and an attack on both the Incrementalist and the Structuralist positions. Two authors have been particularly important in bringing this turnabout—Leslie Gelb and Guenter Lewy. Both men demonstrate that there was much less governmental blundering, indecisiveness, and self-delusion than was formerly believed.

Gelb, in particular, argues that the irony of the Vietnam experience was that "the system worked."[2] Communism was contained for 25 years, just as the president involved aimed to do, and just as the public, the press, and the Congress expected. Gelb adds that American presidents were not taking the nation along with them in a "blind slide down a slippery slope." Nor were American presidents naively expecting an easy military victory in Vietnam. Rather, the presidents involved followed the policy of containment for fear of what would happen domestically and internationally if they did not. Internationally, the presidential fear was that the policy of containment would be badly eroded if Vietnam was lost to the communists. Further, American credibility in the eyes of foreign allies might be lost. Domestically, presidents feared the backlash of voters and politicians on the "right" if they did nothing. Therefore, Gelb maintains, "the costs of raising the ante seemed clearly lower."

Further, Gelb points out that the governmental bureaucracy was not remiss in failing to consider alternatives. Gelb reveals that there was thoughtful and steady questioning of policies regarding Vietnam by the State Department, the Foreign Service, and the military. Particularly surprising is that documentation which shows that CIA analysts began questioning the logic of American intervention in Vietnam as early as 1964. Equally insightful is Gelb's documentation regarding the Gulf of Tonkin resolution. It is now clear that Johnson did not use this resolution as a pretext for escalation of the war. Even after its passage in Congress, Johnson clung to the hope that direct and sustained American intervention might be averted. In sum, Gelb argues that American presidents followed what they considered to be necessary policies, with no illusions as to their success, until the domestic balance of opinion shifted and until Congress finally decided to reduce support to Saigon.

2. Leslie H. Gelb and Richard K. Betts, *The Irony of Vietnam: The System Worked* (Washington, D.C.: The Brookings Institution. 1979).

Lewy is even more supportive of American policies in his writings.[3] For him the new documents prove that from the beginning Hanoi instigated, directed, and led the insurgency in the South. The idea that the rebellion in the South was sponataneous or the result of brutal South Vietnamese governmental policies is incorrect, argues Lewy. The U.S., in light of this North Vietnamese attitude, was not remiss in viewing the Vietnamese situation as analogous to the aggression in Korea in 1950, and was legally warranted, even in light of the Geneva Accords, in interviewing on behalf of the South. In addition, the issue of supposed American war atrocities and war crimes is restudied by Lewy. For Lewy, the new documents support the contention that American atrocities were vastly exaggerated and distorted by the TV and press. Lewy goes so far as to question the inevitability of the final fall of Vietnam in 1975. If President Nixon had not been compromised by the Watergate scandals, and could have provided South Vietnam's government with American air support, the policy of "Vietnamization" might have lasted. Given what has happened since 1975, argues Lewy, this outcome would have been highly beneficial to millions of Vietnamese.

In a way, this academic controversy has a parallel on a more informal, social level. In 1979, two important movies dealt with the Vietnam War. One, *The Deer Hunter,* depicted innocent Americans suffering at the hands of a ruthless enemy. The other, *Coming Home,* starring Jane Fonda, delivered a very frank and virulent anti-war message.

What insights can a historian offer on this controversy and dilemma? I deinitely do not pretend to have all the answers, but the following are thoughts that come to mind. We must first recognize that the recently declassified documents are still only a very small part of the story. The U.S. government usually holds the most crucial "classified" documents, ones that it believes might jeopardize current foreign policy, for 30 years or more before making them available to scholars and the press.

Secondly, any documents that are released are likely to be slanted in two important ways. First of all, they probably are biased because they are White House and Defense Department papers. These types of archives are generally going to be favorable to the executive and military establishment, and to the governmental bureaucracy in general. For instance, consider the documents that Gelb and Lewy were studying. We must understand that it is no accident that these new documents were lately released. The White House and Defense Department are deeply worried about the credibility of American foreign policy in the face of the SALT II negotiations juxtaposed with current Soviet aggression. What subtler way to influence public opinion on these matters than by showing competence, capability, and "morality" in the recent past? It is definitely expedient for our government to act in this manner. Significant questions involving the destiny of our nation are being decided right now, and these decisions are not to be taken without exerting major efforts toward persuasion and influence. A historian attempting to ascertain the truth about the Vietnam War must keep this in mind.

We must be careful, too, of "present-mindedness" in our evaluation of the new works on the Vietnam War. This war was seen as the greatest U.S. policy-failure of the 1960s and early 1970s. Historians and journalists in those years allowed the existence of the war to distort their objectivity regarding many aspects of the American past and present. My warning is that we must not allow current Russian aggression to blind us to mistakes that the U.S. truly *did make* in the past, just as the Vietnam War should not cause us to condemn the U.S. for mistakes that the U.S. *did not make*.

Further, the newly released documents do nothing to negate the critical contention that the U.S.'s policy of "containment" was inherently flawed from the beginning: it required the U.S. to carry out a worldwide policy which was far beyond the capabilities of any one nation or any existing alliance.

Finally, we must recognize that most historians and political scientists still approach the Vietnam War with a characteristic American ignorance. That is, there is the tendency to make very little study of, and pay very little attention to any other country's politics and culture. There was an almost total failure to investigate the feelings and aspirations of the Vietnamese people. Instead, American and alleged Communists actions were seen as the sole motive forces behind these international developments. This is particularly true of the Structuralists, who tend to see nearly all events in the world as almost entirely shaped by the American "counter-revolution."

This last weakness is crucial. The tragic American policy in Vietnam foundered upon one grand imponderable that was beyond our control: the non-Communist Vietnamese were never able to achieve ideological cohesion, organizational discipline, or political legitimacy. They were never able to overcome their differences so as to project one unified policy that would be able to win the support of the peasantry. Given this, America's hopes for success in Vietnam were probably doomed from the beginning.

Comprehension Questions: *Circle the letter of the best answer.*

1. American academicians were fairly unified in their opinion that the Vietnam War was a:
    a. positive move
    b. mistake
    c. political triumph
    d. watershed

2. What did the Incrementalists believe?
    a. the Vietnam War was caused by a series of small miscalculations
    b. the Vietnam War was caused by a series of large miscalculations
    c. the Vietnam War was caused by strong political forces outside the United States
    d. a and b

3. The author believes that most historians and political scientists still approach the Vietnam War with:
   a. insight
   b. a biased attitude
   c. ignorance
   d. forthrightness

Essay Question:

Write a brief answer to the following question.

1. What are your reactions to the evidence presented in this passage?

Time-Rate Conversion Chart

Min:Sec	WPM	Min:Sec	WPM	Min:Sec	WPM	Min:Sec	WPM	Min:Sec	WPM
1:00	1545	4:30	343	8:00	193	11:30	134	15:00	103
1:10	1324	4:40	331	8:10	189	11:40	132	15:10	102
1:20	1159	4:50	320	8:20	185	11:50	131	15:20	101
1:30	1030	5:00	309	8:30	182	12:00	129	15:30	100
1:40	927	5:10	299	8:40	178	12:10	127	15:40	99
1:50	843	5:20	290	8:50	175	12:20	125	15:50	98
2:00	773	5:30	281	9:00	172	12:30	124		
2:10	713	5:40	273	9:10	169	12:40	122		
2:20	662	5:50	265	9:20	166	12:50	120		
2:30	618	6:00	258	9:30	163	13:00	119		
2:40	579	6:10	251	9:40	160	13:10	117		
2:50	545	6:20	244	9:50	157	13:20	116		
3:00	515	6:30	238	10:00	155	13:30	114		
3:10	488	6:40	232	10:10	152	13:40	113		
3:20	464	6:50	226	10:20	150	13:50	112		
3:30	441	7:00	221	10:30	147	14:00	110		
3:40	421	7:10	216	10:40	145	14:10	109		
3:50	403	7:20	211	10:50	143	14:20	108		
4:00	386	7:30	206	11:00	140	14:30	107		
4:10	371	7:40	202	11:10	138	14:40	105		
4:20	357	7:50	197	11:20	136	14:50	104		

Managing Stress and Relieving Tension

Vincent Melograno and
James Klinzing

	Hour	Min.	Secs.
A. Ending time:	___	___	___
B. Starting time:	___	___	___
C. A – B = Reading time:		___	___

Learning to deal effectively with stressors and the resulting muscular tension is important if one wants to achieve total fitness. Unfortunately, some attempts at dealing with stressors and tension do not contribute to good health or fitness at all. Drugs, alcohol, or cigarettes may relieve tension temporarily, but eventually they produce additional, harmful stress when they are relied on. The following are some positive approaches to managing stressors that contribute to long-term personal well-being.

Identifying the Source

A person needs to first identify the stressors in his or her life. Oftentimes we don't realize what it is that is causing an excess of stress in our lives. Once the stressors are identified, however, some of them might be eliminated. When too many demands are made upon a person's time and talents, it is often wise to remove some of these demands. A student may face excessive demands from classes, work, family, friends, athletics, or extracurricular activities. Such a student should ask himself/herself if the stress produced by meeting each of these demands is really worth it. If the answer is no for a particular stressor, then some adjustments must be made. Each stressor needs to be evaluated in this way. A discussion with a friend, parent, academic advisor, or other trusted individual may help a student evaluate his or her priorities and determine which stressors can be eliminated without jeopardizing future goals.

Coping with the Source of Stress

Much of the stress an individual may experience is necessary. Rather than coping with the primary stressor, a person may magnify his or her reaction to it, thus producing secondary stressors. Secondary stressors may include: thoughts about failures or weaknesses, the inability to deal with the stressors, or perhaps procrastination related to an upcoming responsibility (the primary stressor is magnified by delaying effective preparation for it). These negative thoughts or actions can lead to a negative self-fulfilling prophecy. For example, "I know my mind will go blank during the test and I'll fail" . . . sure enough, it happens and a failing grade results.

A simple way to counteract the negative cycle is through the use of positive affirmations. *Positive affirmations* are positively stated thoughts and beliefs about ourselves. They are goal statements phrased in a positive, present-tense format. For example, a student worried about an upcoming examination would first list his or her negative thoughts and/or behaviors associated with this stressor. The negative thoughts might be:

1. I'm not smart enough to understand this material.
2. My mind will go blank during the exam.
3. Studying will not help.

The next step is to generate a list of positive affirmations to counteract the negative statements. For example:

1. I enjoy this class.
2. The course information is orgnanized and I am ready for total recall.
3. I am prepared, so I am going to do well.

By repeating these statements many times in the days prior to the examination, a new level of confidence can be attained. A positive attitude and expectancy can be developed. This will help to eliminate a negative self-fulfilling prophecy and guide an individual in a positive, task-oriented manner. Success is more likely if a negative attitude toward a stressor can be changed to the anticipation of successful fulfillment.

Diversion

Stressors can be forgotten for a period of time through participation in enjoyable, leisure-time pursuits. Such activities divert attention away from sources of stress, thus giving the mind a rest. Each person should develop interests in hobbies and fitness or sports activities and use them to provide a break from life's daily responsibilities. These diversions may be very passive—such as listening to records, collecting coins, or reading—and as active as one prefers—for example, playing golf, hiking through the woods, or taking a long, leisurely bike ride. It is well to develop a variety of leisure-time alternatives; passive and active, indoor and outdoor, individual and team or group, seasonal and nonseasonal, etc.

Exercise

Many people look forward to daily exercise to alleviate tension and anxiety. Aerobic exercises, particularly jogging, swimming, or cycling, allow a person to spend time away from the pressures of work, school, or home. It is difficult to concentrate on problems while performing rhythmic aerobic exercise, thus the mind usually wanders to many other thoughts. Exercise is a very important part of each day for many people because it provides a period of relative tranquility in their otherwise busy schedules.

There is evidence to support the role of exercise in improving psychological well-being. Light levels of aerobic exercise have been shown to have an effect on lessening neuromuscular tension—an effect even greater than that produced by a drug commonly prescribed for relieving tension.[1] Jogging and running programs have resulted in reduced levels of depression among depressed males, females, alcoholics, college students and professors, and people with coronary heart disease.[2] Running is even being used as a form of psychotherapy by some psychiatrists with positive effects.[3] Aerobic exercise appears to induce mood elevations among normal individuals and may have an antidepressant effect on depressed individuals.[4]

Exercise on an aerobic nature lasting 30 minutes or longer at the THR level is the most beneficial for promoting relaxation. Highly competitive sports or activities causing frustration are not recommended for this purpose. There seems to be a sound reason for most people saying they feel better when they exercise regularly.

Comprehension Questions: *Circle the letter of the best answer.*

1. Learning to deal effectively with stress is important if one wants to achieve:
   a. total fitness
   b. relaxation
   c. spiritual awareness
   d. sexual potency

2. Exercise of an aerobic nature lasting at least _____ minutes is most beneficial for promoting relaxation.
   a. 20
   b. 30
   c. 40
   d. 60

---

1. H. A. DeVries, "Tranquilizer Effect of Exercise: A Critical Review," *Physician and Sports Medicine,* 9 (1981): 47–55.

2. C. P. Ransford, "A Role for Amines in the Antidepressant Effect of Exercise: A Review," *Medicine and Science in Sports and Exercise,* 14 (1982): 1–10.

3. L. Barnes, "Running Therapy: Oriented and Moving," *Physician and Sports Medicine,* 18 (1980): 97–100.

4. Ransford.

3. A student may face excessive demands from:
   a. professors
   b. homework
   c. family
   d. him or herself

Essay Question

Write a brief answer to the following question.

1. What are some ways you reduce stress in your life?

Time-Rate Conversion Chart

Min:Sec	WPM	Min:Sec	WPM	Min:Sec	WPM
1:00	890	4:30	198	8:00	111
1:10	763	4:40	191	8:10	109
1:20	668	4:50	184	8:20	107
1:30	593	5:00	178	8:30	105
1:40	534	5:10	172	8:40	103
1:50	485	5:20	167	8:50	101
2:00	445	5:30	162		
2:10	411	5:40	157		
2:20	381	5:50	153		
2:30	356	6:00	148		
2:40	334	6:10	144		
2:50	314	6:20	141		
3:00	297	6:30	137		
3:10	281	6:40	134		
3:20	267	6:50	130		
3:30	254	7:00	127		
3:40	243	7:10	124		
3:50	232	7:20	121		
4:00	223	7:30	119		
4:10	214	7:40	116		
4:20	205	7:50	114		

9–5

Food and Ecosystems

John Christensen

	Hour	Min.	Secs.
A. Ending time:	___	___	___
B. Starting time:	___	___	___
C. A − B = Reading time:	___	___	

An ecosystem is a marvelous thing. Energy flows through and powers the system. Chemicals are continually recycled. A balance exists and we say it is beautiful. However, ecocystems can be disturbed and damaged. A lack of understanding of how they work can result in practices that destroy the delicate innerworkings. Uncontrolled growth is abnormal in an ecosystem. The exponential increase in human population is taxing the ability of our biosphere to provide food for all its people. Before we examine the food crisis, let's look at the essentials of food production.

When organisms eat food, they obtain the energy they need to carry on their life processes and to make body parts. The chemical reactions that take place in an organism as food is utilized are referred to as metabolism. Nutrition is the uptake of materials necessary for metabolism. Essentially, nutrition means eating.

A food chain has three main levels: producers, consumers, and decomposers. Producers make their own food. Consumers rely on what the producers make. Decomposers are special types of consumers that break down plant and animal refuse into simpler chemicals that plants can use. Hence, decomposers are necessary for the recycling of minerals. They also help maintain soil structure and aeration.

A plant's nutrition needs are the following:

1. sunlight
2. carbon dioxide (CO_2)
3. water (H_2O)
4. minerals (elements)
5. oxygen (O_2)
6. heat

In the photosynthesis (energy-trapping) process, plants combine carbon dioxide and water to form organic sugars from which they make their body parts (stems, leaves, etc.) and obtain their energy. In the energy-releasing process (respiration),

From John Christensen: *GLOBAL SCIENCE: Energy, Resources, Environment.* Copyright 1984 by Kendall/ Hunt Publishing Company. Reprinted by permission.

organic minerals are broken down as oxygen is consumed. Heat is given off. In warm blooded animals, heat is necessary to maintain an acceptable body temperature in which chemical (metabolic) reaction can occur.

Minerals are essential for the growth of healthy plants. The necessary minerals must contain 13 different elements. Nitrogen, potassium, and calcium are required in relatively large quantities. The remaining nutrients are needed in lesser amounts. For some only a trace is needed. They are phosphorus, magnesium, sulfur, manganese, boron, iron, zinc, copper, molybdenum, and chlorine.

The minerals a plant needs must be absorbed from the soil. The nutrition of plants is thus dependent on the ability of the soil to store essential elements and to make them available in a biologically active form. This ability can be enhanced to varying degrees with the application of manure and synthetic fertilizers. In nature, this replacement occurs more slowly as rock weathers and organic matter is decomposed. Also, the suitability of a soil for agricultural production depends on its texture and structure. Texture is mainly related to particle size. The most productive soils have a crumbly structure developed when small particles are cemented together by organic materials. Such soils are well aerated and have a large capacity for retaining water.

The nutritional needs of animal are:

1. water (H_2O)
2. oxygen (O_2)
3. minerals (elements)
4. vitamins
5. food (nutrients)
   a. proteins
   b. cabohydrates
   c. fats (lipids)

Animals obtain their food either directly or indirectly from green plants. They obtain their energy and body parts by first breaking down the energy-rich products of photosynthesis into simpler, less energetic molecules. Many of these less energetic molecules become the nutrients that the animal absorbs for the building of its own body parts.

The adult (human) body is 60 percent water by weight. Water serves to regulate the body temperature, transports nutrients, and participates in metabolic reactions.

Oxygen is required for (respiration), the breakdown of food by organisms to release nutrients, energy, carbon dioxide, and water.

Essential minerals elements are involved in the electrochemical functions of nerve and muscle, the formation of bones and teeth, the activation of enzymes (organic catalysts) and in the case of iron, the transport of oxygen. Minerals are so widely distributed in nature that primary dietary deficiencies are unlikely. However, changes in the balance among them may have important consequences for health.

Proteins are broken down by the body into amino acids. The amino acids are then reassembled into body proteins. Some serve to give structure to the organs of the cell. Others acts as enzymes, antibodies, hormones, and metabolically active compounds.

Carbohydrates are broken down to provide our body's main source of energy. Adequate carbohydrate intake prevents the breakdown of protein for energy needs. This is important because protein is best used for body-building functions.

Fats are involved in the maintenance of cell membrane structure and function. They also serve as building blocks for some hormones, provide a concentrated source of energy, carry certain vitamins, and provide insulation and protection for important organs and body structures.

Vitamins are organic molecules that are needed in small quantities in the diet of higher animals to perform specific biological functions. For example, vitamin K is important in blood clotting.

Comprehension Questions: *Circle the letter of the best answer*

1. The chemical reactions that take place in an organism as food is utilized are referred to as:
   a. metabolism
   b. decomposition
   c. exponential increase
   d. aeration

2. Essentially, "nutrition" means:
   a. food
   b. food science
   c. carbohydrate intake
   d. eating

3. The human body is composed of _____ percent water by weight.
   a. 40
   b. 60
   c. 30
   d. 20

Essay Question

Write a brief answer to the following question.

What was the central idea presented in this passage and how did the author back this position?

Time-Rate Conversion Chart

Min:Sec	WPM	Min:Sec	WPM
1:00	783	4:30	174
1:10	671	4:40	168
1:20	587	4:50	162
1:30	522	5:00	157
1:40	470	5:10	152
1:50	427	5:20	147
2:00	392	5:30	142
2:10	361	5:40	138
2:20	336	5:50	134
2:30	313		
2:40	294		
2:50	276		
3:00	261		
3:10	247		
3:20	235		
3:30	224		
3:40	214		
3:50	204		
4:00	196		
4:10	188		
4:20	181		

9-6

Erosion, Drought and Deserts

Unesco

	Hour	Min.	Secs.
A. Ending time:	——	——	——
B. Starting time:	——	——	——
C. A – B = Reading time:		——	——

Soil is a country's most precious natural resource, aptly described as "the bridge between the inanimate and the living." It consists of weathered and decomposed bedrock, water, air, organic material formed from plant and animal decay, and thousands of different life forms, mainly microorganisms and insects. All play their part in maintaining the complex ecology of a healthy soil.

Although soil erosion does occur naturally, the process is slow. Man has increased the rate of natural erosion by at least 2.5 times and, over the centuries, has destroyed an estimated 2,000 million hectares of land. There is good evidence that past civilizations, in the Mediterranean and in Central America, collapsed as a result of soil erosion following the cutting of forests on steep slopes and other destructive practices.

Soil erosion occurs primarily when land is exposed to the action of wind and rain. Unprotected by a cover of vegetation, and the binding action of roots, each raindrop hits the naked soil with the impact of a bullet. Soil particles are loosened, washed down the slope of the land, and either end up in the valley below or are washed out to sea by streams and rivers.

Water erosion is the commonest form of erosion. It is causing massive damage in nearly all developing countries. It is found where steep land is being unwisely farmed where gently sloping land is left exposed to the effects of heavy rain for any length of time.

Worldwide, about 25,000 million tonnes of soil are being washed away each year, ending up in the rivers and finally the oceans. According to a study carried out by the Food and Agriculture Organization of the United Nations (FAO) and the United Nations Environment Programme (UNEP) an estimated 11.6 per cent of Africa north of the equator and 17.1 per cent of the Near East are subject to water erosion. So are 90 million of India's 297 million hectares.

Water erosion causes two sets of problems: an "on-site" loss of agriculture productivity; and a downstream movement of sediment, causing flooding, a loss of river navigability and the silting up of reservoirs.

Reprinted from the Unesco Courier, January, 1985.

While heavy rainfall, prolonged drought or high winds may be the direct cause of soil erosion, they are not the real problem. A landscape can remain stable under all these conditions, whether it is a natural state or being sensibly farmed. Erosion occurs when farming practices are used which fail to take account of the ease with which soils can be washed or blown away.

For example, over-stocking and over-grazing have caused untold damage in much of Africa and Asia in the past few decades. In arid areas, soil is compacted around water holes, the vegetation is stripped and dies, and erosion sets in. Too often the land ends up as desert, the intimate result of soil erosion and degradation. If erosion is the sickness of a land, desertification is its death.

Today, desertification is threatening about 3,200 million hectares of land; the livelihoods of the 700 million people who depend on that land are at stake,

About 30 per cent of the world's exploitable soils are still under shifting cultivation in Africa, Asia and Latin America. The technique is practised by more than 30 million people in Africa alone. Formerly, this use of land served to conserve fertility, as it allowed a long fallow period during which soil fertility would build up to its previous level. Today, population pressure and the struggle for improved yields are cutting the fallow period back to virtually nothing. Under such conditions, the forest soils soon lose their fertility and begin to erode. Essentially, this is because the land is being farmed beyond its capability.

Nearly always, it is exposed land which erodes while land covered in vegetation is stable. The process often starts high in a watershed, on the steep slopes which are traditionally forested. But over the past few decades, there has been mounting pressure on fuelwood resources. Rural people have been forced to travel further and further to find their energy supplies, and to cut wood from higher and steeper ground. Many tropical forests have also been cleared for agricultural development. Between 1975 and 1980, 37 million hectares of forest were destroyed in Africa, 12.2 million in Asia and 18.4 million in Central and South America.

In some countries, an increasingly critical balance of payments situation has forced governments to plant more and more cash crops. If no more arable land is available, the new crops have to be planted in marginal land, previously pasture, which is brought under the plough for the first time. Much of the thin soil may be lost in the first heavy rain which occurs when the field surface is still bare. During a short storm in the United Republic of Tanzania a few years ago, scientists found that a field they were studying lost 5 centimetres of topsoil over its whole surface in just a few hours; rills had cut down to a depth of 15 centimetres.

The problems of soil conservation are closely connected to those of rural development and rural poverty. A farmer who has to struggle to grow even enough food to feed his family cannot devote weeks or months to terracing his land or learning new farming techniques. It follows that successful rural development is an essential precursor to eliminating soil erosion.

Comprehension Questions: *Circle the letter of the best answer*

1. What is the most common cause of erosion?
   a. water
   b. soil
   c. wind
   d. chemical

2. Today, desertification is threatening how many hectares of land?
   a. 5,200 thousand
   b. 3,200 million
   c. 1,100 million
   d. 10 million

3. What is the country's most precious natural resource?
   a. minerals
   b. soil
   c. water
   d. alloys

Essay Question

Write a brief answer to the following question.

The author describes the soil as "the bridge between the inanimate and the living." What does he mean by this?

Time-Rate Conversion Chart

Min:Sec	WPM	Min:Sec	WPM	Min:Sec	WPM
1:00	887	4:30	197	8:00	111
1:10	760	4:40	190	8:10	109
1:20	665	4:50	184	8:20	106
1:30	591	5:00	177	8:30	104
1:40	532	5:10	172	8:40	102
1:50	484	5:20	166	8:50	100
2:00	444	5:30	161		
2:10	409	5:40	157		
2:20	380	5:50	152		
2:30	355	6:00	148		
2:40	333	6:10	144		
2:50	313	6:20	140		
3:00	296	6:30	136		
3:10	280	6:40	133		
3:20	266	6:50	130		
3:30	253	7:00	127		
3:40	242	7:10	124		
3:50	231	7:20	121		
4:00	222	7:30	118		
4:10	213	7:40	116		
4:20	205	7:50	113		

9–7

Nasrudin Hodja: The Man Who Rode His Ass Backwards

Ivan Sop

	Hour	Min.	Secs.
A. Ending time:	____	____	____
B. Starting time:	____	____	____
C. A − B = Reading time:		____	____

Few comic folk heroes in world literature rival Nasrudin Hodja, the author of innumerable pranks and the subject of waggish stories which amuse and delight people from Morocco to the frontiers of China and from Siberia to the Arabian Peninsula. Stories by Nasrudin or about him are found in some forty languages.

For centuries the name of Nasrudin Hodja (Hodja is a term of respect, meaning teacher) has been associated with tales that are amusing, somewhat naive, ribald, and yet imbued with profound folk-wisdom. These stories also exemplify the use of wit and irony as weapons against brutal force and oppression.

But who was Nasrudin?

Some think he never existed and that he is part of the inexhaustible fund of popular legend. Others are convinced that he was a man who actually lived and was born in Turkey, but many countries claim to be his place of birth.

According to tradition Nasrudin was born about eight centuries ago in Turkey, in the little village of Harto near the township of Bivrihisar (to the west of Ankara). For over a century scholars have been trying to discover where he really came from. In Akcheir, another town in Turkey which claims him as a son, a festival is held periodically in his honour. This is where he is supposed to be buried and an inscription on the wall of his mausoleum suggests that he died some time before 1392. But there is no means of proving these assertions and theories.

According to legend, his tomb was surrounded by columns but was without any railings and merely had a massive door with a padlock and no key. This was said to be an example of the wisdom of Nasrudin who used to say that the doors were "closed for his friends and open for his enemies."

He is always popularly represented as an old man with a white beard wearing an outside turban, simply dressed and sitting backwards astride his donkey so as to be sure that he is always facing in the right direction for, as he says: "whatever I tell my donkey to do, he does the opposite."

Reprinted from the UNESCO COURIER, April, 1976.

The character of Nasrudin, an astonishing blend of wisdom and native wit, has long since gone beyond the frontiers of popular Turkish literature. He is part of the folklore of the Balkan peoples, the Serbians, the Croatians, the Macedonians, the Bosnian Muslims, the Bulgarians and the Albanians. His stories are also current in Iran, Armenia, Georgia, the Caucasus, Turkestan, and in many other countries.

Nasrudin exemplifies the humour that is deeply rooted in oral folk traditions, so it is hardly surprising that so many of his "brothers" are to be found all round the Mediterranean.

The Arabs know him as Djuha, Djoha, Djuhi, or Goha, the Berbers as Si Djeha or simply as Djeha, the Maltese as Djahan, the Sicilians as Giufa, the Calabrians as Hioha or Jovani.

In reality, Nasrudin is something of an anti-hero, a parody of the epic hero; he is poor, dirty, shabbily dressed and uses coarse language. He steals without hesitation when he has the opportunity.

One day when he was singing while washing himself, Nasrudin decided that he had a very pleasant voice. When he emerged from the bath house he rushed to the top of the minaret of the mosque and, although it was noon, he called the faithful to evening prayer. Someone shouted up from below: "Fool. With such a horrible voice you should be ashamed to give the call to evening prayer when it's midday." Nasrudin leant over and shouted back, "If some kind person had built a bathhouse on top of the minaret you would see what a fine voice I have."

Innumerable stories illustrate his character and behaviour. When his wife died Nasrudin did not seem very upset. Shortly afterwards his donkey died and he wept bitterly. Someone said to him, "The death of your donkey seems to have upset you more than the death of your wife." Nasrudin replied: "That's quite easy to explain. When my wife died my friends told me, 'We'll find you an even more beautiful wife.' But when I lost my donkey nobody said to me, 'Don't worry, we'll buy you a stronger donkey.' Surely I've every reason to mourn my donkey."

One day Nasrudin was throwing fermented milk into Lake Akshir. A passerby called to him, "What on earth are you doing? "I'm making yoghurt." "Do you think it'll take?" asked the man in astonishment. "I'm quite sure it won't," answered Nasrudin, "but just supposing it did!"

Since folkore is a valuable wellspring of literature, anecdotes about Nasrudin have served as an inspiration for poets and authors of many nationalities, Russian, Ukrainian, Romanian, German, Serbian and Turkish among others. In some cases one adaptation influences another. The Yugoslav writer Slovko Micanovic used a book about Nasrudin by the Soviet author Leonid Golovyov as a model, in writing his novel "Nasrudin Hodja in Istanbul".

Nasrudin appears to have been everywhere as we learn from ubiquitous legends about his life. According to one such story Nasrudin was a sage living in Baghdad around the tenth century, at the time of the Abbasid Dynasty. Having been accused of heresy during a period of religious strife, he is said to have feigned madness in order to save himself from the scaffold.

Other accounts say he lived in Asia Minor, in Anatolia, in the 13th or 14th centuries. Tradition also has it that he lived at the time of Sultan Bayezit and his wars with Tamerlane—in the late 14th and early 15th centuries. And an entire cycle of tales about him and Tamerlane exists in Turkish folklore.

Some stories about Nasrudin and Tamerlane reflect the spontaneous popular resistance to the Mongol conqueror. In the following stories, for example, the dialogue between Nasrudin and Tamerlane initially seems to be merely an exchange of ideas but then a sudden flash of Nasrudin's wit makes Tamerlane seem ridiculous.

Tamerlane said to Nasrudin, "All the Abbasid Caliphs are known by a nickname. Al-Mustansir means 'dependent on God's help', al-Mu'tasim means 'seeking protection in God' and al-Mutawakkil means 'trusting in God'. What would you have nicknamed me if I had been one of them?" Straight away Nasrudin replied, "Tamerlane God-help-us."

One day Tamerlane invited Nasrudin to the bathhouse and asked him, "If I had been a slave what do you think I would be worth?" "Fifty pence" replied Nasrudin. Tamerlane was offended: "Don't you realize that the loin cloth I am wearing is alone worth that?" "Yes, of course", replied Nasrudin smiling. "That's my offer for the lot!"

One day when Nasrudin was with Tamerlane in his palace, a platinum mirror was brought to the conqueror as a gift. Tamerlane looked at himself in the mirror and a few tears came into his eyes. Noticing this, Nasrudin in his turn began to weep. Soon Tamerlane recovered his composure whereas Nasrudin was still sobbing.

"Nasrudin" said Tamerlane, "when I saw how ugly I was in the mirror, I was a bit upset. Knowing how fond you are of me I wasn't surprised to see that you shared my sorrow, and I thank you. But, tell me, why are you still crying now that I have got over it?" "Sire", said Nasrudin, drying his tears, "seeing your face for a moment in the mirror upset you for quite a time. I see you all day long. It's only right that I should weep a little longer."

Variants of these stories occur in which ordinary people get the better of the powerful and in which the "adversary" who is made a fool of is not Tamerlane but a bey or a pasha.

However Nasrudin's witticisms sometimes have quite a different character, as in the following story. A man said to Nasrudin, "Look at that goose running over there." "And what's that to do with me?" Nasrudin replied. "But it's just gone into your house", the man said. "And what's that to do with you?" retorted Nasrudin.

Nasrudin, one of the poorest of men, also stands up for a certain standard of human dignity and moral integrity although it is the comic vein which prevails, as in the following tale.

One day Nasrudin was a guest at dinner and turned up wearing threadbare clothing. Everyone ignored him. Feeling his pride hurt, he slipped out of a side door, hurried home, changed into suitable clothing, put on a beautiful fur-lined cloak and returned to the palace. This time he was welcomed at the door with great ceremony and was ushered to a place at the principal table. He was offered the best dishes and every attention was lavished upon him. After enjoying all his favourite foods, Nasrudin took hold of the fur on the ample sleeve of his cloak, leant towards it and pushed it affectionately towards a well-filled plate saying "Eat, eat, my fur!"

The other guests were intrigued by this prank. "Nasrudin, what are you doing?" With his customary good humour, he described what sort of welcome he had been given on his first arrival and the reception that had been accorded him when he returned a second time. "As it is my fur that has received the honour", he concluded, "it too should share in the feast".

The humour of Nasrudin is not only social satire, it is also a way of looking at life which was obviously not always in agreement with the idology and ruling powers of the time.

The character of Nasrudin is a product of anonymous creators: craftsmen, peasants, shopkeepers, donkey drivers, carters, beggars, shrewd townsmen and countrymen, dreamers, all those who felt social injustice more clearly than they understood the reason behind it, and who expressed their human predicament in stories, tales, jokes and quips.

Nasrudin's stories have a value which is universal: always using the same effect, that of comedy, they approach and sometimes even rival the great works of world literature.

Comprehension Questions: *Circle the letter of the best answer.*

1. The story of Nasrudin would best be described as:
   a. history
   b. a sad story
   c. legend
   d. myth

2. The story of Nasrudin comes mainly from:
   a. India
   b. Turkey
   c. China
   d. Egypt

3. The stories about Nasrudin are almost always:
   a. humorous
   b. sad
   c. tragic
   d. about war and fighting

Essay Question

Why have Nasrudin Hodja stories maintained their popularity over the years?

Time-Rate Conversion Chart

Min:Sec	WPM	Min:Sec	WPM	Min:Sec	WPM
1:00	650	3:00	217	5:00	130
1:10	557	3:10	205	5:10	126
1:20	488	3:20	195	5:20	122
1:30	433	3:30	186	5:30	118
1:40	390	3:40	177	5:40	115
1:50	355	3:50	170	5:50	111
2:00	325	4:00	163	6:00	108
2:10	300	4:10	156	6:10	105
2:20	279	4:20	150	6:20	103
2:30	260	4:30	144	6:30	100
2:40	244	4:40	139		
2:50	229	4:50	134		

Calamity in Vondervotteimittiss (Part I)

Edgar Allan Poe

Everybody knows, in a general way, that the finest place in the world is—or, alas, *was*—the Dutch borough of Vondervotteimittiss. Yet, as few of my readers have ever visited it, it will be only proper that I should enter into some account of it. Indeed, it is with the hope of enlisting public sympathy in behalf of the inhabitants that I here relate a history of the calamitous events which have so lately occurred.

I am able to say positively that Vondervotteimittiss has existed, from its origin in antiquity, in precisely the same condition which it at present possesses. Of the date of this origin, however, I can only speak with that species of indefinite definiteness with which mathematicians must often contend in certain algebraic formulae.

Touching the derivation of the name, I confess myself equally at fault, for among the multitude of opinions upon this delicate point, I am able to select nothing satisfactory.

The village is in a tiny, perfectly circular valley, entirely surrounded by hills, over whose summit the people have never yet ventured to pass for the very good reason that they do not believe there is anything at all on the other side.

Round the circumference of the valley extends a continuous row of sixty little houses. These, having their backs to the hills, must look to the centre of the plain, just sixty yards from the front door of each dwelling. Every house has a small garden before it, with circular paths, a sundial, and twenty-four cabbages. The buildings themselves are all so precisely alike that one can in no manner be distinguished from the other. Their style of architecture is somewhat odd but, at the same time, strikingly picturesque. They are fashioned of hard-burned little bricks, red with black ends, so that the walls look like chessboards upon a grand scale. The windows are narrow and deep, with very tiny panes and a great deal of sash, and on the roof is a vast quantity of tiles with long curly ears. The woodwork throughout is dark-hued, with much carving and only a trifling variety of pattern; the carvers of Vondervotteimittiss have never been able to carve more than two objects—a timepiece and a cabbage—but they do these excellently well and intersperse them with a singular ingenuity wherever they find room for the chisel.

Adapted from *The Devil in the Belfry* by Edgar Allan Poe.

Inside, furnishings and rooms are alike from one dwelling to another. The mantel-pieces are wide and high and have not only timepieces and cabbages sculptured over the front, but a real timepiece, which makes a prodigious ticking, on top in the middle, with a flowerpot containing a cabbage standing on each extremity.

The fireplaces, which are large and deep, always have a rousing fire and, over it, a huge pot of sauerkraut and pork, which the good woman of the house attends. She is a little fat lady with blue eyes and red face and wears a huge cap like a sugar-loaf, ornamented with purple and yellow ribbons. Her dress of orange-colored linsey-woolsey is very short in the waist and, indeed, very short in other respects, not reaching below the middle of the calf of her leg. This is somewhat thick, and so are her ankles, but she has a fine pair of green stockings to cover them; and her shoes of pink leather are fastened each with a bunch of yellow ribbons puckered up in the shape of a cabbage. In her left hand she has a little heavy Dutch watch—in her right she wields a ladle for the sauerkraut and pork.

The boys, all three, are each two feet in height, with three-cornered cocked hats, purple waistcoats, buckskin knee-breeches, red woolen stockings, heavy shoes with big silver buckles, and long coats with large mother-of-pearl buttons. Each has a pipe in his mouth and a dumpy little watch in his right hand; he takes a puff and a look, then a look and a puff. They are in the garden attending the pig, which is corpulent, lazy, and presently occupied in picking up the stray leaves that fall from the cabbages.

Seated right at the front door is the man of the house himself—an exceedingly puffy old gentleman with big circular eyes and a huge double chin; his dress resembles that of the boys, and I need say nothing further about it. The only difference is that his pipe is bigger and makes greater smoke; furthermore, he carries his watch in a pocket, for he has something more important than a watch to attend to, as I shall presently explain. He sits with his right leg upon his left knee, wears a grave coun-tenance, and always keeps one of his eyes resolutely bent upon a certain remarkable object in the centre of the plain.

This object is situated in the steeple of the Town-Council House. The Town-Council, all very little round intelligent men with big saucer eyes, fat double chins, and coats much longer and shoe-buckles much bigger than the ordinary inhabitants, have recently held several special meetings, at which they adopted three important resolutions—

"That it is wrong to alter the good old course of things."

"That there is nothing worth-while out of Vondervotteimittiss."

"That we will stick by our clocks and our cabbages."

In the steeple is a belfry, where exists the pride and wonder of the village—the great clock of the borough, the object of the gaze of all the old gentlemen. The steeple has seven sides, and the clock seven faces so that it can be readily seen from all quar-ters. The belfry man, whose sole duty is to attend it, has the perfect sinecure, for the clock of Vondervotteimittiss was never yet known to have anything the matter with it. Indeed, such is the case with all the other clocks and watches in the borough—never was such a place for keeping the true time! When the large clapper thought proper to say "twelve o'clock!" all its obedient followers opened their throats simultaneously and responded like a very echo.

All people who hold sinecure offices are held in more or less respect, and, as the belfry-man of Vondervotteimittiss has the perfect sinecure, he is perfectly respected; indeed, the very pigs look up to him with a sentiment of reverence. His coat-tail is *very* far longer, his pipe, his shoe-buckles, his eyes, his belly *very* far bigger than any other.

I have thus painted the happy estate of Vondervotteimittiss—alas! that so fair a picture should ever experience a reverse!

Comprehension Questions: *Circle the letter of the best answer.*

1. In Vondervotteimittiss:
   a. everyone carries a watch in one hand
   b. the housewives have a watch in one hand and a broom in the other
   c. only the men and the boys carry watches
   d. the men carry their watches in their pockets

2. The steeple clock has seven faces:
   a. because the villagers are superstitious
   b. so that it can be heard in all directions
   c. so that it can be seen from any part of the village
   d. because the builders made a mistake and the people liked it

3. The most striking characteristic of life among the villagers is the:
   a. spirit of adventure
   b. emphasis on the importance of learning
   c. advanced value system
   d. essential sameness

Essay Question

Write a brief answer to the following question.

1. What is the purpose of this situation?

Time-Rate Conversion Chart

Min:Sec	WPM	Min:Sec	WPM	Min:Sec	WPM	Min:Sec	WPM	Min:Sec	WPM
1:00	1040	3:00	347	5:00	208	7:00	149	9:00	116
1:10	891	3:10	328	5:10	201	7:10	145	9:10	113
1:20	780	3:20	312	5:20	195	7:20	142	9:20	111
1:30	693	3:30	297	5:30	189	7:30	139	9:30	109
1:40	624	3:40	284	5:40	184	7:40	136	9:40	108
1:50	567	3:50	271	5:50	178	7:50	133	9:50	106
2:00	520	4:00	260	6:00	173	8:00	130	10:00	104
2:10	480	4:10	250	6:10	169	8:10	127	10:10	102
2:20	446	4:20	240	6:20	164	8:20	125	10:20	101
2:30	416	4:30	231	6:30	160	8:30	122	10:30	99
2:40	390	4:40	223	6:40	156	8:40	120		
2:50	367	4:50	215	6:50	152	8:50	118		

Calamity in Vondervotteimittiss (Part II)

	Hour	Min.	Secs.
A. Ending time:	___	___	___
B. Starting time:	___	___	___
C. A – B = Reading time:	___	___	

Edgar Allan Poe

An old saying among the wisest inhabitants of Vondervotteimittiss that "no good can come from over the hills" really seemed to have held something of the spirit of prophecy.

It wanted five minutes of noon, on the day before yesterday, when there appeared a very odd-looking object on the summit of the ridge to the eastward. Such an occurrence, of course, attracted universal attention, and every little old gentleman who sat in a leather-bottomed armchair turned one of his eyes with a stare of dismay upon the phenomenon, still keeping the other upon the clock in the steeple.

By the time that it wanted only three minutes of noon, the droll object was clearly perceived to be a very diminutive foreign-looking young man. Since he descended the hills at a great rate, everybody had soon a good look at this strange personage.

His countenance was a dark snuff colour, and he had a long hooked nose, pea eyes, a wide mouth, and an excellent set of teeth, which latter he seemed anxious of displaying, as he was grinning from ear to ear; what with mustaches and whiskers there was none of the rest of his face to be seen. His dress was a tight-fitting swallow-tailed black coat (from one of whose pockets dangled a vast length of white handkerchief), black kersey-mere knee breeches, black silk stockings, and stumpy-looking pumps with huge bunches of black satin ribbon for bows. Under one arm he carried a huge *chapeau* [hat] and under the other a fiddle nearly five times as big as himself. In his left hand was a gold snuff-box, from which as he capered down the hill, cutting all manner of fantastical steps, he took snuff incessantly with an air of the greatest possible self-satisfaction. God bless me! here was a sight for the eyes of the sober burghers of Vondervotteimittiss!

To speak plainly, the fellow had, in spite of his grinning, an audacious and sinister face, and as he danced right into the village, the odd stumpy appearance of his pumps excited no little suspicion; but what mainly occasioned a righteous indignation was that the scoundrelly popinjay, while he cut a fandango here and a whirligig there, did not seem to have the remotest idea in the world of such a thing as *keeping time* in his steps.

Adapted from *The Devil in the Belfry* by Edgar Allan Poe.

The good people had scarcely a chance, however, to get their eyes thoroughly open when, just as it wanted half a minute of noon, the rascal bounced right into the midst of them and, after a *pirouette* and a *pas-de-zephyr,* pigeonwinged himself right up into the belfry of the House of the Town-Council, where the wonder-stricken belfry-man sat smoking in a state of stupefied dignity and dismay.

The little chap seized him at once by the nose, clapped the big *chapeau* upon his head and over his ears and mouth, and, then, lifting the big fiddle, beat him with it so long and so soundly that, what with the belfry-man being so fat and the fiddle so hollow, you would have sworn there was a regiment of double-bass drummers in the belfry.

There is no knowing to what desperate act of vengeance this unprincipled attack might have aroused the inhabitants but for the important fact that it now wanted only half a second of noon. The bell was about to strike, and it was a matter of absolute and preeminent necessity that everybody should look well at his watch and count the strokes.

"One!" said the clock.

"Von!" echoed every little old gentleman in every leather-bottomed armchair in Vondervotteimittiss. "Von!" said his watch also; "von!" said the watch of his vrow and the watches of the little boys.

"Two!" continued the big bell.

"Doo!" repeated the gentlemen and the watches.

"Three! Four! Five! Six! Seven! Eight! Nine! Ten!" said the bell.

"Dree! Vour! Fibe! Sax! Seben! Aight! Noin! Den!" answered the others.

"Eleven!" said the big one.

"Eleben!" assented the little fellows.

"Twelve!" said the bell.

"Dvelf!" they replied, perfectly satisfied, and dropping their voices.

"Und dvelf it iss!" said all the little old gentlemen, putting up their watches. But the big bell had not done with them yet.

"Thriteen!" said he.

"Der Teufel!" gasped the little old gentlemen, turning pale, dropping their pipes, and putting down all their right legs from over their left knees—

"Der Teufel!" groaned they— "Dirteen! Dirteen!—Mein Gott, it is—it is dirteen o'clock!"

What is the use of trying to describe the terrible scene which ensued? All Vondervotteimittiss flew at once into a lamentable state of uproar.

"Vot is cum'd to mein pelly?" reared all the boys— "I've been an ongry for dis hour!"

"Vot is cum'd to mein kraut?" screamed all the vrows— "It has been done to rags for dis hour!"

"Vot is cum'd to mein pipe?" swore all the little old gentlemen— "Donder and Blitzen! It has been smoked out for dis hour!" —and they filled them up again in a great rage, and sinking back in their armchairs, puffed away so fast and so fiercely that the whole valley was immediately filled with an impenetrable smoke.

Meantime the cabbages all turned very red in the face, and it seemed as if the old Nick himself had taken possession of everything in the shape of a timepiece. The clocks carved upon the furniture began dancing as if bewitched, while those upon the mantel-pieces could scarcely contain themselves and kept such a continual striking of thirteen and such a frisking of their pendulums as was really horrible to see. The cats and the pigs were scampering all over the place, squeaking and screeching, cater-wauling and squalling, flying into faces and running under petticoats, and creating altogether the most abominable din and confusion.

All the while, the rascally little scape-grace in the steeple was exerting himself to his utmost. An occasional glimpse through the smoke revealed the scoundrel sitting upon the belly of the belfry-man, bell-rope in his teeth and head jerking to maintain a continuous clatter, while on his lap lay the great fiddle at which he was scraping— out of time and tune—with both his hands, making a great show, the nincompoop!

Affairs being thus miserably situated, I left the place in disgust. I now appeal to all lovers of good time and fine kraut: Let us proceed in a body to the borough, to restore the ancient order of things in Vondervotteimittiss by ejecting that little chap from the steeple.

Comprehension Questions: *Circle the letter of the best answer.*

1. The incidents described in Part II occurred:
   a. in the middle of the night
   b. on a pleasant summer morning
   c. just at supper-time
   d. about noon

2. The villagers' reaction to the visitor at his arrival was based essentially upon his being:
   a. different
   b. colorless
   c. crazy
   d. dangerous

3. The villagers can best be described as:
   a. creatures of habit
   b. highly individual
   c. idealistic
   d. victims of fate

Essay Question

Write a brief answer to the following question.

1. Describe at least 3 characteristics of the mystical apparel of the newcomer.

Time-Rate Conversion Chart

Min:Sec	WPM	Min:Sec	WPM	Min:Sec	WPM	Min:Sec	WPM	Min:Sec	WPM
1:00	1070	3:00	357	5:00	214	7:00	153	9:00	119
1:10	917	3:10	338	5:10	207	7:10	149	9:10	117
1:20	803	3:20	321	5:20	201	7:20	146	9:20	115
1:30	713	3:30	306	5:30	195	7:30	143	9:30	113
1:40	642	3:40	292	5:40	189	7:40	140	9:40	111
1:50	584	3:50	279	5:50	183	7:50	137	9:50	109
2:00	535	4:00	268	6:00	178	8:00	134	10:00	107
2:10	494	4:10	257	6:10	174	8:10	131	10:10	105
2:20	459	4:20	247	6:20	169	8:20	128	10:20	104
2:30	428	4:30	238	6:30	165	8:30	126	10:30	102
2:40	401	4:40	229	6:40	161	8:40	123	10:40	100
2:50	378	4:50	221	6:50	157	8:50	121		

Was It Really Necessary to Use the Atomic Bomb?

	Hour	Min.	Secs.
A. Ending time:	___	___	___
B. Starting time:	___	___	___
C. A – B = Reading time:		___	___

Richard Kezirlan

Ever since revisionist historians ingeniously speculated that the bombs used against Japan in 1945 were dropped mainly as a demonstration against Soviet Russia, scholars and laymen have developed a new interest in the old but perennially debatable questions. Why were the atomic dropped on Japan? Could less drastic alternatives have been implemented? Did the dropping of the bomb contribute to the Cold War? Particularly thought-provoking are the five alternatives that have frequently been put forward as more humane, yet equally efficient substitutes to the military use of the bomb: 1) awaiting Soviet entry and/or declaration of war against Japan; 2) supplying a noncombat demonstration of the weapon; 3) modifying the terms of unconditional surrender so that the Japanese could retain their imperial institution; 4) pursuing alleged Japanese peace feelers; or 5) utilizing conventional warfare for a longer period. The question that concerns us is the current status of this argument. More specifically, what insights do the new documents and the latest scholarly literature have to offer on these perplexing questions and challenging alternatives?

Historians now approach the issue by pointing out that Harry Truman acted largely on the basis of assumptions which the Franklin Roosevelt administration bequeathed to him. Roosevelt initially set the foundation for Truman's later decision by assuming that the bomb was a legitimate weapon to use in wartime, by deciding to build the bomb in partnership with the British, by opting to keep the Soviets officially uninformed (the Soviets had gained some information through their espionage network), and by blocking any effort, in the initial stages, at international control of atomic energy.

When Truman became President on April 12, 1945, he was incompletely informed on many of Roosevelt's most secret policy decisions. As Vice-President, he was not briefed on the exact nature of the Manhattan Project and was not fully aware that it was aimed toward the creation of an atomic bomb. Though Truman was legally free to revise Roosevelt's policies, consider the tremendous personal and political obstacles

From Richard Kezirian: *AMERICAN HISTORY: Major Controversies Reviewed.* Copyright 1987 by Kendall/Hunt Publishing Company. Reprinted by permission.

inhibiting him. The fact that Roosevelt had been such a magnetic and popular President deterred Truman from any rash re-evaluation. Further, he most probably contemplated the electoral catastrophe which potentially awaited him if the American public ever learned that he had unilaterally reversed Roosevelt's policies and shared with the Soviets a secret which had cost the U.S. $2 billion in research and development monies. For Truman, the question was never one of challenging Roosevelt's assumptions and commitments. On the contrary, he was solely concerned with how these policies might be implemented.

By the time of the Potsdam Conference in July 1945, Truman was faced with his first key decision and the following dilemma. According to earlier requests made by the U.S. at Teheran and Yalta, the Soviet Union had agreed to enter the Pacific war on August 8. However, since April 1945 Japan no longer posed as serious a threat. Japan's navy had been swept from the seas, and they could not now shift their Manchurian army to the Japanese homelands to meet an American invasion. Soviet entry was not needed under the new circumstances. More than that, Soviet promises to the U.S. were now an obstacle. Could the U.S. keep the Soviet Union out of the Pacific war? Was this the goal of Truman at Potsdam? Evidence suggests that Soviet exclusion from significant penetration into the Pacific theatre was indeed the aim at Potsdam. Given the difficulties in stopping Soviet advances in Eastern Europe, plus the problems encountered during negotiations with the Soviets over the Polish and German questions, it is doubtful that Truman relished a repeat of this type of confrontation with Stalin in the Far East. The easiest way to avoid this dreaded possibility was to use the atomic bomb to get the war over with as quickly as possible, before the real weight of Soviet influence could be felt.

An additional bonus to this approach was offered by the fact that Truman and his advisers believed that a combat demonstration of the bomb would "impress" the Soviets and make them more amenable to American wishes in the future. Hence, the reasoning behind Truman's failure to invite Stalin to sign the Potsdam Proclamation of July 26 calling for Japan's unconditional surrender, and his very casual statement to Stalin at Potsdam that the U.S. had developed "a new weapon of unusual destructive force" for use against Japan, without explicitly informing Stalin that it was an atomic weapon.

Some historians have suggested that the real reason for Truman's actions with regard to the Potsdam Proclamation and the casual announcement actually reflected a clever strategy: these scholars maintain that Truman wanted to use the bomb and feared that Stalin's signature to a declaration of war, or his knowledge of extensive American progress on the atomic bomb would prompt him to hasten Soviet intervention; thus, catapulting Japan to surrender and thereby making a nuclear attack unnecessary, even impossible. In other words, they argue that Truman was working to delay Japan's surrender specifically to guarantee use of the new weapon. The major difficulty with this revisionist hypothesis is that it exaggerates and claims too much. More explicitly, Truman wanted to avoid requesting any more favors from the Soviets and, further, he was adamantly against discussing atomic energy with Stalin.

In conclusion, let us apply these new insights to the alternatives listed above. We can now understand why Truman's administration did not await Soviet entry and/or a declaration of war, why a noncombat demonstration of the weapon was not provided and why conventional warfare was not relied upon for a longer period of time. Contrary to all these alternatives, Truman was aiming to avert Soviet entry and considered the bomb a legitimate and efficient way both to end the war rapidly and impress the Russians. Truman believed that the bomb would make a significant diplomatic and military impression on the Japanese and Soviet governments only if it had also been shown to have demonstrated military worth on the field of battle.

Further, as to the question of the pursuance of alleged peace feelers, the fact is that the Japanese never approached the U.S. directly to negotiate a peace settlement, but rather these peace feelers were a series of messages from their foreign minister to their ambassador in Moscow asking him to research the possibility of having the Soviets serve as intermediaries in future U.S.-Japanese peace negotiations. Since American intelligence had cracked the Japanese ambassadorial code even before the Pearl Harbor attack, these messages, once intercepted, were quickly decoded and analyzed. As these Japanese proposals included the demand that the Emperor be retained, they were never seriously considered as adequately fulfilling American expectations.

Finally, what about the alternative of redefining unconditional surrender to guarantee Japan's imperial institutions? The evidence suggests that Truman believed that any concession to the Japanese might be interpreted as a sign of appeasement on the part of the American public; even worse it might be considered a grave mistake given the experience with Germany after the First World War. It is here that Truman and his advisers most tragically erred. For neither bomb need have been necessary if the words "unconditional surrender" were removed from the U.S. peace demands. It is now clear that from July 13 onward, the only obstacle in the way of a Japanese decision to surrender was the requirement that it be "unconditional." The importance of this issue to the Japanese can best be measured when one remembers that even after the dropping of the two bombs on Hiroshima and Nagasaki, and after the Soviet declaration of war, the Japanese government still held to their demand that the Emperor and the dynasty be retained. In the end, the U.S. compromised on this issue by implicitly recognizing the Emperor, but requiring him to subject his power to the orders of the Allied supreme commander.

Today, then, the real lament is not what the revisionist historians have suggested in their accusation—that the U.S. used the bomb solely to influence the Russians. Rather, the agony lies in the fact that the Truman administration devoted most of its thought to *how* the bombs would be used, rather than to the moral question of *whether* they should be used. Almost totally neglected by these policymakers was the contaminated fallout which would accompany a nuclear explosion. Practically no one foresaw that war was moving from the deliberate killing and maiming of men and women in the present to the killing and maiming of future generations.

Comprehension Questions: *Circle the letter of the best answer.*

1. Historians now approach the issue of the atomic bomb by pointing out that Harry Truman acted on the basis of:
   a. a deep hate for the Japanese
   b. information given him by the Japanese ambassador
   c. a clear understanding of the situation
   d. assumptions which the Roosevelt Administration handed down to him

2. Truman and his advisors believed that a combat demonstration would _____ the Soviets.
   a. anger
   b. put fear into
   c. impress
   d. b and c

3. Evidence suggested that Truman believed that any concession to the Japanese might be interpreted as:
   a. sign of fear
   b. a war-like stance
   c. a sign of appeasement
   d. none of the above

Essay Question

Write a brief answer to the following question.

What conclusion did the author make concerning the use of the atomic bomb by the Truman administration?

Time-Rate Conversion Chart

Min:Sec	WPM	Min:Sec	WPM	Min:Sec	WPM	Min:Sec	WPM
1:00	1426	4:30	317	8:00	178	11:30	124
1:10	1222	4:40	306	8:10	175	11:40	122
1:20	1070	4:50	295	8:20	171	11:50	121
1:30	951	5:00	285	8:30	168	12:00	119
1:40	856	5:10	276	8:40	165	12:10	117
1:50	778	5:20	267	8:50	161	12:20	116
2:00	713	5:30	259	9:00	158	12:30	117
2:10	658	5:40	252	9:10	156	12:40	113
2:20	611	5:50	244	9:20	153	12:50	111
2:30	570	6:00	238	9:30	150	13:00	110
2:40	535	6:10	231	9:40	148	13:10	108
2:50	503	6:20	225	9:50	145	13:20	107
3:00	475	6:30	219	10:00	143	13:30	106
3:10	450	6:40	214	10:10	140	13:40	104
3:20	428	6:50	209	10:20	138	13:50	103
3:30	407	7:00	204	10:30	136	14:00	102
3:40	389	7:10	199	10:40	134	14:10	101
3:50	372	7:20	194	10:50	132	14:20	99
4:00	357	7:30	190	11:00	130	14:30	98
4:10	342	7:40	186	11:10	128	14:40	97
4:20	329	7:50	182	11:20	126	14:50	96

9–11

Energy Sources

John Christensen

	Hour	Min.	Secs.
A. Ending time:	____	____	____
B. Starting time:	____	____	____
C. A – B = Reading time:		____	____

It at first seems that our energy comes from a great variety of sources. A close analysis reveals that ultimately all our energy comes from only five sources. They are described below.

1. The Sun

Current solar radiation is the largest source. The sun is basically a huge, fusion re-actor that spews forth energy in all directions. Only a tiny fraction of this energy arrives at the Earth. That tiny fraction is still a huge amount of energy. Measurements above the Earth's atmosphere indicate that the Earth intercepts 1.353 kilowatts of power per square meter perpendicular to the sun's rays. That means that the total solar radiation intercepted by the Earth's diametric plane of 1.275×10^{14} square meters is therefore 1.73×10^{17} watts.

We saw earlier that even though 30% of the energy is directly reflected, the re-mainder warms the Earth. It also evaporates water and drives the water cycle. It drives all the winds, waves, and the Earth's weather system. Finally, it provides the energy for all photosynthesis.

At the Earth's surface, the Solar Input is approximately 1.0 kilowatt per square meter. Although very spread out, this power density can accomplish many useful tasks.

Current solar radiation makes possible a variety of energy options that are be-ginning to attract significant interest in the United States. These include solar heating and cooling of homes, solar-powered electric generating plants, wind power and the use of temperature differences in the ocean to generate electricity.

Another large source is stored solar energy. Solar energy is stored in living plants (by photosynthesis) and animals. Significant quantities of energy are available to us from this source. Decomposing plant and animal waste can be converted into methane gas. Methane can be directly substituted for natural gas.

From John Christensen: *GLOBAL SCIENCE: Energy, Resources, Environment.* Copyright 1984 by Kendall/ Hunt Publishing Company. Reprinted by permission.

Solar energy is stored in plants that have recently died (dead wood and hay) and trash.

Solar energy is stored in plants that died many millions of years ago forming fossil fuels (oil, gas, coal, oil shale, and tar sands).

Industrial societies run primarily on oil, gas, and coal. Unless we learn to tap the energy stored in oil shale and tar sands, the stored reserves of solar energy will soon be exhausted.

2. The Tides

This energy originates in the gravitational system of the Earth, the moon, and the sun. The tides offer us a fascinating energy option. The applications are primarily of local interest.

3. The Earth's Heat

The heat stored below the Earth's immediate surface is caused by tremendous sub-surface pressures and heat created by the energetic decay of radioactive substances. This geothermal source can be used to provide steam to turn generators and supply electricity.

4. Fission Fuels

The energy stored in unstable uranium and thorium nuclei can be released and used to produce electricity. Uranium and thorium compounds can be extracted from the Earth's crust like any other minerals.

5. Fusion Fuels

Fusion involves the combining of very light nuclei to make larger atoms. Since stability is gained in the combining process, energy is released. Deuterium (H) and tritium (H) have been found to be the easiest light nuclei to fuse. The supply of deuterium in the world's oceans is huge. Tritium is made from lithium. Lithium can be mined from the Earth's crust. It is very rare.

Comprehension Questions: *Circle the letter of the best answer.*

1. Solar energy is stored in:
   a. plants
   b. humans
   c. animals
   d. all of the above

2. The heat stored below the earth's immediate surface is caused by:
   a. decayed matter
   b. energetic decay of radioactive substances
   c. pressure
   d. b and c

3. The combining of very light nuclei to make larger atoms is called:
   a. fusion
   b. fission
   c. energy
   d. none of the above

Essay Question

Write a brief answer to the following question.

Why is it important for us to understand where our potential energy sources comes from?

Time-Rate Conversion Chart

Min:Sec	WPM	Min:Sec	WPM
1:00	521	4:30	116
1:10	447	4:40	112
1:20	391	4:50	108
1:30	347	5:00	104
1:40	313	5:10	101
1:50	284	5:20	98
2:00	261	5:30	95
2:10	240	5:40	92
2:20	223	5:50	89
2:30	208		
2:40	195		
2:50	184		
3:00	174		
3:10	165		
3:20	156		
3:30	149		
3:40	142		
3:50	136		
4:00	130		
4:10	125		
4:20	120		

9–12

Reflections on the Potato

Nick M. Joaquin

	Hour	Min.	Secs.
A. Ending time:	___	___	___
B. Starting time:	___	___	___
C. A – B = Reading time:		___	___

According to the German writer Günter Grass, the introduction of the potato was a more important event in the history of the German people than all the martial victories of King Frederick the Great. Indeed, Grass considers the potato a crucial factor in the development of Europe. It was the potato, he believes, that made possible the industrialization of Europe and the rise of the proletariat.

We can see what he means. The potato is a highly nourishing food that is also very cheap because it can be grown so quickly and easily. The coming of this "fast food" liberated the masses of Europe from age-old hunger. It developed a sturdier working class. It released more and more people from farm work and made them available for factory labour.

The factories in turn led to the development of a strong labouring class that democratized Europe, and to a science and technology that made Western culture supreme in the modern world.

It can be argued therefore that the identity of the modern European as a highly civilized, cultured and progressive individual can be traced back, partly at least, to the coming of the potato.

But now let us bring in a counter-argument. Let us imagine, say, a European who is rapidly anti-potato because the potato is not indigenous to Europe. As this chauvinist argues, the potato should never have been allowed to change Europe because it, the potato, is so foreign and exotic. By eating the potato, the European lost something of his original nature, with the result that European culture today is a deviation from a pristine original. The true European is the European before the introduction of the potato.

But how can that uncorrupted original be restored?

Our imaginary European chauvinist demands the abolition of the potato.

At once, of course, we see the flaw in his proposal. Abolishing the potato will not restore European man to his pre-potato condition. Why not? Because from the potato have come such developments as industrialization, democratization, modernization, and so forth. And these developments have so radically altered European man that he would still remain what he has become even if he stopped eating potatoes altogether.

Reprinted from the Unesco Courier, May, 1987.

In other words, potatoes are the culture and history that cannot be cancelled in a desire to recover a former innocence.

You may smile at my potato story, which seems to make the potato like the forbidden fruit in the Garden of Eden. But I think that some such story would illustrate the problem of nationalism today in my country, the Philippines—and not only in my country but also in most of Asia, and Third World countries in general. When Adam and Eve ate of the apple, they lost innocence, they lost paradise. And I would say that among the peoples of the Orient, certainly among us Filipinos, there is a feeling that, by tasting of Western science and technology, we lost innocence, we lost a primordial paradise.

Our feelings towards Western culture are therefore ambivalent. We are fascinated by it and we are also repelled. We fear and resist it even as we hanker for it. And though we crave to progress in the Western manner, we wonder at the same time if we should not rather go back—back to the culture we had before we were "corrupted" by the West.

Not long ago I had dinner with a Filipino family whom I admire for their nationalism, although they rather tend to make a display of it. At this dinner, the display consisted of a round grey stone about the size of a baseball. This stone—it was actually a piece of rock salt—was passed around instead of salt because, said my host, that was how the ancient Filipinos salted their food. You pressed the stone on your rice and fish, you rubbed it against your meat, you soaked it in your broth, to obtain the desired saltiness.

I'm afraid they all looked down on me when I said I'd rather have ordinary table salt. That piece of rock salt reminded me of the stones we used in the old days, when bathing, to scrub our bodies with. And I was putting no such stone into anything I was going to eat! Still, I was charmed by the sentiment behind the display, the nationalist nostalgia. What bothered me were the implications behind the sentiment.

In effect, my hosts were saying: "See how truly Filipino we are. Instead of using a saltcellar, which is foreign, we use a salt stone, which is native." The implication therefore is that the more we return to what is native and the more we abolish what is foreign, the more truly Filipino we become.

This may be true—but what I couldn't help noticing then was the inconsistency. Why pick on the poor saltcellar? On the table were fork and spoon, which are not native; and beef and cabbage, which are also not originally Filipino, and I knew that the food had been prepared using the sauté method, which is foreign, and cooked in a saucepan or kettle, both also foreign. To retain these, while abolishing the saltcellar, is tantamount to saying that the saltcellar is a bigger hindrance to becoming truly Filipino than cabbages and kettles.

Of course I know what question was supposedly being answered at that dinner table with the abolition of the saltcellar: the question of identity.

Identity, I would say, is like the river in philosophy. You remember the saying: "You can never step into the same river twice." The river has changed even as you step into it. Nevertheless, the Sumida River remains the Sumida River, though from one moment to the next it is no longer the same river.

This is the dynamic view of identity.

I'm afraid that we in the Orient—or anyway we Filipinos—have a different idea of identity, different because we regard identity as static: something given once and for all, something to which things happen but is itself never a happening, never becoming. We ourselves are, or were, a fixed original identity to which certain things— alien cultures, alien histories—have been added, layer upon layer. Therefore, if such cultures and histories are addition, identity is subtraction. All we have to do is to remove all those superimposed layers and we shall end up with the true basic Filipino identity.

That is the static view of identity.

But culture is not simple addition. Culture is not a stew to which you can add anything and it will still remain a stew. Instead, culture is like those laboratory experiments in physics where the moment you add a new ingredient the original mixture becomes completely transformed into something different.

When history added the saltcellar, the fork and spoon, beef and cabbage to our culture, the identity of the Filipino was so completely transformed that there can be no going back to a pristine original even if we abolished the saltcellar, the fork and spoon, and so on. Culture and history are the flowing waters that make it impossible to step into the same river of identity twice.

Comprehension Questions: *Circle the letter of the best answer.*

1. Gunter Grass believes that the potato made possible:
   a. the change of employment agreements between master and servant in Europe
   b. the industrialization of Europe and the rise of the proletariat
   c. the industrialization of America
   d. the rise of the proletariat in Russia

2. The purpose of Gunter Grass's story about the potato is to illustrate a point about:
   a. the problem of nationalism in Germany
   b. the question of nationalism in the Philippines
   c. potato growing
   d. identity in Europe

3. Culture and history affect:
   a. the waters in a river
   b. what is meant by "identity to one's native country"
   c. what is meant by philosophy
   d. what salt cellars are

Essay Question

Write a brief answer to the following question.

How do the Filipinos view their identity?

Time-Rate Conversion Chart

Min:Sec	WPM	Min:Sec	WPM	Min:Sec	WPM	Min:Sec	WPM
1:00	1192	4:30	265	8:00	149	11:30	104
1:10	1022	4:40	255	8:10	146	11:40	102
1:20	894	4:50	247	8:20	143	11:50	101
1:30	795	5:00	238	8:30	140		
1:40	715	5:10	231	8:40	138		
1:50	650	5:20	224	8:50	135		
2:00	596	5:30	217	9:00	132		
2:10	550	5:40	210	9:10	130		
2:20	511	5:50	204	9:20	128		
2:30	477	6:00	199	9:30	125		
2:40	447	6:10	193	9:40	123		
2:50	421	6:20	188	9:50	121		
3:00	397	6:30	183	10:00	119		
3:10	376	6:40	179	10:10	117		
3:20	358	6:50	174	10:20	115		
3:30	341	7:00	170	10:30	114		
3:40	325	7:10	166	10:40	112		
3:50	311	7:20	163	10:50	110		
4:00	298	7:30	159	11:00	108		
4:10	286	7:40	155	11:10	107		
4:20	275	7:50	152	11:20	105		

Rendezvous with Halley's Comet

Howard Brabyn

	Hour	Min.	Secs.
A. Ending time:	——	——	——
B. Starting time:	——	——	——
C. A – B = Reading time:	——	——	

Like courtiers dancing a stately quadrille, eight instrument-packed space probes (one launched by the European Space Agency, two by the USSR, two by Japan, and three by the USA) are weaving intricate patterns in space in the biggest international astronomic co-operative venture ever mounted—the investigation of Halley's comet.

Two space shuttle missions are also being in part devoted to observation of the comet, the trajectory of which will be continuously monitored by the world's most powerful land-based telescopes. Altogether some 900 professional astronomers from forty-seven countries are taking part in the investigation.

Why all this interest in what veteran US astronomer Fred Whipple has described as "a large, dirty snowball"?

The answer is that astronomers believe that comets consist of the remnants of the building blocks left over from the birth of the solar system some 4,500 million years ago. The history of the solar system is recorded, so it is thought, within their frozen hearts.

Today, for the first time ever, thanks to the genius of two seventeenth-century English scientists, Isaac Newton and Edmond Halley, and the achievements of modern space technology, we have in our hands an unprecidented technology and science with which to observe comets. The 700 or so comets that have been scientifically recorded so far have had nuclei ranging in size from 0.5 to 70 kilometres in diameter.

From time to time a passing star sends a gravitational ripple through the Oort Cloud sending a flurry of these "dirty snowballs" hurtling off into space. Some of them, the "short-period" comets, like Halley's comet, are projected towards the solar system and, influenced by its gravitational pull, become members of the inner solar system, completing their orbits around the sun in less than 200 years. The "long-period" comets can take millions of years to complete their orbital cycles. An average of five new comets are discovered every year.

The outer surface of a comet nucleus is thought to consist mainly of dust. As a comet approaches to within three astronomical units of the sun (one astronomical unit equals the distance between the earth and the sun, roughly 150 million kilometres)

Reprinted from the Unesco Courier, March, 1986.

this outer crust heats up and the sub-surface ice begins to sublimate (a process by which a solid is converted directly into vapour without going through the liquid stage). The resulting gas streams out from the comet carrying dust particles with it to form the coma.

As it gets closer to the sun a comet develops two tails, a yellowish curved tail entrance ticket to one of these refrigerated, flying museums. For Halley's comet is the only vigorously active comet whose orbit brings it relatively close to the earth (this time round, its thirtieth recorded apparition, it is coming to within 62 million kilometres of our planet) and has been determined precisely enough to allow of detailed scientific planning for investigation well in advance; and for the very first time space technology is sufficiently advanced to enable us to go out and meet a comet beyond the blanket of the earth's atmosphere instead of waiting for it to come to us, to penetrate its coma (the fuzzy gaseous cloud, up to 100,000 kilometres across, that shields the nucleus from our sight), to have a close up view of its nucleus and to analyse the components of its tail, in short, to understand the elements from which our solar system was constructed.

In 1950, the Dutch astronomer Jan Hendrik Oort postulated that comets originate from a vast cloud of hundreds of millions of small bodies (now known as the Oort Cloud) that orbits the solar system at a distance of one light-year. The nucleus, or core, of a comet is thought to consist of about 25 per cent dust and lumps of rock or metallic matter and 75 per cent of ice, in which are mixed compounds containing ammonia, methane and carbon dioxide composed of dust particles released during the process of sublimation, and a blueish stream of gas called the plasma tail which is formed when the gases released from the comet's nucleus become charged by solar radiation.

In a few months' time, when all the data have been gathered in, we shall have made a tremendous leap forward in our knowledge of the nature of comets and of the origins of the solar system. We should not, however, forget that this will be due not only to the brilliance of modern astronomers but also to a quite unprecedented effort of international co-operation.

Launched on 15 December 1984, the Soviet space probe *Vega I* flew through Halley's coma on 6 March 1986, at a distance of about 9,600 kilometres from the nucleus, and photographed and analysed the gases around it. Sister satellite *Vega 2* encountered Halley's comet on 9 March 1986 and analysed its coma.

The Japanese probe *Sakigake* (pioneer), launched on 7 January 1985, rendezvoused with Halley's comet on 9 March 1986 and measured the speed and temperature of the solar wind blowing against the comet, whilst on 8 March 1986 its companion satellite *Suisei* (comet) flew past Halley's comet at a distance of 144,000 kilometres and studied the enormous cloud of hydrogen gas surrounding the comet.

Playing supporting roles are the veteran US space probes *Pioneer 12, Solar Max* and *ICE* (International Cometary Explorer). *Pioneer 12* is turning its attention away from its long-term task of observing the effects of the solar wind on planet Venus to focus its spectrometer on Halley's comet during and after the perihelion (the period of the comet's closest approach to the sun). At the same time *Solar Max* is studying the comet's dust and plasma tails for comparison with observations made by *ICE* last September on the nature of the tail of comet Giacobini-Zinner.

Last in the field is the European Space Agency's satellite *Giotto*. Named after the famous fourteenth-century Florentine painter Giotto di Bondone, who included Halley's comet in his Paduan fresco *The Adoration of the Magi* (see colour page 19) after witnessing its apparition in 1301, space probe *Giotto* was launched on 2 July 1985. Basing its trajectory on data supplied by the two Soviet *Vega* probes, *Giotto's* mission was to pass near the comet's nucleus, examining the material streaming from it and transmitting photographs to earth every four seconds.

This might well have been a suicide mission. The slightest error in calculation of its trajectory could have sent *Giotto* crashing into the surface of the comet. As a precaution against the particles which surround the comet, some of them large enough to have inflicted fatal damage, the satellite was fitted with an outer aluminium skin and an inner casing made of Kelvar, the material from which bullet-proof vests are made. As it happened, the spacecraft functioned perfectly until 2 seconds before the scheduled time of closest approach when the telemetry signal was lost owing to dust impacts on the spacecraft. Just over half an hour later, however, the signal was re-covered at ground stations in Australia, and data from all experiments was again being received.

The results will take months to analyse fully but first impressions are that they are spectacular. The Halley Multicolour Camera on board *Giotto,* appears to have determined the size of the nucleus as approximately fifteen by eight kilometres, and the spacecraft has contributed a mass of other information to the International Halley Watch, perhaps the most complex international astronomical project ever undertaken. And as scientists sit down to assess the information as it comes flooding in from the space Armada, they will surely sense the presence of two great figures from the past peering eagerly over their shoulders—Isaac Newton, the man who first propounded a workable theory of the orbits of comets, and Edmond Halley who applied this theory to the comet named after him, which he had seen in 1682 and which he accurately predicted would return at regular seventy-six-year intervals, thus blazing the trail for the amazing adventure we are living through today.

Comprehension Questions: *Circle the letter of the best answer.*

1. How did astronomer Fred Whipple describe the comet?
   a. a large, dirty snowball
   b. a large crater
   c. an icicle made of metal and ice
   d. a large rock

2. What do astronomers believe comets consist of?
   a. a combination of carbon, zinc, and telluride
   b. remnants of space vehicles that have been destroyed in space
   c. pieces of ice, carbon and other minerals
   d. remnants of the building blocks of the solar system

3. On the average, how many new comets are discovered each year?
   a. 50
   b. 20
   c. 1,000,000
   d. 5

Essay Question

Write a brief answer to the following question.

Why is it important for scientists to study events like Halley's comet?

Time-Rate Conversion Chart

Min:Sec	WPM	Min:Sec	WPM	Min:Sec	WPM	Min:Sec	WPM
1:00	1270	4:30	282	8:00	159	11:30	110
1:10	1089	4:40	272	8:10	156	11:40	109
1:20	953	4:50	263	8:20	152	11:50	107
1:30	847	5:00	254	8:30	149	12:00	106
1:40	762	5:10	246	8:40	147	12:10	104
1:50	693	5:20	238	8:50	144	12:20	103
2:00	635	5:30	231	9:00	141	12:30	102
2:10	586	5:40	224	9:10	139	12:40	100
2:20	544	5:50	218	9:20	136	12:50	99
2:30	508	6:00	212	9:30	134		
2:40	476	6:10	206	9:40	131		
2:50	448	6:20	201	9:50	129		
3:00	423	6:30	195	10:00	127		
3:10	401	6:40	191	10:10	125		
3:20	381	6:50	186	10:20	123		
3:30	363	7:00	181	10:30	121		
3:40	346	7:10	177	10:40	119		
3:50	331	7:20	173	10:50	117		
4:00	318	7:30	169	11:00	115		
4:10	305	7:40	166	11:10	114		
4:20	293	7:50	162	11:20	112		

The Great Depression: Could It Have Been Avoided?

Richard Kezirian

	Hour	Min.	Secs.
A. Ending time:	____	____	____
B. Starting time:	____	____	____
C. A – B = Reading time:	____	____	

It has been over fifty years since Black Thursday, the dreariest day of the great Stock Market Crash of 1929. Fifty years, indeed! The current ebb and flow of economic events make its shadow ever more ominous. The situation then was catastrophic. In September 1929, industrials stood at 452; by November they had crashed to 224; on July 8, 1932, at the depths of the Great Depression, they had sunk to 58. In that same period, such blue chip stocks as General Motors fell from 73 to 8, U.S. Steel from 262 to 22 and Montgomery Ward from 138 to 4. Fifty years ago shanty towns of the dispossessed and hungry were called "Hoovervilles;" the newspapers which covered the impoverished who slept on park benches at night were called "Hoover blankets;" a trouser pocket turned inside out was called a "Hoover flag." In the Southwest, country singers were crooning the popular song, "Hoover Made a Soup-hound Outa Me."

All this, of course, was grossly unfair to Herbert Hoover. The causes of the Depression were not his fault. But it was natural for people to look for a scapegoat for these ills. And it was easy for them to pick Hoover. Later, others were to blame Franklin Roosevelt for his actions and his demagoguery, which they claimed made matters even worse. Whatever may be said about each man personally, we must recognize that neither knew how to solve the problems of the Depression. Who did? Now it is generally recognized that they were victimized by uncontrollable circumstances. In the end, it was World War II which brought prosperity back to this nation.

Historians, then, are not so narrow-minded as to blame one President or the other. But that is not to say that the argument is less emotional; it is just depersonalized. Nor can one say that the lines of the argument have shifted very much since the 1930s. Generally, historians today spread the blame much the same way that people did back then: liberals with one theory and conservatives another. These main schools of thought have fancier names now, however, the "structuralists" (or fiscal theorists) and the "monetarists." Their names reflect the essence of their arguments. The structuralists are indebted to the intellectual and economic writings of John Maynard Keynes. They argue that the Crash and Depression resulted from serious structural flaws in the American economy. The rival "monetary" theory has been gaining more and more converts lately, due to the writings of Milton Friedman, Clark Warburton, Phillip Cagan and Elmus Wicker. The monetarists argue that the nation required wiser monetary policy rather than structural reforms.

Let us look into these arguments more closely. Given the nature of today's economy, a historical perspective surely will not hurt that much, and might even offer some insights into our current economic problems. First, the structuralists argue that the immediate cause for the turndown of economic activity and the decline of the Stock Market in 1929 was the "inventory recession" which plagued the nation that summer. That is, production of industrial products had outrun consumer and investment demand. After that, structural weaknesses in the economy became apparent and were so extensive that they prohibited recovery.

For instance, there was a disastrous maldistribution of income. Structuralists point out that in 1929 the rich were indubitably rich and the poor lamentably poor. In that year, the top 5 percent of the population owned 33 percent of all personal income. What that added up to was that 26 million of the total 27.5 million American families earned less than $2,500 per year, which in 1929 was deemed necessary for a decent standard of living.

Further, our nation's corporate structure was oligopolistic in some areas, monopolistic in others. How could capitalist competition be maintained, structuralists ask, when one-tenth of 1 percent of American corporations earned nearly half of the net income and owned over half the assets of all corporations in the United States? Corporations were insulated from the public they served, and from the natural laws of supply and demand.

Financially, the Stock Exchange was a problem area. Wall Street was weakly regulated, and the vogue of buying stock "on margin" jeopardized the future of the American economy. America's banking system was equally unsound. There were few of the protective safeguards of today and the actions of many banks were, as a result, speculative and fraudulent. As one contemporary noted: "Banks provided everything for their customers but a roulette wheel."

Finally, structuralists point to the poor state of foreign trade. World War I made the U.S. a creditor nation and saddled most of Europe with tremendous war debts. Europeans, face with the problems of debt payments and an unfavorable trade balance, eventually began to curtail purchases of American products. This especially hurt American agriculture, which was consequently burdened by surpluses and overexpansion.

To summarize, structuralists argue that the American economy was fundamentally unstable. For prosperity to return, domestic reforms were needed. A massive redistribution of income was needed to support enough purchasing power to keep the economic wheels turning fast enough. Banks needed to be regulated and individual deposits insured. Wall Street had to be more carefully monitored and forced to curtail reckless practices. More importantly, the Republican Party's policies of the 1920s—tax cuts for the highest incomes, high tariffs, etc.—had to be abandoned.

The monetarists vehemently disagree. For the monetarists, the Great Depression is just another example of how government mismanagement can damage an inherently healthy system of private enterprise. In this case, the culprit was the Federal Reserve System, whose monetary policies turned what would otherwise have been a mild recession into a major catastrophe. According to monetarists, the Stock Market Crash and the inventory recession of 1929 could not in themselves have produced a major collapse in economic activity. Indeed, for the first year after the crash, they argue, the recession showed signs of recovery. This recovery was thwarted, however, when the Federal Reserve System allowed the supply of money to decline by nearly 3 percent from August 1929 to October 1930. As a result, in November 1930 a series of major bank failures occurred. Again, instead of quickly moving to provide banks with more cash so that the public demand for liquid assets could be met, and the monetary debacle averted, the Fed did nothing.

Another great failure of the Fed was its panic when Great Britain went off the gold standard in 1931. Though the gold reserves of the U.S. were at a high point, the Fed raised the discount rate sharply to arrest our gold drain. The result was another spectacular increase in the number of bank failures. All told, from July 1929 to March 1933, one-third of America's banks went out of existence, the money supply had fallen by one-third, and an economic system, which was essentially stable, was damaged dramatically. What is particularly irksome to monetarists is that the Federal Reserve System was established, in large part, to prevent just this type of occurrence. The moral which Milton Friedman draws from this experience is: "Any system which gives so much power and so much discretion to a few men that mistakes—excusable or not—can have such far-reaching effects is a bad system."[1]

1. Milton Friedman and Anna Schwartz, *A Monetary History of the United States* (Princeton, N.J.: Princeton University Press, 1963).

These are the two sides of the argument. It is impossible at this time to find a concensus on this issue; besides, tangling with Keynes and Friedman is beyond the abilities of most students of the Great Depression. Nonetheless, one might doubt if leaving troublesome issues to the "fate" of the market system is the answer. Crucial questions involving America's economic destiny have never been left to the strictures of laissez-faire. Men and women have always found ways to step in to make sure that those questions were resolved one way or another. When the government did not take political and economic responsibility, the maneuverings of the most opportunistic, and the most conniving were often given free reign. For better or worse, it would seem preferable to accept the limitations of intelligent management through democratically-controlled institutions.

Comprehension Questions: *Circle the letter of the best answer*

1. What was the dreariest day of the great Stock Market Crash of 1929 called?
   a. Blue Monday
   b. Black Monday
   c. Red Tuesday
   d. Black Thursday

2. What major event brought prosperity back to this nation after the Depression?
   a. The Crimean War
   b. World War II
   c. World War I
   d. The Depression

3. The structuralists argue that the immediate cause for the turndown of economic activity and the decline of the Stock Market in 1929 was:
   a. the 1928 Drought
   b. World War II
   c. the "inventory recession"
   d. the low standard of living among city dwellers

Essay Question

Write a brief answer to the following question.

What arguments did the structuralists make as to why the depression took place?

Time-Rate Conversion Chart

Min:Sec	WPM	Min:Sec	WPM	Min:Sec	WPM	Min:Sec	WPM
1:00	1343	4:30	298	8:00	168	11:30	117
1:10	1151	4:40	288	8:10	164	11:40	115
1:20	1007	4:50	278	8:20	161	11:50	113
1:30	895	5:00	269	8:30	158	12:00	112
1:40	806	5:10	260	8:40	155	12:10	110
1:50	733	5:20	252	8:50	152	12:20	109
2:00	672	5:30	244	9:00	149	12:30	107
2:10	620	5:40	237	9:10	147	12:40	106
2:20	576	5:50	230	9:20	144	12:50	105
2:30	537	6:00	224	9:30	141	13:00	103
2:40	504	6:10	218	9:40	139	13:10	102
2:50	474	6:20	212	9:50	137	13:20	101
3:00	448	6:30	207	10:00	134	13:30	99
3:10	424	6:40	201	10:10	132	13:40	98
3:20	403	6:50	197	10:20	130	13:50	97
3:30	384	7:00	192	10:30	128		
3:40	366	7:10	187	10:40	126		
3:50	350	7:20	183	10:50	124		
4:00	336	7:30	179	11:00	122		
4:10	322	7:40	175	11:10	120		
4:20	310	7:50	171	11:20	119		

America Creates a Literature

Leonard Pitt

		Hour	Min.	Secs.
A. Ending time:		——	——	——
B. Starting time:		——	——	——
C. A – B = Reading time:			——	——

Independence from British rule did not instantly create a distinctly American culture. That took time. But after 1815 a greater sense of national identity did begin to develop. And there soon emerged a literary culture that was not merely an echo of the European tradition.

From about 1815 to 1840 a number of writers based in New York City began exploring native American themes. Among them were Washington Irving, William Cullen Bryant, and James Fenimore Cooper. Cooper's *Leatherstocking Tales,* published from 1823 to 1841, were the first important novels to use the frontier as a setting and to depict the contrast between civilization and the wilderness.

In the 1840s and 1850s New England became the scene of such extraordinary literary productivity—by poets, historians, novelists, and essayists—that the period came to be known as the New England Renaissance. This flowering of thought and letters was brightest in and around Boston. At Concord, Henry David Thoreau wrote *Walden* (1854), and at Salem, Nathaniel Hawthorne produced *The Scarlet Letter* (1850). Many of the better-known poets of the era were New Englanders: Henry Wadsworth Longfellow, Oliver Wendell Holmes, John Greenleaf Whittier, and James Russell Lowell. And at the heart of the intellectual ferment was the essayist Ralph Waldo Emerson, leader of the movement known as Transcendentalism. With its emphasis on the sacredness of the individual and the power of self-reliance, Transcendentalism suited the romantic spirit of the times.

Walt Whitman, who was born on Long Island, produced one of America's greatest literary classics, *Leaves of Grass* (1855). He was greatly influenced by Emerson's ideas, and his poetry goes far beyond that of his contemporaries in ignoring literary tradition and convention and relying on his own inspiration. Although his work shocked readers at the time, its informality, its outpouring of emotion, and its celebration of the common man all marked it as distinctively American.

Herman Melville, born in New York City, wrote about his experiences on American whaling ships and on the islands of the South Pacific. *Moby Dick* (1851), a failure in Melville's lifetime, has since become a world classic. It is a multilevel novel that, while describing the whaling industry in detail, explores the tragic and the heroic in human nature.

Although born in Boston, Edgar Allan Poe grew up in the South and worked there during much of his brief career. As literary critic, poet, and short story writer, he exerted a powerful influence both at home and abroad. Some of the most popular works about the South were the songs of a northerner, Stephen Foster.

The most popular novel of its time—also written about the South by a northerner—was *Uncle Tom's Cabin* (1852) by Harriet Beecher Stowe. Stowe condemned slavery for its cruelty and its destruction of black families. Although a huge amount of fiction was written by women for women in America, no other work had the influence of *Uncle Tom's Cabin.*

In 1835 a young French nobleman, Alexis de Tocqueville, published *Democracy in America.* Many still consider it the most remarkable book ever written about this country. For nine months Tocqueville journeyed throughout the nation, meeting citizens, both distinguished and ordinary. He seemed to notice everything—religion, marriage, prison management, vigilante justice, agriculture, the cities, the wilderness. Above all, he was impressed by the leveling trend in American life and by the strength and flexibility of popular government. Yet he did not fail to see some of the flaws in the democratic jewel. Slavery prompted him to make this gloomy forecast: either the country would grant full equality for blacks, which seemed unlikely, or it would crack open on the slavery issue. He saw early and clearly America's greatest problem.

Comprehension Questions: *Circle the letter of the best answer.*

1. The period in which there was a lot of literary output in New England was called:
   a. The Leatherstocking period
   b. The Intellectual Renaissance
   c. The Democratic Revival
   d. The New England Renaissance

2. What literary failure of Herman Melville has since become a success?
   a. Wind in the Willows
   b. Scarlet Letter
   c. Moby Dick
   d. Uncle Tom's Cabin

3. Harriet Beecher Stowe's most popular novel was:
   a. Uncle Tom's Cabin
   b. Scarlet Letter
   c. Leaves of Grass
   d. Evangeline

Essay Question

Write a brief answer to the following question.

In your opinion, why did it take fifty years before America found its own literature and began to produce leading writers?

Time-Rate Conversion Chart

Min:Sec	WPM	Min:Sec	WPM
1:00	660	4:30	147
1:10	566	4:40	141
1:20	495	4:50	137
1:30	440	5:00	132
1:40	396	5:10	128
1:50	360	5:20	124
2:00	330	5:30	120
2:10	305	5:40	116
2:20	283	5:50	113
2:30	264	6:00	110
2:40	248	6:10	107
2:50	233	6:20	104
3:00	220	6:30	102
3:10	208	6:40	99
3:20	198	6:50	97
3:30	189		
3:40	180		
3:50	172		
4:00	165		
4:10	158		
4:20	152		

The Impact of Television

Ronald Lovell and
Philip Geraci

	Hour	Min.	Secs.
A. Ending time:	___	___	___
B. Starting time:	___	___	___
C. A – B = Reading time:		___	___

It would be accurate to say that television affects the lives of virtually everyone in the United States nearly every day. Statistics on television viewing reveal that, since 1980, each home with at least one television receiver has kept it on more than seven hours every day! And each year since records have been kept, the per-day listening period has grown.

It has been estimated by the Television Bureau of Advertising that 48 percent of leisure time is spent watching television, as opposed to 32 percent listening to radio, 13 percent reading newspapers and seven percent reading magazines. However, some question this figure since it totals 100 percent and does not allow room for people who read books, listen to records or go to the theater.

According to *Broadcasting/Cablecasting Yearbook '84,* television is viewed in American homes for 24-hours-and-five-minutes each week. Fourteen of those hours are during prime time. Television watching grows in winter, and drops in summer. Watching is at its lowest in July—vacation month—and at its highest in January, when more people stay indoors.

This does not precisely follow the curve produced by the release of new shows in the fall. The television "year" is actually only half a year, since only 26 shows make up a complete season. Then the networks go into reruns. The fall season begins in October and ends somewhere around March or April. One might expect viewing to be at its height in October, when programming is new, yet October viewing is only slightly above September, seeming to indicate that the lives of individuals—at least, their television lives—are influenced as much by other factors as by the newness of television programming.

A. C. Nielsen figures for 1983 show TV households to be 83.8 million, an increase of half a million over the previous year; this figure represents 98 percent of all American homes. Ninety percent of all TV homes had color receivers.

Weekday TV watching begins early, with statistics showing the average viewer watching approximately six-and-one-half hours per week, between 7 A.M. and 1 P.M. Viewing drops by 75 minutes in the afternoon, but picks up again at 4:30—the evening news span—and climbs to its highest level during "prime time"—8 to 11 P.M.—when viewing averages more than 14 hours per week. Viewing drops significantly after 11 P.M., and falls to its lowest point (three hours) between 1 and 7 A.M.

Women watch more daytime TV than men, a fact that seems obvious since the male audience is largely at work, whlie most women are still at home, despite the recent tremendous increase in the numbers of women who work outside the home. Even so, 26 percent of all watchers between the weekday hours of 10 A.M. and 1 P.M. are men; fifty seven percent are women. (The remainder are teens and children.)

The numbers change at night, during prime time, when, in 1983, 38 percent of all watchers were men, 45 percent women. Even during prime time, women outpull men in time spent in front of the tube. This fact does not worry advertisers a bit, since women do most of the buying.

Situation comedies draw the largest audiences on a continuous, week-by-week basis, followed by general drama, mystery and suspense, adventure and feature films, according to *Broadcasting/Cablecasting Yearbook, '84.* The networks are well aware of statistics such as these, and plan their formats accordingly. In 1980, 39 percent of all programming was situation comedy. Special events—the moon walk, Watergate hearings, JFK's funeral, bowl and Olympic games—attract larger audiences, and audiences that include a large percentage of men.

Many television viewers criticize the networks for scheduling popular programs at the same viewing hour. But television programming is as much finding subject matter that has as much mass appeal as that being shown on the other networks at the same time as it is finding programs that people want to see. Network programmers deliberately schedule shows of high interest against competing shows of high interest, not worrying that many potential viewers would like to see both. It's maddening to viewers, but that's the way television's economic game is played.

Network programmers seek to build an audience that stays with the network all evening. Analysis of Nielsen figures suggests that once a viewer leaves one network, the set is not likely to be turned back to that network for the rest of that evening. So programming must be not so much the presentation of shows that have excellent viewer appeal as shows thaat are merely "less objectionable" to viewers than that which is on the other networks. Some critics say this is the networks' way of "backing into" show quality. Unfortunately, it often guarantees excellent prime-time ratings for shows that, in the views of many critics, are of poor quality but, nevertheless, are better than the other networks' presentations at that hour.

Because television is so tightly tied to the rating system, it has been criticized for appealing to the lowest common denominator in society. More men and women over age 55 watch than of younger ages; more young children watch than older children; and more children who are from minority or lower socioeconomic status watch than children from more affluent white families. Younger viewers with lower IQ and test scores watch more than viewers of the same age who are brighter.

The conclusion to be drawn from this is that since television is a passive medium, it requires little from the viewer except "being there." Television does not require much mental effort (but neither do motion pictures or recordings). Consequently the majority of television viewers would appear to be less discriminating in matters of taste than persons with more education.

Despite its status as the leading medium of communication—reaching more people with sight and sound than any other process, either written or broadcast—the newness of television may be wearing off, as growing numbers of people seem to be turning to other pursuits. The more discriminating turn to books, magazines and specialized record or radio listening, returning to TV only when programs they consider worthwhile are scheduled. The steady growth of low-power, subscription and cable television, and of video movies indicates a mounting interest in media over which the individual has at least some programming control.

A continuing study of television listeners being conducted at Walt Disney's Epcot Center has disclosed that, according to *TV Guide,* listeners are "watching less . . . and liking less of what they see on network TV" and they feel TV is "bad for children."

In 1984, 47,000 persons responded to a set of questions drawn up by editors of *TV Guide* by punching keys on a computer console built into the arms of their chairs. Although the poll was not scientific because the Epcot visitors voluntarily chose to participate, nevertheless it offers an insight into the views of, at least, the kind of people who visit Epcot (generally more affluent, better educated and politically conservative). Among the findings:

1. More than a third perceive bias in television's reporting of business and labor stories, with labor coverage more negative than business.
2. Only 28 percent see TV as *politically* slanted, but of those, all but 7 percent feel that the Republicans are usually the group that is depicted negatively.
3. Dan Rather was judged the most reliable of the three regular nightly news anchormen, with Peter Jennings second and Tom Brokaw third.
4. Fifty-two percent said they are watching less TV today than five years ago. This was especially true of younger and college-educated viewers.
5. On programming, a third said the networks are too dependent on ratings, 28 percent said shows are too similar, and nearly half complained that there is too much sports on the air.
6. By more than two to one, respondents said that television has had a negative impact on children.

So what alternatives to network television did the respondents suggest? Forty percent said they liked the greater number of choices offered by cable, and 30 percent said they might buy or rent a videocassette recorder in the future.

According to another survey, the number of TV households tuning in to one of the three major networks dropped by 6 percent in 1984, despite an increase of 1.1 million in the number of homes with sets. However, even though millions of disenchanted viewers may forsake television for media that they consider more stimulating, television is likely to remain this nation's leading medium of information as well as entertainment for some time to come.

Comprehension Questions: *Circle the letter of the best answer.*

1. What percent of an American's leisure time is spent watching T.V.?
   a. 20
   b. 48
   c. 56
   d. 67

2. What type of T.V. show draws the largest percentage of viewers?
   a. comedy
   b. movies
   c. suspense
   d. variety

3. What T.V. news anchor person is most respected?
   a. Tom Brokaw
   b. Dan Rather
   c. Peter Jennings
   d. Jane Polly

Essay Question

Write a brief answer to the following question.

Based on what you have read, what conclusions can you make?

Time-Rate Conversion Chart

Min:Sec	WPM	Min:Sec	WPM	Min:Sec	WPM	Min:Sec	WPM
1:00	1420	4:30	316	8:00	178	11:30	123
1:10	1217	4:40	304	8:10	174	11:40	122
1:20	1065	4:50	290	8:20	170	11:50	120
1:30	947	5:00	284	8:30	167	12:00	118
1:40	852	5:10	275	8:40	164	12:10	117
1:50	775	5:20	266	8:50	161	12:20	115
2:00	710	5:30	258	9:00	158	12:30	114
2:10	655	5:40	251	9:10	155	12:40	112
2:20	609	5:50	243	9:20	152	12:50	111
2:30	568	6:00	237	9:30	149	13:00	109
2:40	533	6:10	230	9:40	147	13:10	108
2:50	501	6:20	224	9:50	144	13:20	107
3:00	473	6:30	218	10:00	142	13:30	105
3:10	448	6:40	213	10:10	140	13:40	104
3:20	426	6:50	208	10:20	137	13:50	103
3:30	406	7:00	203	10:30	135	14:00	101
3:40	387	7:10	198	10:40	133	14:10	100
3:50	370	7:20	194	10:50	131	14:20	99
4:00	355	7:30	189	11:00	129	14:30	98
4:10	341	7:40	185	11:10	127	14:40	97
4:20	328	7:50	181	11:20	125	14:50	96

9–17

What Is a Newspaper?

Ronald Lovell and
Philip Geraci

	Hour	Min.	Secs.
A. Ending time:	____	____	____
B. Starting time:	____	____	____
C. A – B = Reading time:		____	____

The Random House *Dictionary of the English Language* defines "news" as "a report of a recent event" or "a report on current events in a newspaper or on radio or television." A newspaper is defined as "a publication, usually issued daily or weekly, containing news, comment, features, photographs and advertising."

The dictionary definition of news, however, leaves much to be desired in the context of newspapering, because much of any newspaper's content has *nothing* to do with reports of recent events. For example, the crossword puzzle that is a staple in many newspapers and the first thing some readers turn to hardly qualifies as news. The same is true of comics. These are features, and in most newspapers they occupy greater space than news. Perhaps a newspaper should be called a "news and feature paper."

Newspapers also contain advertising, and the accepted ratio of news to advertisements is 60 percent ads, 40 percent news. So maybe a newspaper should be called an "adpaper."

There is really much more to the modern newspaper than reports of recent events. Some of this can be traced to the *Acta Diurna* of Roman times when daily bulletins were posted on walls for everyone to read. "Diurna" means "daily" and these daily bulletins established one of the principle standards of a newspaper: regular, consistent publication. Six centuries later, the Chinese *Tsing Pao* began a long period of publishing, lasting until this century.

But the roots of modern newspapers really lay in Europe in somewhat more recent times. Although there were brief attempts at publishing on the continent during the 17th century, it was in England that the newspaper really took root. William Caxton, a printer, is credited with one of the first examples. But many freedoms were lost under the autocracy of Henry VIII and subsequent rulers, and freedom of the press was one of them.

It was largely because of such oppression that America was founded, and it wasn't long before printers in the American colonies—Benjamin Harris in Massachusetts and Benjamin Franklin in Philadelphia—began using their presses to speak out against curbs on individual freedoms.

Thus early newspapers were not as much reports of recent events as examples of what have come to be known today as expressions of editorial opinion. Some publications appeared infrequently, not regularly and consistently. But they did contain some aspects of the 20th century newspaper, and established a legacy that has come to nurture the modern "press." Print media have even taken the name of the machine that produces them as a generic label.

What constitutes a "newspaper?" Here are some of the commonly accepted characteristics.

1. It must be published at regular intervals. Daily newspapers appear every day, weeklies every week. Some community newspapers appear at less-frequent intervals; nevertheless, they appear consistently and continuously.
2. It must be devoted to the masses. In other words, it must contain general, not specialized, information, although it may have specialty sections with information that doesn't interest every reader, such as sports or food.
3. It must be available to everyone who wants it, and not to a select few. If not, it becomes a specialized publication, not a newspaper.
4. It must contain news. That means, according to the Random House dictionary, reports on "current events."
5. It must champion the interests of its geographic constituency. That means that a newspaper in New York should contain news of New York, not Philadelphia, for the most part. But geographic constituency can be narrowly defined. It could mean a suburban area, a highway, an inner-city neighborhood. The *Village Voice* was created to serve the interests of residents of New York's Greenwich Village. The Charlevoix *Courier* serves 3,287 residents of Charlevoix, Michigan, and nobody else.

One big way in which a newspaper differs from a news *magazine* is in its geographical constituency. Magazines may carry news, but their geographical constituency is the entire nation; most newspapers have a more narrow geographical focus. An exception is *USA Today,* which is something like a national news-magazine (i.e., *Time* or *Newsweek*) and is printed on newsprint at plants in Atlanta, Minneapolis-St. Paul, Pittsburgh, Chicago, Denver, Houston, Los Angeles, Miami, New York, Philadelphia and Washington, with new locations being added as the paper grows.

There are also legal definitions of a newspaper. The state of Maryland, for example, has defined a newspaper in very specific terms. Article 81 of the Annotated Code of Maryland states that a publication is *not* a newspaper unless

1. it is published and distributed no less frequently than once each week;
2. it does not, when its successive issues are put together, constitute a book;
3. it is intended for circulation among the general public; and
4. it contains news items, legal and general intelligence, reports of current events, editorial comments, advertising matter, and other miscellaneous information of public interest generally found in the ordinary newspaper.

The definition of what a newspaper is really lies in the uses to which it will be put. Every big newspaper of substance tries to keep its readers informed on events that concern them. Part of that elusive quality called "editorial judgment" is the ability or the art of its editors to feel, almost instinctively, what is news and what isn't. Press releases by the millions pour through the mails to the editorial offices of newspapers around the world. Many are boldly headlined NEWS. To some people, they are, but an editor must decide if they are news to the readers of a specific newspaper.

Many editors of metropolitan newspapers consider themselves historians. Laboring with an innate sense of history born of long hours of editing the day's news, they know that in future years, scholars will pour over microfilmed records of newspapers, putting their special interpretation on events of a specific period. This seemed especially to be the case with the *Washington Star,* no longer published. Headlines from this famous newspaper, once the nation's leading chronicle of U.S. government actions, read like a history book: "War Declared on Axis"; "Europe Invaded"; "War Ends"; "Russia Launches Sputnik"; "JFK Dies of Gunshot Wound"; "Nixon Resigns"—headlines like these are like pages of American history. It's all there, in newspapers.

Comprehension Questions: *Circle the letter of the best answer.*

1. What percentage of print in the newspaper can be classified as news?
   a. 20
   b. 40
   c. 60
   d. 80

2. The modern newspaper can be traced to the:
   a. early monasteries
   b. Roman Senate
   c. Acta Diurna
   d. Animus Motus of England

3. The definition of a newspaper lies in:
   a. how it will be used.
   b. who reads it.
   c. who prints it.
   d. no answer is given.

Essay Question

Write a brief answer to the following question.

What are the five commonly accepted characteristics of a newspaper?

Time-Rate Conversion Chart

Min:Sec	WPM	Min:Sec	WPM	Min:Sec	WPM	Min:Sec	WPM
1:00	1220	4:30	271	8:00	153	11:30	106
1:10	1046	4:40	261	8:10	149	11:40	105
1:20	915	4:50	252	8:20	146	11:50	103
1:30	813	5:00	244	8:30	144		
1:40	732	5:10	236	8:40	141		
1:50	665	5:20	229	8:50	138		
2:00	610	5:30	222	9:00	136		
2:10	563	5:40	215	9:10	133		
2:20	523	5:50	209	9:20	131		
2:30	488	6:00	203	9:30	128		
2:40	458	6:10	198	9:40	126		
2:50	431	6:20	193	9:50	124		
3:00	407	6:30	188	10:00	122		
3:10	385	6:40	183	10:10	120		
3:20	366	6:50	179	10:20	118		
3:30	349	7:00	174	10:30	116		
3:40	333	7:10	170	10:40	114		
3:50	318	7:20	166	10:50	113		
4:00	305	7:30	163	11:00	111		
4:10	293	7:40	159	11:10	109		
4:20	282	7:50	156	11:20	108		

9–18

Ecology and Ecosystems

John Christensen

	Hour	Min.	Secs.
A. Ending time:	___	___	___
B. Starting time:	___	___	___
C. A – B = Reading time:		___	___

It is possible to study organisms without giving much consideration to how and where those organisms live. For example, an anatomist may study the structure of an animal's bones, muscles, and organs without caring much about the life of the animal in its environment. It is also possible to study environments without worrying about the animals, plants, and other kinds of organisms that live there. For example, one may describe a desert in terms of its nonliving or *abiotic* parts. These would include sand, wind, temperature, rainfall, or elevation. A physical geologist or meteorologist might take this view.

An *ecologist* is a different kind of scientist. The ecologist is interested in both the living (biotic) and nonliving (abiotic) parts of the ecosystem. Perhaps more important, an ecologist studies the *interactions* that occur in ecosystems. Interactions occur between living things. This occurs when an animal eats a plant or another animal. Interactions also occur between the biotic and abiotic parts of the system. This happens when waste materials from living things decompose returning minerals to the soil. The study of such interactions is the science of *ecology*.

Human ecology is especially interesting to some scientists because human populations are so numerous, diverse, and widespread on planet Earth. Human beings are much more than biological animals. We socialize with each other. We exist in and interact in our neighborhoods. We are part of society as a whole. Human ecology seeks to bring together physiological, behavioral, sociological, political, economic, ethical, and religious factors.

Ecologists usually deal with five main levels of organization—organisms, populations, communities, ecosystems, and the ecosphere.

In some ways, ecosystems are defined for convenience. The definition may change depending on what a person wants to study. The interactions occurring within a jar of pond water make up a rich and fascinating ecosystem. One might define all of Lake Michigan as a single ecosystem. An ecosystem may be studied within any area of space. All that is necessary is some boundary across which inputs and outputs of materials and energy may be measured. Thus, a student of ecology may investigate ecosystems like a forest, a pond, a rotting log, a garden, a culture of bacteria in a test tube, or the entire Earth!

Ecologists generally group ecosystems on Earth under a few major types. *Aquatic ecosystems* include lakes, ponds, rivers, springs, swamps, estuaries, coral reefs, seas, and oceans. On land, the major ecosystems—often called *biomes*—are forests, grasslands, savannahs (combinations of grasslands with scattered trees), chaparrals (shrublands), tundra, and deserts. These groupings are handy. Although no two forests are exactly alike, they have enough in common. An understanding of the natural laws at work on one type of forest helps predict what goes on in another.

All of the various ecosystems on Earth are connected to one another. If we group all of the ecosystems on the planet, we have the largest life unit of all—the *ecosphere*. The ultimate goal of ecology is to find out how everything in the ecosphere is connected to everything else.

Comprehension Questions: *Circle the letter of the best answer.*

1. An ecologist is interested in:
    a. learning about city life
    b. understanding living and nonliving parts of the ecosystem
    c. creating living environments that support exotic life
    d. developing new ecosystems that support a variety of plant life

2. The study of interactions between biotic and abiotic parts of the ecosystem is called:
    a. the study of relationships
    b. the understanding of nature
    c. the science of ecology
    d. the creation of habitats

3. One can conclude from this article that:
    a. ecosystems are fragile
    b. ecologists are interested in establishing new ecosystems
    c. understanding ecosystems helps us deal with the environment in a better way
    d. establishing interactions is the ultimate goal of ecologists

Essay Questions

Write a brief answer to the following question.

Why is it important for us to understand the workings of the various ecosystems in our environment?

Time-Rate Conversion Chart

Min:Sec	WPM	Min:Sec	WPM
1:00	507	4:30	113
1:10	435	4:40	109
1:20	380	4:50	105
1:30	338	5:00	101
1:40	304	5:10	98
1:50	277	5:20	95
2:00	254	5:30	92
2:10	234	5:40	89
2:20	217	5:50	87
2:30	203		
2:40	190		
2:50	179		
3:00	169		
3:10	160		
3:20	152		
3:30	145		
3:40	138		
3:50	132		
4:00	127		
4:10	122		
4:20	117		

The Desert as a Way of Life

Hamidou A. Sidikou

	Hour	Min.	Secs.
A. Ending time:	____	____	____
B. Starting time:	____	____	____
C. A – B = Reading time:		____	____

To survive in a harsh world man has no option but to adapt to the physical and climatic conditions of his environment. In doing so he must develop strategies which are often reflected in salient features of his culture and society.

The peoples of Niger, and especially the Tuareg, the Tubu, the Kanuri, the Gué-zébida and the Arabs who live in the difficult conditions that prevail in the arid and semi-arid regions of the country, are no exception to this universal rule. Individually and collectively, their way of life is influenced, if not determined, by the need to adapt to the rigours of a climate in which the dominant factors are wide temperature variations, their duration and intensity.

Over two-thirds of Niger's total area of 1,267,000 square kilometres consists of desert and semi-desert zones situated between latitudes 15° and 23° North. Of this vast expanse, the Ténéré Desert, bounded to the west and north-west by the Aïr massif and to the north and north-east by high plateaux whose southern limits are marked by impressive cliffs, itself covers more than 350,000 square kilometres.

In these climatic zones, a combination of factors related to rainfall, atmospheric humidity and seasonal temperature variations normally gives rise to four distinct seasons of varying length.

The rainy season, which lasts from July–August to September, is short and irregular. When it does rain, the precipitation is often slight, but sudden violent storms are a threat to those whose houses are made of low-quality earth containing a large proportion of salts which dissolve rapidly in the wet.

From the end of September to the end of October there is a short intermediate season characterized by both a high atmospheric humidity level and very high temperatures. This is followed by a dry, cold season lasting from November to March when an east wind, the Harmattan, brings dry mists which are liable to be transformed into violent sandstorms, and temperatures fall below zero at night.

Finally, there is a hot dry season which extends from March to June or July. This is the season of very great heat, with temperatures reaching 45° C or more.

Reprinted from the Unesco Courier, January, 1987.

The maximum daily temperature range which is generally experienced at the beginning and end of the dry season may be as great as 20° C, while the range between the absolute minimum and maximum temperatures may even reach 40° C, if not more. An extraordinary capacity for adaptation is required of peoples subject to such rigorous climatic conditions. This adaptation is reflected in every aspect of their lives. The strategies they adopt are in many cases indissociable from the organization of society and from housing, clothing and diet.

In this setting, human activity is strictly ruled by the existence of watering places. Because they are so rare, they have great economic value and are decisive factors in the determination of social status. Three branches of human activity—stock-raising, agriculture and manual labour—appear to be directly determined by the harsh climatic conditions.

Stock-raising activities not only fulfil economic requirements but also meet the need to adapt to the climate with its great variations of temperature. Camels and cattle are the main species raised, primarily for the production of milk which is the basic element of the diet. Since camels are more hardy than cattle, they can be raised in wide open rangelands and are able to adapt more easily to variations in soil composition and grazing vegetation.

The available quantity of milk, which serves as both food and drink, varies from season to season, and this is why two complementary species are chosen for its production. Thus camel's milk, which is available in adequate quantities during the hot, dry season, is appreciated both for its very rich vitamin content and for its low fat content, characteristics which are thought to increase endurance and resistance to hunger. It is also said to have remarkably beneficial effects on eyesight. The absence or very low proportion of visually handicapped people among populations whose diet is based on camel's milk may be partly due to its high mineral content.

Camel-herders also engage in trans-Saharan trading. One reason for this is the need to reconcile the differing demands of life in complementary ecological zones. Until it declined following successive droughts which decimated the herds and destroyed the vegetation on which they depended for grazing, the caravan trade, in which tens of thousands of camels were still involved only a few years ago, was of more than just economic significance. It was one of many responses to the particular environmental conditions and perpetuated a whole way of life through a wide-ranging network of social relationships.

Knowledge of the location of watering places is a key factor in this way of life in areas where the water supply is a matter of fundamental and permanent concern. Agricultural activity is thus limited to the area around oases where a permanent supply of water is available. Date-growing is the mainstay of this irrigation agriculture adapted to the seasons. Dates, which are an important item of trade with the regions to the south, are a source of food, according to their quality, for both man and beast.

Manual labour is primarily concerned with the exploitation of salt and natron. The latter, a hydrous sodium carbonate, is an essential element in animal feed since it meets the animals' salt requirements and also rids them of intestinal parasites, thus boosting their milk production.

The concern to adapt diet to environmental conditions, which always underlies human behaviour, is also apparent in the unusual, some would say immoderate, consumption of tea. A beverage that both quenches thirst and staves off hunger, tea is served ceremonially. It plays a part in creating physiological mechanisms for adapting to the variations in temperature.

Dress is another important indication of adaptation to the environment. The wearing of the veil and the turban are not only of social significance (attainment of adult status, for example), they also serve to protect the head, and in particular the eyes, nose and ears against the effects of low temperatures, the stinging blast of hot or cold winds and sandstorms. The wearing of voluminous clothing, usually made of cotton, is a form of adaptation to high temperatures.

Finally, housing, its conception, the materials used in its construction, and the use made of it in relation to the seasons, is another important element in adaptation to climatic conditions. In the Kawar region of Niger, for example, where, in past centuries, fortified villages were constructed for security reasons, four main types of dwellings are found.

Stone houses, the last relics of those troubled times, are used during the dry, cold season because they offer better protection against sharp drops in temperature.

During the hot, dry season, houses constructed of date-palm leaves come into their own. Cool, airy and well ventilated, they are divided into rooms designated for different functions. A room reserved for the head of the household adjoins the entrance; there is a room for the women and children, a store-room for food or for animal fodder, a kitchen, and a living-room in which meals are taken.

Tents, which are made of skins or of rush matting, vary in size according to the means of the occupants. They are always put up on a north-south axis with one or two openings on the east and west sides to allow air to circulate and the rays of the sun to enter. Tents are all-the-year-round dwellings which can easily be dismantled. They are set up on top of dunes during the hot season and in spots protected by vegetation among the dunes in the cold season. The tent is the perfect example of a dwelling fully adapted to the climate.

Straw huts, whose dimensions vary according to economic considerations and to the availability of straw, itself dependent upon rainfall, are used both as temporary shelters and permanent dwellings. In the latter case they are used mainly during the rainy season and in the hot season since they offer the best protection against rain and great heat.

These are some of the strategies developed by the peoples of Niger who live in very hot desert areas. Their purpose is to provide a minimum of comfort by adaptation to temperature conditions which remain, throughout the year, a matter of primordial concern.

Comprehension Questions: *Circle the letter of the best answer.*

1. One could describe Niger as a place:
    a. where a temperate climate exists
    b. that is harsh
    c. where people thrive on the land
    d. that is heavily inhabited

2. The clothing worn by the people in Niger:
    a. is colorful and heavy
    b. requires extensive care
    c. helps them adapt to the climate conditions
    d. is purchased basically from other countries

3. One can conclude from reading this passage that:
    a. the people of Niger live a comfortable life
    b. Niger's people have learned to adapt to the temperature conditions
    c. climatic conditions have little impact on the region
    d. vast resources exist in the region

Essay Question

Write a brief answer to the following question.

How do the peoples of Niger adapt to the living conditions in the arid and semi-arid regions of the country?

Time-Rate Conversion Chart

Min:Sec	WPM	Min:Sec	WPM	Min:Sec	WPM
1:00	1401	4:30	311	8:00	175
1:10	1201	4:40	300	8:10	172
1:20	1051	4:50	290	8:20	168
1:30	934	5:00	280	8:30	165
1:40	841	5:10	271	8:40	162
1:50	764	5:20	263	8:50	159
2:00	701	5:30	255	9:00	156
2:10	647	5:40	247	9:10	153
2:20	600	5:50	240	9:20	150
2:30	560	6:00	234	9:30	147
2:40	525	6:10	227	9:40	145
2:50	494	6:20	221	9:50	142
3:00	467	6:30	216	10:00	140
3:10	442	6:40	210	10:10	138
3:20	420	6:50	205	10:20	136
3:30	400	7:00	200	10:30	133
3:40	382	7:10	195	10:40	131
3:50	365	7:20	191	10:50	129
4:00	350	7:30	187		
4:10	336	7:40	183		
4:20	323	7:50	179		

9–20

The Articles of Confederation and the Constitution

Unesco

	Hour	Min.	Secs.
A. Ending time:	___	___	___
B. Starting time:	___	___	___
C. A – B = Reading time:		___	___

The Continental Congress ran the Revolutionary War, but it was not really a national government. At first the rebels operated under state constitutions, most of which were drafted during the Revolution. A national system of government, called the Articles of Confederation, was adopted in 1781. Since the aims of the Revolution included independence and the overthrow of Britain's centralized monarchy, the rebels wanted power divided among the various state governments. So under the Articles the national government was quite weak. There was no executive branch that might become a new monarchy. National laws could be passed only if nine of the thirteen votes in Congress agreed; amendments to the Articles took all thirteen. Congress lacked the power to create an army, impose taxes, or regulate commerce. As a result, money and an army could be raised only by getting the states to agree to meet certain quotas.

The Articles of Confederation made sense for a people that had just gotten out from under a strong central government. It protected the authority of each state and placed local self-determination above all else. But it left the nation unable to deal with either domestic or foreign crises. Right after the Revolutionary War, the nation fell into an economic depression that resulted in part from Britain's refusal to grant the Americans shipping rights in the British empire. The decentralized national government under the Articles was unable to negotiate a settlement with the former motherland. Hard times caused the debtor farmers of western Massachusetts, led by Captain Daniel Shays, to rebel against legal punishments for nonpayment of debts. Shays' Rebellion scared many property owners. They, along with other people in various states, began to press for a new structure of national government that would be truly national but still protect individual rights.

The Congress of the Confederation responded to the pressure by arranging for a convention to revise the Articles of Confederation. At Philadelphia, in the sweltering summer of 1787, fifty-five delegates debated the reshaping of the American Republic.

The discussions brought to light the intense conflicts between big states and small ones, northerners and southerners, slave owners and those who owned no slaves, farmers and merchants, westerners and easterners, debtors and creditors. But the delegates did not give up until they had forged a new constitution. It severely limited the powers of the states and elevated those of the central government. It provided for a two-house federal legislature, for a president chosen by a college of electors appointed by the states, and for separate executive, legislative, and judicial branches. It did not just revise the Articles of Confederation; it totally replaced them.

Ratification of the Constitution took place amid bitter debate in special state conventions. Resistance to the new document was greatest in the large states: Virginia, Massachusetts, Pennsylvania, and New York. Opponents of the Constitution feared the centralization of power would destroy the states and curtail personal liberty. Some undecided delegates to the ratifying conventions were finally won over when supporters of the Constitution promised that a Bill of Rights would be added to protect individual freedom. Those favoring the new system were called Federalists. Three of their leaders—Alexander Hamilton, James Madison, and John Jay—produced a series of penetrating essays favoring the new government, which were later collected and published as *The Federalist*. Federalist eloquence and the fact that more and more people were realizing the nation could never survive without a stronger central government finally brought about ratification. In June 1788 the Constitution of the United States of America became the law of the land.

The following February, in the first national election, General Washington received all sixty-nine electoral votes to become the first president. John Adams of Massachusetts was chosen vice president. Washington was sworn in April 30, 1789, on the balcony of Federal Hall on Wall Street in lower Manhattan. New York City, with its Dutch gabled roofs and cobbled streets, became the first capital of the new United States.

Comprehension Questions: *Circle the letter of the best answer.*

1. Under the Articles of Confederation:
   a. most power was centralized in the federal government
   b. power was divided among the state governments
   c. central government controlled the economy
   d. state governments could not overrule the central government

2. The reason why the Articles of Confederation made sense right after the Revolutionary War was that:
   a. people needed to feel free from a central authority
   b. the central government needed to have control to maintain order
   c. individuals needed to have the protection of a national army
   d. Congress needed to have control of foreign affairs in order to maintain peace

3. Hamilton, Madison and Jay produced papers called "The Federalists" which:
   a. denounced having a strong central government
   b. supported having a weak central government
   c. proposed the idea that a strong central government was needed
   d. criticized the proposal of having a constitutional convention

Essay Question

Write a brief answer to the following question.

Why were the Articles of Confederation necessary at the beginning of our new nation?

Time-Rate Conversion Chart

Min:Sec	WPM	Min:Sec	WPM
1:00	663	4:30	147
1:10	568	4:40	142
1:20	497	4:50	137
1:30	442	5:00	133
1:40	398	5:10	128
1:50	362	5:20	124
2:00	332	5:30	121
2:10	306	5:40	117
2:20	284	5:50	114
2:30	265	6:00	111
2:40	249	6:10	108
2:50	234	6:20	105
3:00	221	6:30	102
3:10	209	6:40	99
3:20	199	6:50	97
3:30	189		
3:40	181		
3:50	173		
4:00	166		
4:10	159		
4:20	153		

Crossing Paths with a Snake

Ellen Hale

	Hour	Min.	Secs.
A. Ending time:	___	___	___
B. Starting time:	___	___	___
C. A – B = Reading time:		___	___

In all the history of man, no creature has evoked more attraction and repulsion, more fear or fascination, than the snake. From drawings etched in stone caves to masterful marble carvings, the serpent has always been accorded special spiritual and mystical meaning.

The reasons for this obsession are many. Graceful and able to move effortlessly, the snake appears to defy nature. Impeccably clean and clad in stunning or subtle colors, it mysteriously sheds its skin regularly. But most of all, the fascination with the snake can be traced to its venom and poisonous bite.

Not all snakes are venomous, of course. Of an estimated 3,000 species of snakes in the world, only 375 are considered poisonous.

In the United States, there are two families of native poisonous snakes—the Elapidae and Crotalidae—and only about 20 species of venomous snakes. But that does not make a snakebite any less of a danger here.

Indeed, world-renowned pharmacologist and snakebite expert Dr. Findlay E. Russell estimates that 45,000 snakebites from all kinds of snakes occur each year in this country. About one-third of those he sees are among professional herpetologists, zoo workers, and other snake handlers. But most bites happen to the unsuspecting "civilian."

Of all snakebites, about 8,000 a year are from venomous snakes. From nine to 15 people die each year from those bites, according to Russell, professor of pharmacology and toxicology at the University of Arizona in Tucson, and author of the best-known textbook on the subject of snakebites, *Snake Venom Poisoning*.

Despite the progress of modern medicine and the age-old problem of snakebites, much controversy still surrounds the treatments for bites by venomous snakes.

In the past two or three decades, a host of treatments have been tried, most only to be discarded as useless. Even now, the debate continues over the use of a surgical procedure called fasciotomy, with some doctors recommending its use and others vehemently criticizing it.

Reprinted from FDA Consumer, July/August, 1987.

Meanwhile, antivenin—the antidote to venom—remains the most popular treatment. But its use has pitfalls as well. Most notable are painful and sometimes dangerous side effects. Attempts to purify the antivenin, which now is produced from horse serum, to prevent sickness have been promising. But they've progressed slowly because the demand for improved products is too small to make their production profitable.

The great bulk of snakebites in the United States—as much as 98 percent—comes from snakes in the Crotalidae family, more commonly known as pit vipers. So called because of a heat-sensitive "pit" found between each nostril and eye, pit vipers include the notorious rattlesnakes, copperheads and cottonmouths.

The Elapidae are represented by the coral snake, which has short and fixed fangs. Bites from them account for only 2 percent to 4 percent of all snakebites. In 1986 in the United States, there were only five bites by coral snakes.

The highest incidence of snakebites occurs in North Carolina, with nearly 19 venomous bites reported each year for each 100,000 people. Arkansas, Texas, Georgia, West Virginia, Mississippi and Louisiana, successively, report the next highest rates.

That most bites occur in the South—rather than the West—can be explained by the fact that the copperhead snake, responsible for so many bites there, lives well in populated areas where rattlesnakes often get killed, says Dr. Sherman A. Minton, professor emeritus of microbiology and immunology at Indiana University School of Medicine in Indianapolis.

To confuse matters of medical treatment, researchers have found that when venomous snakes bite they don't always release venom—or envenomate, as scientists say. Nor do all venomous bites involve release of enough venom to prove dangerous.

For example, Russell estimates that one-fourth of bites from rattlesnakes are not envenomated and that another 15 percent aren't sufficiently envenomated to constitute a medical emergency.

In ancient times, snakebites were typically treated with incantations and rituals that bordered on exorcism. But medicine had become a little more progressive by the time, 800 years ago, that the famed Jewish philosopher and physician Maimonides wrote:

"When someone is bitten, one must strive to immediately tie and bind a ligature above the site of the bite as tightly as possible so that the poison not disseminate throughout the body . . . another person should make incisions with a knife at the site of the bite and suck with his mouth as strongly as he is able. He should spit out all that he sucks. He should first rinse his mouth with olive oil or wine and oil . . . and if there is no one available to do the sucking, one should strive to apply cupping glasses."

In fact, Maimonides' centuries-old prescription is still pretty up-to-date. While the "cut-and-suck" method of snakebite treatment may not be the most preferable, it still can play a lifesaving role.

The treatment of snakebites varies with the kind of snake involved and the amount of venom released, but the most important step, all physicians agree, is to get the patient to a hospital as soon as possible. In recommendations made in 1977 by the National Research Council of the National Academy of Sciences and subsequently published by the American Red Cross, experts say a snakebite should receive immediate medical attention whether it's poisonous or not and even in cases where a snakebite "is only suspected."

In the process of getting the victim to medical care, it's crucial to keep him or her motionless and to immobilize the part of the body that's been bitten—steps intended to slow the venom's spread to other parts of the body. If no symptoms develop, these steps should be sufficient until the victim can get to a hospital, even if it takes four or five hours.

Surveys show that most snakebites occur within close range of medical care. Russell's studies show that the average time from bite to hospital in California is 34 minutes; in Arizona it's 42 minutes; in Idaho, over an hour.

The symptoms of a snakebite, like the treatment of it, vary widely and depend on the location of the bite, the age and health of the victim, the kind of snake, and, of course, the amount of venom released. Snakebites in children, for example, are often very serious because their smaller blood supply makes for a higher concentration of venom.

Pain and swelling are the most common symptoms; studies show they occur in three-fourths of envenomated rattlesnake bites, usually within minutes of the bite. Pain, changes in pulse rate, dimmed vision, nausea, and shortness of breath are among other symptoms considered "moderate" by the National Academy of Sciences and the American Red Cross.

Symptoms rated as severe are: blurred vision, convulsions, shock, paralysis and unconsciousness.

When symptoms occur and medical care is not within immediate reach, Maimonides' advice begins to apply: If mild to moderate symptoms appear, a wide constriction bandage, from three-fourths of an inch to one-and-a-half inches wide, should be wrapped from two to four inches above the bite—but never around a joint or around the head, neck or trunk. The band should be tight, but not so tight as to interfere with blood flow; the rule of thumb is to make it loose enough to slip a finger under. Don't remove the band until the victim reaches medical care, but check the victim's pulse near the bite regularly to make sure blood flow has not been stopped.

If severe symptoms develop, more immediate and intensive treatment is needed. Many ranchers, forest rangers and hikers carry special snakebite suction cups when they work outdoors. Most popular is one called the Sawyer extraction kit, says Russell, who swears by it.

The extractor cups are put over the fang punctures and within three minutes can remove 23 percent of the venom. Within 30 minutes, one-third of it can be removed, according to Minton.

How fast must you act? "The sooner the better," says Indiana University's Minton.

However, he adds, "some of the recent work we've been doing suggests that venom stays localized around the bite for several hours." The cups should be used for about 30 minutes.

If severe symptoms develop, and no such device is carried, then the famous cut-and-suck treatment should be used immediately. Cuts shold be made with a sterilized blade through the fang marks, about half an inch long and no deeper than the skin itself. The cuts should be parallel and *not* crisscrossed.

There's little danger to the individual who rescues the snakebite victim this way, but experts nonetheless don't recommend swallowing the venom.

There's no way of knowing whether the venom is successfully being drawn out, and Russell estimates that mouth suction can probably extract only about one-tenth of the venom. "But, it's better than nothing," he says.

At the same time, if it can be safely done, the snake should be killed and brought to the hospital so experts can identify it.

If the individual is more than four hours from a hospital and shows any symptoms at all, even mild ones, the constriction band and suction procedure should be followed, the Red Cross recommends.

It should be noted that different experts have their own advice. Russell and Minton, for example, generally believe that if the patient is more than 30 minutes from medical care, suction treatment should be initiated.

First aid for a snakebite becomes more difficult if the victim is alone and must seek out help by himself or herself. "It's a potentially bad situation," says Minton. If it is a leg bite, immobilizing the leg would make it impossible to walk to medical care. In such a case, and if the bite appears to be a bad one, he suggests an individual attempt the cut-and-suck treatment on himself. Russell recommends the victim walk slowly and rest every five minutes or so. If the bite occurs on an upper extremity, try and keep the limb below heart level.

If it's a rare coral snake bite, constriction bands, incision and suction will do little, if any, good because the most toxic ingredients of the venom are absorbed directly into the bloodstream and are quickly disseminated throughout the body. The best bet, says Russell, is to take no food or drink and get to medical care fast.

Another first-aid alternative for snakebites is the "Australian treatment," in which an elastic bandage is wound around the bite, in much the way a sprained ankle is treated, to try and keep the venom localized.

The Australian treatment, so called because it originated in Australia where snakes are particularly poisonous, is not used much in this country "because everyone is afraid of it," says Minton. Side effects could include loss of a limb or development of areas of dead tissue that could require skin grafting.

Once first aid has been rendered, it's time for official medical care, and in this arena there is still much controversy.

Antivenin is the most common treatment, but, over the years, its use has been challenged—unsuccessfully—by a few other therapies.

Experts now largely discount the use of steroids in any primary treatment of snakebites. Russell's own experiences suggest they may do more harm than good: Most of the snakebite death reports he has studied have involved use of big doses of steroids. The only role of steroids, he and others say, is in the treatment of reactions to antivenin. In the operation, surgeons cut through the fascia, the dense planes of connective tissue that support and separate muscles, to release pressure underneath it.

Russell admits he "is not a great lover of fasciotomy" and therefore does not recommend it, particularly in light of studies showing that 90 percent or more of snakebites only reach just beneath the skin.

Minton believes "it may be called for in some cases." Such cases would be rare and would involve only deep bites where swelling is so severe it could cause nerve damage. Even then, however, the procedure should only be done at medical centers properly equipped with the right instrumentation—specifically, a certain kind of catheter that can be inserted into tissue to measure pressure.

So, the treatment of choice for serious snakebite remains antivenin. Antivenin is a combination of antibodies to some of the toxic antigens in venom. In the body, the antibodies combine in tissue and blood with the antigens in the venom, thus immobilizing them.

Antivenins are regulated as biological products by FDA's Center for Drugs and Biologics and must meet certain standards of safety, purity and effectiveness before they can be marketed.

Most people who must take the treatment suffer what is known as "serum sickness," reactions to the foreign proteins and chemicals in the dose of antivenin. Most common symptoms are: itching, swelling of the face and eyelids, anxiety, rash, and a feeling of increased skin temperature. More severe but less common are shock and abnormally rapid heartbeat.

A recent study by Russell of 200 snakebite victims revealed that 74 percent had some reaction to antivenin. Three percent of those had to be hospitalized. The most common treatment for reactions to antivenin is administration of the antihistamine Benadryl.

Snake venom is too complex a substance to use new genetic engineering techniques to produce a safer antivenin, but other approaches show promise.

Russell and his colleagues at the University of Arizona have actually produced a much purified antivenin for use in pit viper bites.

The new purified antivenin has been tested in a few cases and worked very well, but probably will never be commercially developed because it would not be profitable, says Russell.

Comprehension Questions: *Circle the letter of the best answer.*

1. Treatment for snake bites is:
    a. well understood by doctors
    b. limited to one basic procedure
    c. surrounded in controversy
    d. very difficult to perform

2. Most of the snakebites in the United States comes from the:
    a. Crotalidea family
    b. Elapidea family
    c. Faciotomy family
    d. Minton family

3. This article was written to:
    a. impress the reader of the author's knowledge about snakes
    b. convince the reader to avoid desert areas
    c. create fear in people concerning snake bites
    d. inform people about snakes and what to do in case of an emergency

Essay Question

Write a brief answer to the following question.

What specific techniques did you learn about treating snake bites from this article?

Time-Rate Conversion Chart

Min:Sec	WPM	Min:Sec	WPM	Min:Sec	WPM	Min:Sec	WPM	Min:Sec	WPM
1:00	2471	4:30	549	8:00	309	11:30	215	15:00	165
1:10	2118	4:40	530	8:10	303	11:40	212	15:10	163
1:20	1853	4:50	511	8:20	297	11:50	209	15:20	161
1:30	1647	5:00	494	8:30	291	12:00	206	15:30	159
1:40	1483	5:10	478	8:40	285	12:10	203	15:40	158
1:50	1348	5:20	463	8:50	280	12:20	200	15:50	156
2:00	1236	5:30	449	9:00	275	12:30	198		
2:10	1140	5:40	436	9:10	270	12:40	195		
2:20	1059	5:50	424	9:20	265	12:50	193		
2:30	988	6:00	412	9:30	260	13:00	190		
2:40	927	6:10	401	9:40	256	13:10	188		
2:50	872	6:20	390	9:50	251	13:20	185		
3:00	824	6:30	380	10:00	247	13:30	183		
3:10	780	6:40	371	10:10	243	13:40	181		
3:20	741	6:50	362	10:20	239	13:50	179		
3:30	706	7:00	353	10:30	235	14:00	177		
3:40	674	7:10	345	10:40	232	14:10	174		
3:50	645	7:20	337	10:50	228	14:20	172		
4:00	618	7:30	329	11:00	225	14:30	170		
4:10	593	7:40	322	11:10	221	14:40	168		
4:20	570	7:50	315	11:20	218	14:50	167		

White Greed for Indian Land

Leonard Pitt

	Hour	Min.	Secs.
A. Ending time:	——	——	——
B. Starting time:	——	——	——
C. A – B = Reading time:	——	——	

Of the thousands of cowboy-and-Indian movies made in Hollywood, the one that was never filmed shows the whites honoring a treaty "so long as the grass grows green." Imagine a script in which, after the peace pipe is smoked, the Indians establish a self-governing nation on their own land inside the United States, where they are free to follow their own traditions. They are assisted, of course, by the U.S. calvary, which prevents white frontiersmen from raiding Indian land and Indian braves from attacking white settlements. This fantasy nearly became a reality in Indiana about 1812. Only the end of British rule there after the War of 1812 and the death of the great Shawnee chief Tecumseh prevented it from happening.

The United States in 1789 could not claim that it *owned the land* occupied by the Indians of the Old Northwest, but it did assert that it *held political sovereignty* there. As Washington's secretary of war, Henry Knox, explained: "The Indians being the prior occupants possess the right of the soil. It cannot be taken from them unless by their free consent, or by right of conquest in case of a just war." This peculiar relationship was reaffirmed later by the U.S. Supreme Court. The Court described Indian tribes as "distinct, independent, political communities" to be dealt with like all other foreign nations, according to the treaty provision of the Constitution. Although these "domestic dependent nations" occupied areas within the United States and were subject to its will, the Indians kept title to their land according to natural law. Secretary Knox hoped to deal with the Indians under this fair doctrine. But administration of the policy was placed in the hands of underlings and left up to the states or territorial governors to enforce. Here the system broke down. Pioneers cared little for the law and pressed to have the "hell hounds of death" removed by any means possible. So the border warfare continued.

The most troubled Indian-white frontier was the Northwest Territory—the triangular region formed by the Ohio and Mississippi rivers and the Great Lakes. White settlers and speculators coveted the area and demanded government help. Beset by a variety of governmental difficulties, Presidents Washington and Adams moved haltingly in the matter of Indian affairs. The Indians, protected by British forts in the Great Lakes region, stoutly resisted white attackers. In 1791, at the headwaters of the Wabash River, various Indian tribes led by Chief Little Turtle, a Miami Indian, destroyed the six-hundred-man army of General Arthur St. Clair. This remains the greatest single defeat ever suffered by the U.S. army at the hands of Indians. Retribution came three years later at the Battle of Fallen Timbers, near present-day Toledo, Ohio. There General Anthony Wayne defeated the tribes of the Maumee River region and opened Ohio to settlement. The following year the main Indian tribes signed the Treaty of Greenville, which stripped them of much of what is now Ohio and Indiana, cut their alliance with Britain, and opened the Northwest Territory to white settlement. Ohio entered the Union as a state in 1803.

To obtain land U.S. treaty commissioners tried every trick in the book. Often they took advantage of the Indians' desire for muskets and rum. The government also played the Indian tribes off against one another. As General Harmer said, he liked to set the Indians "at deadly variance." Treaties were signed with the most willing Indian chiefs, often deliberately "mellowed" by whiskey or rum at the treaty powwow. But the treaties covered even those tribes that were not represented or had refused to sign. Sometimes Indians agreed to delayed purchases whereby they signed away their children's rights to the land but continued to occupy it during their own lifetime.

Jefferson began to shape a new policy. As a humane individual and a student of Indian languages and customs, he sympathized with their plight. "It may be regarded as certain," he wrote in 1786, "that not a food of land will ever be taken from the Indians without their consent. The sacredness of their rights is felt by all thinking persons in America as much as in Europe." But his outlook changed when he became president in 1801. In organizing the Louisiana Territory, he encouraged a policy of Indian removal. And when Georgia began to move the Cherokees off twenty million acres of prime land and a Cherokee delegation came to protest to the Great White Father, Jefferson sided with the state of Georgia.

Often when diplomacy failed to dislodge the Indians, warfare followed. Sometimes whites attacked the unyielding Indians. Other times the Indians retaliated against whites for breaking promises that were supposed to last "as long as the rivers shall run." Indians who were determined to survive and preserve their independence were faced with a dilemma. If they accepted the white man's payment and moved off the land, they soon found that they were being pushed even further from their native soil. If they stood their ground it still might cost them dearly in the end—unless, perhaps, they could forge an alliance with other tribes. But such alliances were hard to create, since tribal differences were many.

Comprehension Questions: *Circle the letter of the best answer.*

1. The United States could not claim they owned the land that the Indians had but did claim they held:
   a. economic rights to the land
   b. political sovereignty there
   c. territorial rights to the area
   d. claims against the land for damages done in the war

2. The United States Supreme Court held that:
   a. settlers could move onto Indian land without payment
   b. Indians did not have a right to the land after defeat
   c. the Indian nations needed to be treated like other foreign nations
   d. states could annex Indian territory in exchange for payment

3. From reading this passage you could conclude:
   a. Indians were treated fairly concerning their territory
   b. Indians were willing to settle with the U.S. Government
   c. Indians were willing to negotiate a peaceful settlement of the issues
   d. Indians received harsh and unjustified treatment at the hands of the white men

Essay Question

Write a brief answer to the following question.

Red Cloud of the Ogala Sioux said: "When the white man comes to my country he leaves a trail of blood behind him." Is this still true today concerning the American Indians?

Time-Rate Conversion Chart

Min:Sec	WPM	Min:Sec	WPM
1:00	873	4:30	194
1:10	748	4:40	187
1:20	655	4:50	181
1:30	582	5:00	175
1:40	524	5:10	169
1:50	476	5:20	164
2:00	437	5:30	159
2:10	403	5:40	154
2:20	374	5:50	150
2:30	349		
2:40	327		
2:50	308		
3:00	291		
3:10	276		
3:20	262		
3:30	249		
3:40	238		
3:50	228		
4:00	218		
4:10	210		
4:20	201		

The Career and Life Planning Process

	Hour	Min.	Secs.
A. Ending time:	___	___	___
B. Starting time:	___	___	___
C. A – B = Reading time:		___	___

Fred Hecklinger and B. Curtin

What is career and life planning and how can it help you? It enables you to make decisions about the time you spend in your career and your life. By following an organized approach to career and life decision-making, you will be able to make more effective decisions now, and in five years, ten years, or twenty years. You will feel that you have more control over the course of your life. You may not always know exactly where you are headed, but by knowing and using the career and life planning process, you can make better decisions when you come to each junction along the way and have to choose between two or more routes.

The career and life planning process involves gathering information so that you can make realistic decisions based on facts and self knowledge rather than on feelings and suggestions of others. Think back to your last major purchase, perhaps a home or a car. How much time and energy did you spend researching and uncovering information about this purchase? What did you do to get the information you needed?

Home	**Car**
• ask neighbors	• research written evaluations
• building inspection	• talk with other owners
• self inspection	• talk with salesperson
• talk with owners	• talk with a mechanic
• talk with real estate agent	• test drive
• talk with former owners	• go to other showrooms
• spend time in neighborhood	• look at competition
• research home values	• talk with loan officer
• talk with mortgage officer	• self-inspection

If you are employed full time five days a week, 50 weeks a year, for forty years, you will spend approximately 10,000 days or 80,000 hours at work. This is a major part of your life, certainly more important than any house or car purchase. Therefore, it is essential for you to take the time and action that is necessary to plan your career. In addition, take time to plan your nonworking hours so that you can have a fulfilling lifestyle. Your career and lifestyle are basic to your achievement of happiness and satisfaction with life. The investment of your time in the career and life planning process can have great rewards.

The importance of this process has been demonstrated by people who have studied the work life, career patterns, and personal needs of adults. Abraham Maslow concentrated his studies on human needs, which he classified in a hierarchy. Basic needs such as food, water, and safety are in the lower part of the hierarchy, while the satisfaction needs such as love, knowledge, self-respect, and self-actualization form the upper part. People work not only to satisfy the more basic needs, but also to fulfill their need for a sense of purpose, for self-worth, and for success. It is important to recognize work as an integral part of this sense of fulfillment. Realize that it is difficult to deal with the higher level needs if the lower level needs have not been met. In practical terms, it is difficult to deal with career satisfaction if one has no job and does not know where the money will come from to put food on the table.[1]

John Holland's approach to the study of career choice could be nicknamed "birds of a feather stick together." Holland concluded that people in similar occupations have similar personalities and personal preferences. In making a career decision, therefore, it would be helpful for a person to consider careers which attract people with similar interests and personality characteristics. Interest in a career and in the people with whom one works is often the key to motivation.[2] This is the basis of the extensive use of interest inventories in the career planning process. The two names most often associated with these inventories are Edward K. Strong and G. Frederick Kuder.

Donald Super's evolutionary view of career development illustrates the dynamic nature of this process. Super identified two major stages in career development: the exploratory stage and the establishment stage. Within these stages, he defined five major tasks:

1. crystallization—considering career goals and formulating general preferences.
2. specification—investigating career options and looking internally at one's self.
3. implementation—setting out to achieve the career goals and obtaining a job in the field.
4. stabilization—maintaining a position and developing competence in one's career.
5. consolidation—planning ahead for future career growth.

It is important to note that this is an ongoing process, involving continual change and evaluation throughout one's life.

1. Abraham Maslow, Motivation and Personality, 2e (New York: Harper & Row, 1970).
2. John Holland, *Making Vocational Choices: A Theory of Careers* (Englewood Cliffs, N.J.: Prentice-Hall, 1985).

Comprehension Questions: *Circle the letter of the best answer.*

1. The purpose of this passage is to:
   a. tell you how to go about getting a job
   b. create a system of job hunting techniques
   c. indicate the importance of interviewing techniques
   d. discuss the importance of career planning

2. John Holland's idea of "birds of a feather stick together" refers to:
   a. people in similar positions have similar personalities/personal preferences
   b. individual who see things in life differently
   c. people who cannot get along with one another because of personality differences
   d. groups working together for the betterment of the whole group

3. Career planning can be said to be:
   a. a one time decision one makes
   b. an ongoing process throughout life
   c. difficult to reach for most persons
   d. a once in a life time decision

Essay Question

Write a brief answer to the following question.

Why is career and life planning important to you?

Time-Rate Conversion Chart

Min:Sec	WPM	Min:Sec	WPM
1:00	736	4:30	164
1:10	631	4:40	158
1:20	552	4:50	152
1:30	491	5:00	147
1:40	442	5:10	142
1:50	401	5:20	138
2:00	368	5:30	134
2:10	340	5:40	130
2:20	315	5:50	126
2:30	294	6:00	123
2:40	276	6:10	119
2:50	260	6:20	116
3:00	245	6:30	113
3:10	232	6:40	110
3:20	221	6:50	108
3:30	210	7:00	105
3:40	201	7:10	103
3:50	192	7:20	100
4:00	184	7:30	98
4:10	177	7:40	96
4:20	170	7:50	94

The World's Homeless Millions

Unesco

	Hour Min. Secs.
A. Ending time:	___ ___ ___
B. Starting time:	___ ___ ___
C. A – B = Reading time:	___ ___

The General Assembly of the United Nations has declared 1987 the International Year of Shelter for the Homeless. More than 1,000 million people—a quarter of the world population—are either literally homeless or live in extremely poor housing and unhealthy environments. About 100 million people have no shelter whatsoever; they sleep in the streets, under bridges, on waste ground, in alleys and doorways.

The problem of inadequate housing is universal. It is common to industrialized and developing countries, to urban and rural areas. Because of an unprecedented urban explosion, the developing countries are faced with the formidable task of providing shelter, services and work in cities for an additional 150,000 people every day.

In the shanty-towns the urban poor live in helpless insecurity, evicted repeatedly from homes which are demolished before their eyes and confronted by hostile officials who refuse to recognize their existence. Hostility breeds hostility. In these mush-rooming squatter colonies, a generation of city-dwellers is growing up with no stake in the present social order, which they find unrelentingly oppressive. Many of them hold society responsible for their degraded lives; many also have learned to live by preying upon it.

City after city has therefore turned into a powder keg of crime and violence. Governments have responded by increasing the numbers and powers of the police, a policy which has at best treated the symptoms of the crisis and not its causes. As a result social peace has become more and more fragile.

Many of the remedies chosen have aggravated the disease. For example, the authorities perceive that the quality of housing in the cities is poor and that living conditions are unhygienic. The solution they adopt is to raise housing standards through stricter enforcement of more exacting building codes.

However, higher standards increase the cost of construction and place legal housing even further beyond the reach of the urban poor, more and more of whom are forced into shanty-towns and inner-city slums. The authorities find that there are too many squatters, clear their colonies and raze their hovels to the ground.

Reprinted from the Unesco Courier, January, 1987.

Most governments have tried to rehouse squatters in State-built housing. This has not solved the problem either. Not only has the pace of public construction lagged far behind the growth of the cities, but even State-built dwellings of this kind have proved far too expensive for the poor. The authorities have therefore been forced to subsidize the poor and have quickly found that the cost is far too high. This dismal failure has often led them to avoid the problem of providing shelter by pretending that it has ceased to exist.

Hectic urban growth and the rising demand for housing push up rents to levels far higher than what the poor, and even large sections of the middle class, can pay. The authorities respond by imposing rent control, a solution which makes investment in housing uneconomic and dries up the supply of new dwelling units, thus increasing the pressure on existing units and accelerating the growth of squatter colonies.

Most obstacles to the provision of shelter are man-made, rooted in laws and economic conditions. The removal of these hurdles involves first of all guaranteeing the urban poor a secure title to plots of land, however small these may be; secondly, allowing them to build whatever kind of housing they can afford and leaving them free to improve it when their means permit; thirdly, meeting their need for sanitation and safe drinking water in the cheapest way possible; and lastly giving them access to financial and technical assistance in building their homes.

In the search for low cost options, architects and shelter planners have found that the best way to start is by taking a hard look at a country's traditional architecture and construction methods. This approach, once practised exclusively by imaginative architects, has now been widely adopted by shelter planners and is yielding rich dividends. Unbaked clay bricks are, for example, not only considerably cheaper than cement blocks or fired bricks, they are also much better thermal insulators.

The second important lesson that planners have learned is that if shelter can be brought within the means of the poor, then instead of being a drag on the economy, investment in housing for low-income groups can become a powerful and sustained stimulus for economic growth in a developing country.

If they are to solve the shelter problem the developing countries must mobilize the savings of the poor to finance the construction of their own homes. Not only must private builders become involved as entrepreneurs in building houses for low-income groups, but the output of the building materials industry must be reoriented to meet the need for cheap building materials.

This does not mean that the industry should accept low profit returns on the production and sale of these materials. It implies that the industry must be given the technological support needed to produce cheap building materials for low-cost housing. A final but very important point is that the success and viability of shelter projects depend heavily on the involvement of the beneficiaries.

The urban and rural poor have shown a tremendous capacity to improve their housing conditions with little or no external assistance—thus demonstrating the need for policies aimed at "helping the poor to help themselves", a need being increasingly recognized by governments in their development policies and programmes.

This approach to human settlement policies is increasingly being adopted by the governments of developing countries. Thus there is hope that current trends can be reversed, that present conditions are not unchangeable and that this formidable challenge can still be met.

Comprehension Questions: *Circle the letter of the best answer.*

1. The author believes the remedies used by government agencies have:
   a. solved most of the housing problems for the poor
   b. increased the chances of new housing in the areas
   c. caused people to have hope that their housing needs will be met
   d. aggravated the disease

2. The author believes the solution to housing for the poor is:
   a. found in developing inexpensive building materials
   b. through writing grants that will provide money for building projects
   c. by having big business take a smaller profit to keep the costs down
   d. through government intervention

3. In this passage, the author is:
   a. trying to convince us that government needs to take more action
   b. explaining the need for more money to build low-cost housing
   c. helping us understand the dilemma faced by millions of homeless people
   d. defending the position that the poor could improve their own housing conditions

Essay Question

Write a brief answer to the following question.

What have planners learned concerning how to improve and make housing for the poor more attainable?

Time-Rate Conversion Chart

Min:Sec	WPM	Min:Sec	WPM	Min:Sec	WPM
1:00	937	4:30	208	8:00	117
1:10	803	4:40	201	8:10	115
1:20	703	4:50	194	8:20	112
1:30	625	5:00	187	8:30	110
1:40	562	5:10	181	8:40	108
1:50	511	5:20	176	8:50	106
2:00	469	5:30	170	9:00	104
2:10	432	5:40	165	9:10	102
2:20	402	5:50	161	9:20	100
2:30	375	6:00	156	9:30	99
2:40	351	6:10	152	9:40	97
2:50	331	6:20	148	9:50	95
3:00	312	6:30	144		
3:10	296	6:40	141		
3:20	281	6:50	137		
3:30	268	7:00	134		
3:40	256	7:10	131		
3:50	244	7:20	128		
4:00	234	7:30	125		
4:10	225	7:40	122		
4:20	210	7:50	120		

9–25

Who Decides What Is News?

	Hour	Min.	Secs.
A. Ending time:	——	——	——
B. Starting time:	——	——	——
C. A – B = Reading time:		——	——

Ronald Lovell and Philip Geraci

The process of selection, is almost always the same. The decision that something is newsworthy is based on the experience, biases and gut feelings of those in gate-keeping positions who are almost always influenced by competitive pressure as well. Beyond using the hypothetical, how do actual media people decide what news is and then set out to cover it?

In 1964, Herbert J. Gans, a professor of sociology at Columbia University, began a study of what he called "what this society tells itself about itself through the news and why." To do so he concentrated on domestic news as reported by the national news media, specifically the "CBS Evening News," "NBC Nightly News," *Newsweek* and *Time*.[1]

As outlined by Gans in his subsequent book, *Deciding What's News,* the typical television network news program is structured like a newspaper: the most important story of the day comes first, followed by two additional sections (separated by commercial messages) of other hard news stories, most of them domestic and taking place in Washington. The final sections consist of features. The broadcast ends with a human interest piece that is usually humorous.

The newsmagazines, each containing about 50 pages of news columns a week, combine dramatic narrative with dramatic still pictures. Both divide stories into "front of the book"—national, international and business news of the week—and "back of the book"—sections appearing only once or twice a month and dealing with specific subjects such as law, religion, sports, film, theater, art and the press. Unlike a newspaper front page and the lead story on a television news program, news magazines do not always place the most important story in their most prominent spot, on the cover. Although the cover story is always important, it does not always deal with a subject in the same way a newspaper front page and a lead item of a TV news show do.

From Ronald Lovell and Philip Geraci: *THE MODERN MASS MEDIA MACHINE.* Copyright 1987 by Kendall/Hunt Publishing Company. Reprinted by permission.

1. Herbert J. Gans, *Deciding What's News* (New York: Pantheon Books, 1979).

In deciding who makes news, Gans divided people into "knowns" (incumbent presidents, presidential candidates, leading federal officials, state and local officials, and alleged and actual violators of the law and the mores) and "unknowns" (protestors, rioters and strikers; victims; alleged and actual violators of the laws and mores—differing from the "knowns" in the same category by the nature of their crime and the victim; participants in unusual activities; and voters, survey respondents and other aggregates).

But news is also made up of activities, according to Gans: government conflicts and disagreements; government decisions, proposals and ceremonies; government personnel changes; protests, violent and nonviolent; crimes, scandals and investigations; disasters, actual and averted; innovations and traditional activities; and national ceremonies.

But Gans also thinks that news decisions are made on the basis of values held by journalists working in news organizations: values based on ethnocentrism, altuistic democracy, responsible capitalism, small-town pastoralism, individualism and moderatism.

With this as a background, Gans then moves into the real heart of his study: how and why the people responsible for story selection do their jobs. "Story selection is essentially composed of two processes: one determines the availability of news and relates journalists to sources," he writes, "the other determines the suitability of news, which ties journalists to audiences."

Under availability, Gans sees what he calls a "tug of war" emerging between journalists who see people mainly as potential sources and sources who see themselves as people with the chance to provide information that promotes their interests, publicizes their ideas or just gets their names and faces into the news. While sources make themselves available, it is journalists who decide if they are suitable. The access to journalists is shaped by incentives, power, the ability to supply suitable information, and geographic and social proximity. Suitability decisions are made by journalists on the basis of sources' past suitability, productivity, reliability, trustworthiness, authoritativeness and articulateness.

Gans discusses other factors in the process of deciding what is news: objectivity, values and ideology; profits and audiences; and pressures, censorships and self-censorship. "A simple summary . . . would suggest that news is about the economic, political, social and cultural hierarchies we call nation and society," Gans writes. He says that most news reports are about those at the top of the hierarchy and those on the bottom who threaten those on the top. The reports go to those in the middle.

The journalist in the United States is a person with the leeway to make the choices for everyone else as to what to cover and present as news. Gans calls this activity one of the journalist's prime functions. Unlike other countries in which the government does the managing, the United States allows news organizations and their journalists to do so. In the process, he concludes, "they also regulate individuals and groups with messages; and, in so doing, they maintain order in the symbolic arena." And that, if nothing else, reveals the vast power and responsibility of American media, day after day, year after year.

Comprehension Questions: *Circle the letter of the best answer.*

1. In deciding what news will appear, Gans indicates that:
   a. stories are divided between the knowns and the unknowns of the day
   b. features are decided upon for their explosive nature
   c. news reports are chosen for their audience appeal
   d. anchor men and women make the choices for their news cast

2. Most news reports are aimed at:
   a. the people at the top of the society
   b. the general population in the middle
   c. the bottom group so they can react to what is happening to them
   d. to a divergent audience made up of all segments of the population

3. In this passage, the author is attempting to:
   a. convince us that reporting is unbiased
   b. inform us about the nature of choosing news stories
   c. point out the inconsistencies of news stories in the different media
   d. develop the point that reporting is scientific

Essay Question

Write a brief answer to the following question.

What are the major factors a journalist looks at to determine if a story is worth pursuing?

Time-Rate Conversion Chart

Min:Sec	WPM	Min:Sec	WPM	Min:Sec	WPM
1:00	843	4:30	187	8:00	105
1:10	723	4:40	181	8:10	103
1:20	632	4:50	174	8:20	101
1:30	562	5:00	169	8:30	99
1:40	506	5:10	163	8:40	97
1:50	460	5:20	158	8:50	95
2:00	422	5:30	153		
2:10	389	5:40	149		
2:20	361	5:50	145		
2:30	337	6:00	141		
2:40	316	6:10	137		
2:50	298	6:20	133		
3:00	281	6:30	130		
3:10	266	6:40	126		
3:20	253	6:50	123		
3:30	241	7:00	120		
3:40	230	7:10	118		
3:50	220	7:20	115		
4:00	211	7:30	112		
4:10	202	7:40	110		
4:20	195	7:50	108		

An Energy History of the United States and the World

	Hour	Min.	Secs.
A. Ending time:	___	___	___
B. Starting time:	___	___	___
C. A – B = Reading time:		___	___

John Christensen

In the beginning, people relied on renewable sources of energy. The first humans lived on solar energy stored in food and other plant parts. They ate fruits and vegetables and animals that ate plants (and other animals). They burned wood from fallen trees. Even when they learned to broaden their energy base and use the winds to move ships and flowing water to drive their machines, these early civilized humans were still a solar-powered society.

Even though the energy stored in fossil fuels was discovered early in human history, the fossil fuel age really began with the Industrial Revolution. During that period, coal was used extensively for heating buildings. As the mines went deeper seeking that coal, problems with flooding arose. Spurred by the demand for power to pump water out of the mines the steam engine was invented. Powering these steam engines consumed even more coal. As a result, a whole host of industrial applications of the perfected steam engine were discovered.

A dependence on fossil fuels came more slowly in the United States. Europe was already well into the Industrial Revolution at the end of the 19th century. On the other hand, the U.S. was still operating with renewable energy sources—wind, wood, and water.

Wood alone accounted for about 90 percent of U.S. energy consumption in 1850. The average consumption (mostly for home heating) by the frontier American was 17½ cords per year. (A cord of wood is a stack 4 ft. by 4 ft. by 8 ft.) This wood was used inefficiently. Its total energy content is 2½ times the average amount of energy used to heat a home today.

Most of the wood (140 million cords in 1850) was used in houses. Wood also was an important source of energy for the country's young industry and transportation system. Trains and steamboats burned 7 or 8 million cords of wood annually. Almost 2 million cords were turned into charcoal for smelting iron. This consumption of charcoal, amounting to about 750,000 tons, is now almost matched by the consumption of charcoal in outdoor barbeque grills.

The conversion to coal began to take place at the end of the 19th century. Virgin forests were cut down and it became necessry to transport energy to its point of consumption. Wood, when burned, produces about 6.3 MJ per pound while coal has more than twice that energy density—13.0 MJ per pound. If you are going to transport energy, you want to carry as much per pound as you can. Thus, coal replaced wood. Later, oil replaced coal.

The switch from wood to coal began at the end of the 19th century. By 1910, coal accounted for three quarters of the total. The use of oil and natural gas began to grow during the 1920's. Petroleum is easier to use and it is cleaner. At the end of World War II the petroleum age arrived. It now appears that the dominance of the petroleum products (oil and natural gas) may also be drawing to a close. In 1974, they made up 77 percent of the total. In 1982, the share of oil and natural gas fell to 69 percent.

Is a transition to a new dominant source beginning? The 1983 data are tantalizingly unclear. We see two small surges. Nuclear energy's contribution has grown from less than 1 percent in 1970 to about 4 percent in 1983. There are those who see in this growth the beginning of a nuclear age. Also coal is showing a renaissance. It contributed 17 percent of the total in 1975. That rose to 23 percent in 1983.

It would be foolhardy to try to predict the future of either source right now. What happens will depend on the outcome of a complicated and interrelated set of environmental, economic, and political considerations.

Comprehension Questions: *Circle the letter of the best answer.*

1. The United States in the late 1800's depended mainly on:
    a. coal for heating and industry
    b. solar energy
    c. wood for heating and industry
    d. wind and water for energy

2. The author of ths passage is attempting to:
    a. convince you that nuclear energy will replace other forms of energy in the next decade
    b. inform you that the history of energy from early times to today
    c. predict the coming problems with energy sources in the future
    d. create a picture of gloom and doom for coming generations

3. In 1983 we discovered an increase in:
    a. the consumption of wood for fuel
    b. the use of petroleum products
    c. the renaissance of coal
    d. the use of natural gas

Essay Questions

Write a brief answer to the following question.

What potential problem could the world community face in the coming decades concerning energy consumption?

Time-Rate Conversion Chart

Min:Sec	WPM	Min:Sec	WPM
1:00	618	4:30	137
1:10	530	4:40	132
1:20	464	4:50	128
1:30	412	5:00	124
1:40	371	5:10	120
1:50	337	5:20	116
2:00	309	5:30	112
2:10	285	5:40	109
2:20	265	5:50	106
2:30	247		
2:40	232		
2:50	218		
3:00	206		
3:10	195		
3:20	185		
3:30	177		
3:40	169		
3:50	161		
4:00	155		
4:10	148		
4:20	143		

Diversity in Ecosystems

John Christensen

	Hour	Min.	Secs.
A. Ending time:	———	———	———
B. Starting time:	———	———	———
C. A – B = Reading time:		———	———

Diversity is an important characteristic of all natural cosystems. Diversity means simply how many different kinds of living things there are, how great their numbers, and how they are spread out in a particular geographic area. Suppose you construct a relatively simple ecosystem in an aquarium. You put in only one kind of fish and only one kind of water plant. This ecosystem would not be very diverse. If you let your aquarium sit open to the air for a while, the ecosystem would change. Many different kinds of microscopic organisms would probably grow in the water. After a month or two, you might look at a drop of aquarium water under the microscope and find algae, fungi, protozoans, tiny crustaceans, and numerous insect larvae. The ecosystem would have become much more diverse. Why? There would now be many more kinds of organisms present.

Suppose you planted a garden plot with only one hybrid species of squash. What would happen after awhile if you did not attend your garden very carefully? Your garden which started out as a *monoculture* of a single plant species would become more diverse. Many different kinds of weeds would sprout up. Many different insects and other consumers would come to feed on the fruits of your labors.

Human gardeners and farmers usually strive for ecosystems of less diversity. Weeds are pulled. Pests are killed for good reason. The farmer wants to capture as much energy as possible in the form of food fit for humans. Farmers want to lose as little as possible to other organisms. Weeds competing for space, water, and sunlight or pests actively consuming desired crops are eliminated.

There is a price to be paid. Less diverse ecosystems are not as stable as more diverse ones. A diverse system conserves its nutrients, is resistant to pest and disease invasion, and can withstand a fairly wide range of climatic variation. This strength results from diversity. If one species is wiped out, there are many others to take its place.

Monocultures, such as an orange grove or a wheat field, must have their nutrients replaced by fertilizers. They lack resistance to pests and disease. They are usually protected by chemical herbicides and pesticides. They are also threatened by unusual changes of climate (dry spells and cold snaps) and are likely to require artificial and expensive irrigation and shielding.

From John Christensen: *GLOBAL SCIENCE: Energy, Resources, Environment.* Copyright 1985 by Kendall/Hunt Publishing Company. Reprinted by permission.

Limiting Factors in Ecosystems

What determines the combination of plant and animal types found in a particular ecosystem? Why is one area a desert, another a forest, and still another a grassland? The kind of biome occurring in a particular place at a particular time is primarily a result of temperature, precipitation, and soil type. Note that little moisture and high average temperatures result in a desert. How might human activity change this picture?

One important ecological principle may help answer that question. The *law of limiting factors* applies here. The factor that is most *deficient* in an ecosystem determines the presence (or absence) of any given plant or animal. It is said that people can live without air for three minutes, without water for three days, and without food for three months. Whether or not those time estimates are accurate, the law of limiting factors is in effect. A human being can perish very quickly in an environment where water and food are abundant, but air is in short supply. Similarly, where air and food are plentiful but water scarce, death is just as certain. In this case, water (not air) is the limiting factor.

Comprehension Questions: *Circle the letter of the best answer*

1. Human gardners and farmers seek:
   a. highly diverse ecosystems on their land
   b. complicated ecosystems for their land
   c. ecosystems of less diversity
   d. monocultures in which to grow their crops

2. You can conclude from reading this passage that:
   a. the more diverse an ecosystem the better
   b. the use of pesticides is needed to yield good crops
   c. monocultures are the ideal condition for land areas
   d. artificial irrigation is the way to keep land abundant

3. The law of limiting factors says:
   a. abundant supplies of nutrients are needed to sustain life
   b. most organisms are limited in their growth potential
   c. the factor that is most deficient in an ecosystem determines the existence of an organism
   d. human activity is determined by the amount of energy expanded by the specific species

Essay Question

Write a brief answer to the following question.

What factors determine the make-up of an ecosystem?

Time-Rate Conversion Chart

Min:Sec	WPM	Min:Sec	WPM
1:00	620	4:30	138
1:10	531	4:40	133
1:20	465	4:50	128
1:30	413	5:00	124
1:40	372	5:10	120
1:50	338	5:20	116
2:00	310	5:30	113
2:10	286	5:40	109
2:20	266	5:50	106
2:30	248	6:00	103
2:40	233	6:10	101
2:50	219	6:20	98
3:00	207	6:30	95
3:10	196	6:40	93
3:20	186	6:50	91
3:30	177		
3:40	169		
3:50	162		
4:00	155		
4:10	149		
4:20	143		

9-28

Protecting Tots From Drug Poisonings

Bill Rados

	Hour	Min.	Secs.
A. Ending time:	___	___	___
B. Starting time:	___	___	___
C. A – B = Reading time:		___	___

Parents should not rely on child-resistant packaging alone to protect their youngsters from accidentally swallowing prescription drugs. According to a government survey, in some cases the safety packages do not work as they should, or the caps have been left off or are loose. In other cases, the pharmacist may have filled the prescription in a non-child-resistant package without the buyer's knowledge.

These are some of the findings of a 1986 study of 2,015 cases in which children under 5 accidentally swallowed oral prescription drugs. The study was done by the American Association of Poison Control Centers (AAPCC) for the U.S. Consumer Product Safety Commission (CPSC). Parents or other adults who were in the house at the time were interviewed to learn how and where the accidents happened.

Childhood poisonings from prescription drugs have dropped markedly since a federal regulation requiring child-resistant packaging was passed in 1974. Still, more than 60,000 cases of children under 5 accidentally swallowing prescription drugs were reported to the 56 AAPCC poison control centers in 1985, the last year for which figures are available.

To see if the child-resistant packages involved in the accidents were working properly, those interviewed were asked to send the drug containers to CPSC for testing. Of the 306 child-resistant packages received, 65 percent were not working properly. The study report stated that although the small number of child-resistant packages received by CPSC could not be considered a representative sample of all prescription drug packages, the high failure rate is "of concern." The report noted that "the problem suggests the continuing need for surveillance and enforcement of special packaging standards."

"Because the data show that some child-resistant packaging in the home may not be functioning properly, parents cannot rely upon packaging alone to prevent access by young children," the report warned.

Also alarming is the finding that 17 percent of the drugs involved were in no container at all, but were found loose by the child.

Reprinted from FDA Consumer, March, 1987.

Almost one-third of all medicines that were in a prescription container at the time of the accident were not in child-resistant packaging. Yet, many of the people surveyed said they had not asked for non-child-resistant containers when the prescription was filled. Additionally, over half the containers that weren't child-resistant had been dispensed to parents of children under 5, and 18 percent had been dispensed for the child. These facts indicate that pharmacists may have dispensed non-child-resistant containers without a request from the purchaser or a physician, in violation of the Poison Prevention Packaging Act, according to CPSC.

Ninety-one percent of the children involved in the accidents were between 1 and 3. Forty-three percent were age 2. These findings indicate that "the normal developmental characteristics of children are important risk factors," CPSC stated.

The survey also asked about the types of drugs involved, who they belonged to, and where the medicine was stored when the accident happened.

Antibiotics were the most common drug, representing 23 percent of all drugs in the study. These were often liquid antibiotics that had been prescribed for the child or a brother or sister. Birth control pills and other hormones were the second most common drugs, representing 15 percent of the cases. The next three categories were painkillers (10 percent), heart drugs (9 percent), and sedatives (6 percent). These three are important because "they present substantial risk due to their potent toxicity," according to CPSC.

It was the child's mother to whom the drugs most often belonged (27 percent), followed by the child (22 percent). Thirty-one percent of the drugs belonged to someone not in the child's immediate family. This includes grandparents (17 percent) and other older adults who often are taking highly toxic drugs and are not always aware that they should take extra precautions to keep their medicine out of the reach of young children.

The kitchen was the most common storage place for medicines (48 percent of the cases), followed by the bedroom (24 percent) and the living room (10 percent). Interestingly, the bathroom was fourth on the list (8 percent). "These findings indicate that medication is stored where it is convenient to take, which makes it readily accessible to children as well," CPSC stated.

"The results of the survey show that all consumers, regardless of whether they have young children of their own or not, should take care to obtain their prescriptions in child-resistant packaging and to always resecure the caps tightly," CPSC concluded. "Additionaly, care must be taken to keep the medicine stored out of sight and out of reach, especially medicine being taken on a regular basis."

Comprehension Questions: *Circle the letter of the best answer.*

1. It appears from the information in this passage that:
   a. child-resistant packaged drugs has virtually eliminated drug poisonings of children
   b. the government is satisfied with the results of reducing the number drug poisonings in the United States
   c. the high failure rate of child-resistant packaging is of concern to the Consumer Product Safety Commission
   d. the American Association of Poison Control Centers is doing all it can to insure safety in packaging drugs

2. The author in this passage is attempting to:
   a. Inform the reader about the concerns about the packaging of drugs
   b. scare the public into believing little is being done to protect children from unnecessary drug poisonings
   c. convince the reader that all is well in the drug industry
   d. analyze the ability of the government to create a safety net for consumers of prescription drugs

3. The area that is the most common place to store medicines is the:
   a. bathroom
   b. living room
   c. the bedroom
   d. the kitchen

Essay Question

Write a brief answer to the following question.

Why is it important to use child-resistant packaging for prescription drugs?

Time-Rate Conversion Chart

Min:Sec	WPM	Min:Sec	WPM
1:00	781	4:30	174
1:10	669	4:40	167
1:20	586	4:50	162
1:30	521	5:00	156
1:40	469	5:10	151
1:50	426	5:20	146
2:00	391	5:30	142
2:10	360	5:40	138
2:20	335	5:50	134
2:30	312	6:00	130
2:40	293	6:10	127
2:50	276	6:20	123
3:00	260	6:30	120
3:10	247	6:40	117
3:20	234	6:50	114
3:30	223	7:00	112
3:40	213	7:10	109
3:50	204	7:20	107
4:00	195	7:30	104
4:10	187	7:40	102
4:20	180	7:50	100

9-29

What Makes the Cascade Volcanoes Hazardous?

Ann Harris and Esther Tuttle

	Hour Min. Secs.
A. Ending time:	___ ___ ___
B. Starting time:	___ ___ ___
C. A – B = Reading time:	___ ___

In March 1975, Mount Baker began belching out clouds of steam from Sherman Crater, located on the southeast side of the cone about 1,150 feet down from the glacier-covered summit. For several months thermal activity increased, melting some of the ice in the crater. Sulfurous ash came out with the steam and polluted the air downwind of the volcano.

Public campgrounds in the area were closed because of the possibility of a mudflow being triggered by melting snow mixed with hot ash and other debris. The level of Baker Lake, a reservoir at the foot of the mountain, was lowered because U.S. Geological Survey geologists feared that a mudflow might cause the dam to break, which would devastate the communities farther down the valley. Thermal activity subsided after a time, but the possibility of a dangerous eruption is still very real as recent events at Mount St. Helens (170 miles to the south, air distance) have demonstrated.

Composite volcanoes, like those in the Cascades, sometimes have explosive eruptions, depending upon the amount of gas in the lava and its *viscosity,* or resistance to flow. The viscosity of a lava controls the ease or difficulty with which the gas escapes into the atmosphere. Composite cones are built up by lava that is predominantly intermediate, or andesitic, in composition. Andesitic lava is ordinarily more viscous than basaltic lava; but if the temperature of an andesite lava is extremely hot, then it becomes more fluid, or nonviscous, and is able to flow easily from a crater or vent. If a vent becomes clogged and gas pressure builds up, then an explosion occurs which ejects pyroclastic debris, clouds of ash, etc. Usually eruptions of composite volcanoes are intermittent, with periods of possibly violent activity followed by many years of apparent dormancy. Thus volcanoes of this type are long-lasting and tend to construct very large, lofty cones over a long span of time.

Sudden release of intense heat is the immediate danger when a volcanic explosion occurs. All living things on the volcano's flanks may be incinerated by the blast. As hot ash, gas, and steam spew out, snow and ice turn to hot water and steam that mix with ash and pour down the mountain as a mudflow which buries everything in its path.

The water storage reservoirs that have been constructed on the lower slopes of most of the Cascade volcanoes may serve as catch basins for mudflows—providing enough warning has been given so that the water can be drawn down. Whether or not the dams can hold is uncertain. A large enough mudflow could overtop or destroy a dam, endangering all the communities downstream as hot mud and water race down a river valley. Such a flood would be catastrophic.

Hot falling ash carried rapidly downwind may start fires over a wide area, contaminate water supplies, collapse roofs, render highways impassable, clog storm drains, endanger aircraft, damage crops, etc.

Can eruptions be predicted? The monitoring program of the U.S. Geological Survey, in cooperation with state surveys, seeks to interpret data and issue warnings based on several types of indicators: (1) increases in thermal activity; (2) increases or changes in seismic activity; (3) gravity and magnetic measurements; (4) remote sensing and infrared studies; (5) gas and temperature monitoring; and (6) observations of actual changes (i.e., bulges, tilting, etc.) in the volcano's outward conformation through comparison of photographs or use of time-lapse photography.

In the Cascades, volcanic eruptions have been infrequent in terms of human life spans. In fact, before Mount Baker started heating up and steaming, many residents did not believe the geologists and other scientists who warned of potential hazards. However, Mount St. Helens's behavior since 1980 has succeeded in making believers out of skeptics. What is now recognized is that major evacuations are really the only adjustment that human beings can make when a volcano becomes threatening.

Comprehension Questions: *Circle the letter of the best answer.*

1. After reading this passage you can conclude:
   a. composite volcanoes are generally inactive and cause little disruption
   b. composite volcanoes like the Cascades have been dormant for many years
   c. composite volcanoes are long-lasting and tend to construct very large, lofty cones
   d. composite volcanoes have erupted on a frequent basis over the past fifty years

2. Volcanic eruptions can be:
   a. predicted as to when and where an eruption will take place
   b. determined by a series of specific tests
   c. prevented by the use of explosives
   d. monitored for certain indicators that help predict an eruption

3. Volcanic eruptions often lead to:
    a. massive destruction in the immediate area
    b. short term damage to the wilderness in its path
    c. difficulties for decades
    d. damages to plant, animal, and human life in the region

Essay Question

Write a brief answer to the following question.

What are some indicators that a volcano may erupt?

Time-Rate Conversion Chart

Min:Sec	WPM	Min:Sec	WPM
1:00	641	4:30	142
1:10	549	4:40	137
1:20	481	4:50	133
1:30	427	5:00	128
1:40	385	5:10	124
1:50	350	5:20	120
2:00	321	5:30	117
2:10	296	5:40	113
2:20	275	5:50	110
2:30	256	6:00	107
2:40	240	6:10	104
2:50	226	6:20	101
3:00	214	6:30	99
3:10	202	6:40	96
3:20	192	6:50	94
3:30	183		
3:40	175		
3:50	167		
4:00	160		
4:10	154		
4:20	148		

Myths and Facts of Generic Drugs

FDA Consumer

"Generic drugs" is the term for prescription drugs that are the same as brand-name drugs. (There are generic versions of nonprescription drugs, too, but this article is concerned only with prescription medications.) As with any new type of product, most brand-name prescription drugs are developed under a patent. This patent serves to protect a drug firm's investment in developing the drug by giving the company the sole right to sell the drug while the patent is in effect. Thus, generic versions of that drug may be sold by competing drug companies only after the patent expires—generally about 17 years after the original drug was discovered.

Because competition enters the picture when a patent expires, generic drugs usually sell for less than the brand-name product from the original manufacturer. The fact that generics generally sell for less has led many people to believe that generics are in some way inferior to brand-name products. That's not true; generic drugs contain exactly the same active ingredients as the brand-name drug and must be just as safe and effective.

Here's some more information to clarify the record on generic drugs:

MYTH: A new law permits the Food and Drug Administration to ignore safety and effectiveness requirements for generic drugs while brand-name drugs still must meet these rigid tests.

FACT: The new law, the 1984 Drug Price Competition and Patent Restoration Act, does not lower any standards for generic drugs. Previously, generic manufacturers had to perform their own tests to prove that the active ingredients in their products were safe and effective. But since that had already been proven when the equivalent brand-name drug was first marketed by the original manufacturer, there was really no need to test all over again. However, generic drugs must go through scientific testing to show that they work just as well as the original drug. Although the law is new, generic drugs are not. They've been around for many years. The new law just makes them available for many more drugs.

Reprinted from FDA Consumer, September, 1987.

MYTH: Generic drugs just won't do the job as well as brand-name drugs.

FACT: Under the new law, generic drugs must be bioequivalent to their brand-name counterparts to gain FDA approval. That means that the generics must contain the same active ingredients and must be identical in strength, dosage form (tablet, solution, etc.), and route of administration (for example, taken by mouth or through injection). Further, they must release the same amount of drug into the body as the brand-name drug.

MYTH: Generic drugs are not as potent as brand-name drugs.

FACT: Generic drug manufacturers have to ensure that their products are of the same quality, strength, purity, and stability as the brand-name products.

MYTH: Generics take longer to act in the body.

FACT: In seeking FDA approval for their products, generic makers must submit evidence that their drugs will have the same therapeutic effect as the brand-name counterparts. This means that a generic product can be expected to deliver to the bloodstream, or other site where the drug does its work, the same amount of active ingredient as the original product.

MYTH: Generics are not as safe as brand-name drugs.

FACT: FDA requires that all *drug products be safe and effective. Since generics use the same active ingredients as their brand-name counterparts and work the same way in the body, generics are as safe and effective as their brand-name equivalants.*

MYTH: FDA requires that brand-name manufacturers test new drugs in thousands of patients, but it lets generic firms get by with tests in only 20 or 30 healthy volunteers.

FACT: Generic drugs are duplicates of products that have already been tested for safety and effectiveness. Therefore, generic manufacturers need only prove to FDA that their drug behaves the same way in the body as the original version. That requires only small-scale tests. In fact, the same small-scale testing is done for brand-name drugs whenever they are reformulated.

MYTH: Generic manufacturers only have to prove that the active ingredients in their products get to the bloodstream. That doesn't mean that their products are used by the body in the same way.

FACT: When the same amount of the active ingredients of the generic version gets into the bloodstream at the same rate as the brand-name version, there is no scientific reason to believe that the effects of the two drugs will differ.

MYTH: Most drugs are tested for bioequivalence in healthy young volunteers, yet 25 percent of all prescription drugs are taken by the elderly who don't react the same to drugs.

FACT: While the elderly may often absorb and process (metabolize) drugs differently than younger people, there is no proof that drugs will perform differently in them. Further, it isn't ethical to force already weakened or disabled patients to give blood samples and face the other discomforts of bioequivalence testing. Further, such patients cannot be used in bioequivalence testing because they are virtually always taking other drugs concurrently.

MYTH: Brand-name drugs are made in modern facilities, while generics are often made in substandard facilities. Thus, generics are generally inferior.

FACT: FDA allows no drugs to be manufactured in substandard facilities. FDA officials inspect more than 5,000 drug plants a year to ensure that standards are met. Generic firms have state-of-the-art plants that compare favorably with those of brand-name firms. (In fact, brand-name firms account for an estimated 70 percent to 80 percent of generic drug production, making duplicate versions of their own or other brand-name companies' drugs, but selling them without the brand name.)

MYTH: Patients using generic products are more likely to suffer side effects than those using brand-name drugs.

FACT: There is no evidence of this. FDA monitors reports from doctors and others of adverse drug reactions and has found no difference in the rates of adverse reactions between generic and brand-name drugs.

Comprehension Questions: *Circle the letter of the best answer.*

1. One fact about generic drugs is:
   a. they are usually more expensive
   b. they are of poorer quality
   c. they are exactly like the original drug
   d. they frequently replace the original drug

2. After reading this passage you could conclude that:
   a. generic drugs are easier to get than original drugs
   b. generic drugs go through the same testing as the original drugs
   c. original drugs are more effective than generic drugs
   d. generic drugs are more available to the public than original drugs

3. By and large doctors tend to:
   a. prescribe original drugs more often because they are safer
   b. leave it up to the patient to determine what brand of drug they will purchase
   c. tell their patients not to use generic drugs
   d. use generic drugs more often because they are more effective

Essay Question

Write a brief answer to the following question.

What are your attitudes about generic drugs now that you have completed this passage?

Time-Rate Conversion Chart

Min:Sec	WPM	Min:Sec	WPM	Min:Sec	WPM
1.00	1000	4:30	222	8:00	125
1:10	857	4:40	214	8:10	122
1:20	750	4:50	207	8:20	120
1:30	667	5:00	200	8:30	118
1:40	600	5:10	194	8:40	115
1:50	545	5:20	188	8:50	113
2:00	500	5:30	182		
2:10	462	5:40	176		
2:20	429	5:50	171		
2:30	400	6:00	167		
2:40	375	6:10	162		
2:50	353	6:20	158		
3:00	333	6:30	154		
3:10	316	6:40	150		
3:20	300	6:50	146		
3:30	286	7:00	143		
3:40	273	7:10	140		
3:50	261	7:20	136		
4:00	250	7:30	133		
4:10	240	7:40	130		
4:20	231	7:50	128		

9-31

Learning to live

Nicole Friderich

	Hour	Min.	Secs.
A. Ending time:	____	____	____
B. Starting time:	____	____	____
C. A – B = Reading time:		____	____

Perseverance is a quality shared by all concerned with the problem of drugs. The men and women involved in law enforcement do not let themselves be disheartened by the fact that only between 10 and 15 per cent of the illicit drug traffic is intercepted as a result of their work. They continue their efforts, seek new methods, draw benefit from modern techniques, and realize the importance of active cooperation with those who are engaged in scientific research into the different drugs, treat drug users, or attempt through education to limit the harm caused by drugs and prevent drug abuse.

The scientists who study the chemical composition of legal and illegal drugs and their physical and psychological effects (about which in many cases we still know very little), therapists, doctors and psychologists, are continuing their work and in some cases making essential discoveries, such as that of endorphins a decade ago.

Neither these specialists nor social workers allow themselves to be discouraged by the fact that their devotion only achieves a "cure" in 30 percent of treated cases of dependence on so-called hard drugs or on alcohol, which may be put in this category. They reflect on experiments that have been carried out, learn from their failures as well as their successes, compare their results, improve their methods, and unflaggingly help those who are trying to free themselves from the grip of drugs. Organizations such as Alcoholics Anonymous, whose members have succeeded in overcoming their dependence on certain substances, support and encourage those who have been unable to do so, and consider that their work should be a continuing effort. The families and friends of drug users often search unremittingly for a solution, sometimes ready to believe in a miracle; their task is a hard one.

Educators, teachers, parents and youth leaders are playing an active role in these joint efforts. Their cooperation is sought by everyone, from therapists to enforcement agents and government authorities, since the importance of their preventive efforts is appreciated. Nothing if not constructive, their role is to help the young and less young to develop their character and strengthen their intellectual, emotional and moral resources, to learn to learn and to learn to be.

Reprinted from the Unesco Courier, July, 1987.

Professional educators have been trained to do this; they understand the theory and practice of teaching, psychology and technical skills. Family members have usually not had such an initiation. In their day-in, day-out task of bringing up young children, possibly not their own, to live a life which in many cases they hope will be better than theirs, they rely on their personal experience, their love, their moral or religious principles.

Efforts, notably those carried out by Unesco, to encourage all those involved in education in the broadest sense to take part in what has been called preventive education, are already bearing fruit. Those concerned with education have become aware of the role they can play and have spared neither their efforts nor their good will. Most of them have volunteered their help but have often asked "What can we do?"

One of the first tasks has been to show them the preventive effects of what they were already doing: character training, the development of a critical approach, decision-making capacities, respect for principles, and understanding of psychological mechanisms; and, of course, the transmission of knowledge of the nature and the effects of certain substances which are already studied as part of some school programmes or which have a domestic use.

It has also been necessary, and this is an essential task, to demystify the idea of drugs as magical and evil substances which have incomprehensible effects and are totally alien to their experience. Many parents and educators have come to understand the problems more fully after thinking honestly and frankly about the use of legal drugs which they take or see others take. Why do people smoke, drink, take tranquilizers, stimulants and medicines which give them a sense of well-being? Are they seeking energy, relaxation, pleasure, an escape from stress? The phenomenon of dependence is not unfamiliar to those who have watched someone try to stop smoking or drinking, or have witnessed the anguish of a person deprived of his or her usual sleeping pill or tranquilizer.

Educators have thus become more fully aware of what they already knew and have defined what they want to find out. They are not by any means seeking an encyclopaedic knowledge of the world's countless drugs (new drugs to cure illness appear every day and each one is potentially beneficial or dangerous). But they do wish to be fully informed about the substances used in their own countries and environments, products which certain groups or younger generations know more about than they do "from their own experience, however biased or incomplete such "knowledge" may be.

Parents and teachers have also made it clear that they want to know how to act in time, before it's "too late". They have asked to be informed about the signs and symptoms of drug taking and quickly realized that the most important thing they can do is to be supportive.

Techniques for opening up channels of communication have been put forward to educators and they have developed others for themselves. Some have discovered the importance of active education methods, pupil participation and learning by doing.

This has had a beneficial effect on their teaching as a whole. The efforts made by educators to confront an immediate problem have committed them to action and in some cases encouraged them to adopt less theoretical approaches.

But their work has not always been crowned with success. Their methods, some imported from other cultures or borrowed from other contexts, have not always been effective. In some cases quick and easily quantifiable results were expected. "Evaluations" have been made without taking into account the objectives which had been set and which could have been achieved with the means available. The authorities, in some cases, and, very often, those who agreed to finance preventive education experiments, have insisted on rapid and spectacular results—forgetting that the education of a human being takes years and that people are free agents—and have attempted to apply to prevention strict cost-benefit criteria.

Far from being discouraged, parents and educators have continued their work. They have formed groups, shared their discoveries, experiences, disappointments and successes. They have exchanged their ideas—and the role of an organization like Unesco has been of inestimable value in this respect. This role is still developing. In all the world regions, in situations where the pattern of drug use varies widely, a growing number of initiatives in favour of preventive education are being taken. Experience and innovation are complementary. No one ever claims that a definitive solution has been found. Problems are being patiently solved as and when they arise.

Educators, families and youth leaders will continue their work. They will not abandon their efforts to prevent drug abuse since in the final analysis their motivation is love for those in their care and whom they wish to help through education to "learn to live".

Comprehension Questions: *Circle the letter of the best answer.*

1. Law enforcement agents are:
   a. satisfied with the arrest rate of drug dealers
   b. concerned that too many people continue to use drugs
   c. not disheartened by the fact that only 10–15% of the illicit drug traffic is stopped
   d. pleased with the high rate of arrests of major distributors of drugs into the United States

2. You can conclude from reading this passage that:
   a. all forms of drug addiction are easily overcome through therapy
   b. drug addiction is a long lasting and difficult problem to cure
   c. law enforcement agents are on top of the drug trafficking in the United States
   d. psychologists and counselors feel the treatments used are long lasting for most patients

3. The most important ingredient others can provide in the recovery of a drug dependent person is:
   a. support
   b. pity
   c. chastisement
   d. dependence

Essay Question

Write a brief answer to the following question.

What is the central message of this passage?

Time-Rate Conversion Chart

Min:Sec	WPM	Min:Sec	WPM	Min:Sec	WPM
1:00	1086	4:30	241	8:00	136
1:10	931	4:40	233	8:10	133
1:20	815	4:50	225	8:20	130
1:30	724	5:00	217	8:30	128
1:40	652	5:10	210	8:40	125
1:50	592	5:20	204	8:50	123
2:00	543	5:30	197	9:00	121
2:10	501	5:40	192	9:10	118
2:20	465	5:50	186	9:20	116
2:30	434	6:00	181	9:30	114
2:40	407	6:10	176	9:40	112
2:50	383	6:20	171	9:50	110
3:00	362	6:30	167	10:00	109
3:10	343	6:40	163	10:10	107
3:20	326	6:50	159	10:20	105
3:30	310	7:00	155	10:30	103
3:40	296	7:10	152	10:40	102
3:50	283	7:20	148	10:50	100
4:00	272	7:30	145		
4:10	261	7:40	142		
4:20	251	7:50	139		

The Myth of Superabundance

	Hour	Min.	Secs.
A. Ending time:	____	____	____
B. Starting time:	____	____	____
C. A − B = Reading time:		____	____

Leonard Pitt

On the settled side of the frontier—on farms and in towns and cities—the colonials also altered their environment, although less radically. The relationship of the people to the land differed markedly from what it was in the Old World. Most of western Europe's forests had long since been cut and its bogs drained of water. By the sixteenth and seventeenth centuries Europeans had learned to preserve wooded areas, terrace hilsides, spread manure for fertilizer, build stone fences to protect crops against grazing animals, construct dikes, and alternate crops to replenish the soil. English agriculture in particular was "geared to the *flow* of nature, not to its sudden exhaustion."

In America the situation was reversed. New land was relatively abundant and cheap. The Chesapeake tobacco planters were faced with the continuous problem of using up the land, for tobacco is an acid crop that quickly exhausts the soil. By the eighteenth century, planters had opened new plots in the West, or were planning to do so. For them soil conservation was time-consuming and costly. The Germans of Pennsylvania perpetuated the old-fashioned habits of husbandry, but most other farmers, as they planted their crops, chopped down trees, shot birds out of the sky, or felled deer, had one eye on the horizon. There, they assumed they would find more and better land and resources when the old land gave out. This created what Stewart Udall, a leading conservationist, calls the "Myth of Superabundance."[1]

The spendthrift use of soil and other farm resources amazed the Swedish botanist Peter Kalm. On a visit to America in 1750 he noted:

> [The] easy method of getting a rich crop has spoiled the English and other settlers . . . in a word the grainfields, the meadows, the forests, the cattle, etc. are treated with equal carelessness; and the characteristic of the Enligh nation, so well skilled in these branches of husbandry, is scarcely recognizable here . . . their eyes are fixed upon the present gain, and they are blind to the future.

1. *The Quiet Crisis* (New York: Avon, 1964).

Farming is essentially an effort to increase the food supply by controlling certain natural forces. Inevitably the process brings with it some negative results. Benjamin Franklin described one such situation:

> In New England they once thought Black-birds useless and mischievous to their corn, they made [laws] to destroy them, the consequence was, the Black-birds were diminished but a kind of Worms which devoured their Grass, and which the Black-birds had been used to feed on encreased prodigiously; Their finding their Loss in Grass much greater than their savings in corn they wished again for their Black-birds.

Here is a classic instance of what biologist Barry Commoner would consider a violation of two basic laws of ecology: "Nature Knows Best" and "There Is No Such Thing as a Free Lunch."

City dwellers faced their own ecological problems. From the beginning, a water supply, home sanitation, and garbage collection were among the most troublesome aspects of city life. Only New York had a regular garbage collection system: hogs roamed the streets eating garbage and trash, and a hogreeve patrolled them. Later, garbage collectors were hired to care for some streets, and men hauled away refuse in carts at the price of sixpence a load. Penalties existed for obstructing public thoroughfares with refuse or filth, but the laws were seldom obeyed. Drinking water came from wells that were often uncomfortably close to privies. In Newport and Charleston, privies sometimes emptied into the streets. Passersby complained of "Spoiling & Damnifying" their clothes, "especially in ye Night when people cannot see to shunn them." In nature there is no such thing as waste, but cities have the most difficult time coping with what Commoner terms "The Second Law of Ecology: Everything Must Go Somewhere." Nevertheless, European visitors found American cities astonishingly clean and healthy, with the exception of Charleston, which suffered from "country fever."

The vast majority of colonists were farmers who, despite their transgressions against the forest, remained very much in touch with nature and nature's rhythms. They were attuned to the change of seasons, to the shortening and lengthening of daylight. They perceived the readiness of the soil for planting, of the trees for pruning, and of the crops for harvesting. They sensed the smells, sounds, textures, and colors of the outdoors. The majority of towns retained a rustic aspect that pleased the townspeople of the eighteenth century. There were fish in the streams, wild birds in the treetops, and cattle and sheep—and sometimes deer—grazing on the meadows. The nation was still innocent of railroads, tenements, mill towns, and slag heaps. And science had not yet linked up with technology to produce the industrial-urban order that would profoundly change the landscape.

Comprehension Questions: *Circle the letter of the best answer*

1. The myth of superabundance was evident in the early years of our country because:
   a. land, water, and animal life was in great supply
   b. people didn't care about the environment
   c. conservation was not heard of at this time
   d. farming was the way to employ many people

2. One can conclude from reading this passage that:
   a. we are practicing good conservation techniques at this time
   b. we have not learned the lessons of the past
   c. ecologists have the situation under control
   d. city dwellers are not involved in contributing to the problem

3. The second law of ecology is:
   a. all men must return what they take
   b. nature is in charge of herself
   c. man needs to clean up his act
   d. everything must go somewhere

Essay Question

Write a brief answer to the following question.

What was meant by the "myth of superabundance" during our early history as a nation?

Time-Rate Conversion Chart

Min:Sec	WPM	Min:Sec	WPM
1:00	791	4:30	176
1:10	678	4:40	170
1:20	593	4:50	164
1:30	527	5:00	158
1:40	475	5:10	153
1:50	431	5:20	148
2:00	396	5:30	144
2:10	365	5:40	140
2:20	339	5:50	136
2:30	316	6:00	132
2:40	297	6:10	128
2:50	279	6:20	125
3:00	264	6:30	122
3:10	250	6:40	119
3:20	237	6:50	116
3:30	226	7:00	113
3:40	216	7:10	110
3:50	206	7:20	108
4:00	198	7:30	105
4:10	190	7:40	103
4:20	183	7:50	101

9-33

Was the "Relocation" of Japanese-Americans Defensible?

Richard Kezirian

	Hour	Min.	Secs.
A. Ending time:	___	___	___
B. Starting time:	___	___	___
C. A – B = Reading time:		___	___

One of the most lamentable episodes in America's past has been the treatment accorded Japanese-Americans during World War II. There is hardly an American historian today who does not believe that the actions taken against Japanese-Americans during the harried days after Pearl Harbor were unconstitutional and motivated by unwarranted hysteria. Newly-opened historical archives make this story clearer now than ever before. So, in light of recent documents, this essay aims to present the background and reasons which prompted the decision to evacuate, relocate and detain Japanese-Americans.

Of approximately 127,000 persons of Japanese ancestry residing in the continental United States, more than 112,000 were imprisoned, including almost all of those residing in the West Coast states. This is a story which too few Americans know, despite recent publicity. In fact, an informal survey of leading college textbooks revealed that, on the average, less than a quarter of one page was devoted to this tragedy, if it was mentioned at all.

The first point to recognize is that the story does not begin at Pearl Harbor, but goes back to the 1970s when Japanese immigrants first came to this country. It was then that the Japanese were first exposed to the anti-Oriental prejudice which already was raging against the Chinese. As with all prejudice, at the heart of the matter were misperceptions, misunderstandings, fears, unwarranted stereotyping and jealous hatred. Organized labor feared that the Japanese would displace native Americans in key jobs. School officials and parents worried that the integration of Japanese children into the schools would be a pernicious influence on white youths. Business and farming interests worried that Japanese competition and expertise would decrease profits. Space does not allow for the use of the facts and statistics to prove these contentions wrong, but other more degraded fears can be easily disposed of—that the Japanese were intellectually inferior, that Japanese men were a menace to white women, and that the Japanese were unassimilable into America's traditions.

Basic prejudices were further heightened by international events, especially the Russo-Japanese War of 1904–05. Here the Japanese fought the Russians to a stalemate, the first time that white military supremacy had been challenged by a nonwhite people in modern history. Such events not only worsened official diplomatic and commercial relations between the U.S. and Japanese governments, but they intensified prejudice at home. For instance, California's Alien Land Law of 1913 and Congress's Quota Immigration Law of 1924 were passed with the Japanese specifically in mind. Later foreign events—the invasion of Manchuria in 1931, the "accidental" Japanese attack on the American gunboat *Panay,* and the outbreak of the Sino-Japanese War in 1937—proved even more dramatic in their effects. But the surprise attack at Pearl Harbor was the catalyst which set this chemically-explosive mixture boiling. The popular hysteria after Pearl Harbor seemed to know no bounds. There was inordinate fear of a Japanese invasion of the Pacific Coast and the feeling that Japanese-Americans would abet the enemy in an invasion of this sort.

Many newspapers played upon the stirred and angry emotions. A sampling of the headlines after Pearl Harbor from the hitherto moderate *Los Angeles Times* gives an idea of the proportions of these fears: "Enemy Planes Sighted Over California Coast;" "Caps on Japanese Tomato Plants Point to Air Base;" "Japanese Here Sent Vital Data to Tokyo." While American newspapers attributed the belligerent actions of Germany to the deeds of evil leaders, the tendency was to attribute the actions of th Japanese government to the deeds of an evil race.

Soon important political and civic leaders succumbed to the popular hysteria. Noted examples included California's liberal governor, Culbert L. Olson; California's attorney general, Earl Warren; and columnist Walter Lippmann. Before long, Congressional representatives from California, Oregon, and Washington met to plan to pressure for drastic actions.

At the source of a growing movement for relocation were key West Coast military officials stationed at the Presidio in San Francisco, particularly General John L. DeWitt, General Allen W. Gullion and Colonel Karl R. Bendetsen. It was these prominent Army officers who were responsible for leaking to the newspapers false information about supposed Japanese-American espionage units working in the Pacific Coast states and supposed enemy attacks at various locations along the western coast.

We know now that these reports were completely incorrect, and that anti-Japanese prejudice, short-sightedness and incompetence were the determining factors behind the actions of the Presidio team. Records of phone conversations and daily decision-making documents are available now and the indictments against these men can be made on a personal basis. The documents emphasize how influential a handful of misinformed and misguided bureaucrats can be as they set about creating a more important role for themselves in the governmental and military structure. On their behalf, one must recognize that the fallacious Roberts Report had just been published by the U.S. government, indicting certain Japanese residents in Hawaii for collaborating with the Pearl Harbor attackers. Hence, these Presidio officers feared being disgraced by inadequate precautions, such as happened to Lieutenant general Walter C. Short, who was in charge of the defense of Hawaii before the air invasion of December 7. However, in their zealousness, they over-reacted. This fact, in combination with their prejudices, incompetence and ambitions, caused them to misread the whole situation.

The influence of a competent commander who could recognize the true realities of the military situation should not be underestimated. For example, in Hawaii, where the Japanese populaton made up over 37 percent of the total, General Delos C. Emmons staunchly refused to go along with relocation plans. He argued that such policies would have more negative repercussions logistically than positive, and he believed that the danger of espionage was exaggerated. Hence, relocation plans were scuttled and, as Emmons predicted, no significant disloyalty resulted. If West Coast officials had shown equal military foresight, the same could have occurred on the mainland. This is borne out by the fact that, to the end, Army Chief of Staff George C. Marshall and FBI Director J. Edgar Hoover argued that the mass relocation of the whole Japanese-American community was unnecessary. Finally, but reluctantly, they conceded to West Coast pressure.

Of course, no such unconstitutional and prejudiced decisions could have been implemented against Japanese-Americans if public opinion in the continental U.S. itself had been more balanced. Decisions made by key politicians and military officials were fearlessly executed because they knew that they would be popular with the general public. In fact, President Franklin Roosevelt's final acquiescence was because of popular opinion and his own anti-Japanese prejudices. He believed that the decision for relocation would receive bipartisan support and would help to promote national solidarity behind the war effort.

Another factor in the relocation issue was the performance of the federal judiciary. The U.S. Supreme Court constitutionally validated the actions of the federal executive by refusing to inhibit the president's broad war and police powers. In the key court cases of *Hirabayashi v. U.S., Korematsu v. U.S.* and *Ex parte Endo,* the court accepted the premise of "collective ancestral guilt." For whites, cases of treason were to be decided on individual basis during the war; for the Japanese, guilt was decided collectively. so, in the end, the Supreme Court offered Japanese-Americans no legal protection.

Finally, and sadly, Japanese-Americans filled the need for a national scapegoat. The first six months after Pearl Harbor were months of unmitigated military disaster for American fighting units, particularly in the Pacific. As defeat piled upon defeat, hatreds at home were whetted and it was no accident that the process of relocation coincided almost exactly with America's greatest military disasters.

For these reasons, then, relocation plans were implemented without regard for the human costs and economic losses involved. A conservative estimate shows that the economic losses of Japanese-Americans because of the relocation process were in the neighborhood of $400 million. The total claims finally paid to Japanese-Americans by the U.S. government totalled merely 38 million. Furthermore, claims were made on the basis of 1942 prices and payment was made in inflated postwar dollars.

In the long run, of course, all Americans were the losers. For a precedent was set, both legally and historically, for the evacuation, relocation and detention procedure. Both a state of emergency and an "acceptable" target group would have to exist. But those requirements being met, the whole process could occur at the mere issuance of a presidential executive order.

Comprehension Questions: *Circle the letter of the best answer.*

1. In this passage the author attempted to:
   a. justify why the Japanese-Americans were set to camps
   b. defend the governments actions during this time
   c. convince the reader that what was done was in the best interests of the United States
   d. present the background and reasons why this occurred

2. FBI Director J. Edgar Hoover argued that:
   a. Germans should also be sent to holding camps
   b. supported the government's actions against the Japanese-Americans
   c. the mass relocation of Japanese-Americans was unnecessary
   d. most Japanese should be deported to Japan

3. The author concludes that:
   a. relocating the Japanese-Americans was the right thing to do
   b. sending Japanese-Americans to camps helped calm the people
   c. Americans in general were losers because of this happening
   d. the U.S. Government was justified in what it did to the Japanese-Americans at this time

Essay Question

Write a brief answer to the following question.

Why did the Supreme Court agree to "collective ancestral guilt" for all Japanese-Americans during World War II?

Time-Rate Conversion Chart

Min:Sec	WPM	Min:Sec	WPM	Min:Sec	WPM	Min:Sec	WPM
1:00	1404	4:30	312	8:00	176	11:30	122
1:10	1203	4:40	301	8:10	172	11:40	120
1:20	1053	4:50	290	8:20	168	11:50	119
1:30	936	5:00	281	8:30	165	12:00	117
1:40	842	5:10	272	8:40	162	12:10	115
1:50	766	5:20	263	8:50	159	12:20	114
2:00	702	5:30	255	9:00	156	12:30	112
2:10	648	5:40	248	9:10	153	12:40	111
2:20	602	5:50	241	9:20	150	12:50	109
2:30	562	6:00	234	9:30	148	13:00	108
2:40	527	6:10	228	9:40	145	13:10	107
2:50	496	6:20	222	9:50	143	13:20	105
3:00	468	6:30	216	10:00	140	13:30	104
3:10	443	6:40	211	10:10	138	13:40	103
3:20	421	6:50	205	10:20	136	13:50	101
3:30	401	7:00	201	10:30	134	14:00	100
3:40	383	7:10	196	10:40	132	14:10	99
3:50	366	7:20	191	10:50	130	14:20	98
4:00	351	7:30	187	11:00	128	14:30	97
4:10	337	7:40	183	11:10	126	14:40	96
4:20	324	7:50	179	11:20	124	14:50	95

Skimming-Rate Progress Chart

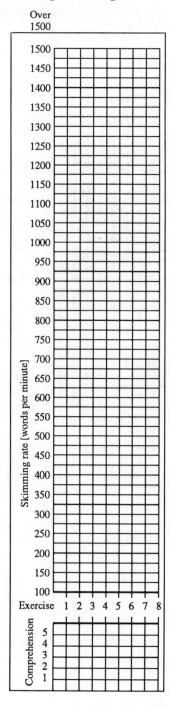

Rate Boost Progress Report

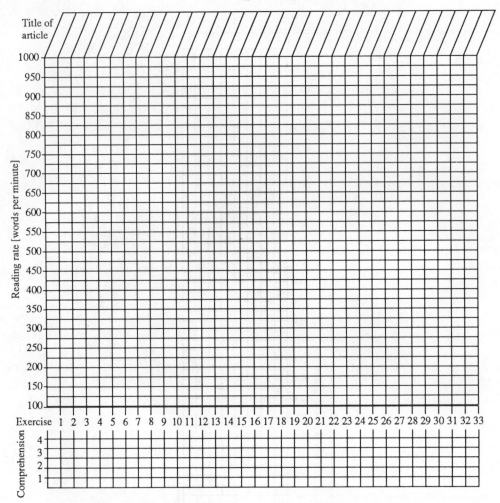

Title of article

Reading rate [words per minute]

1000
950
900
850
800
750
700
650
600
550
500
450
400
350
300
250
200
150
100

Exercise 1 2 3 4 5 6 7 8 9 10 11 12 13 14 15 16 17 18 19 20 21 22 23 24 25 26 27 28 29 30 31 32 33

Comprehension
4
3
2
1

Rate-Boost Answer Key

9-1 The Kennedy Legacy: Will It Endure?

1. b   2. a   3. b

Q. Why does the author believe it will be difficult to judge the Kennedy Presidency?
A. Because Kennedy was president for so short a time and the other unique problems associated with it: the gap between expectations and performance, and the fact that the assassination evokes sympathy and pathos.

9-2 The Mississippi River and 1542

1 d   2. c   3. a

Q. What attitude does Mark Twain seem to have toward organized religion. Cite two examples to support your claim.
a. He seems to have a low opinion of it. Some possible examples include: (a) associating the "absurd" practices of the lax court with religion since it was the "passion" of the ladies. (b) Spansh Inquisition is spoken of in uncomplimentary terms (c) the English church was shown as being started by Henry VIII who is described in uncomplimentary terms (d) the Spanish and French are said to have taken advantage of the Indians as well as converting them.

9-3 Was the U.S.'s Involvement in Vietnam a Success or a Failure?

1. b   2. d   3. c

Q. What are your reactions to the evidence presented in this passage?
A. Answers will vary.

9-4 Managing Stress and Relieving Tension

1. a   2. b   3. c

Q. What are some ways you reduce stress in your life?
A. Answers will vary.

9-5 Food and Ecocystems

1. a 2. d. 3. b

Q. What was the central idea presented in this passage and how did the author back this position?

A. The central idea of this passage is that organisms need food to obtain energy to carry on their life processes and to make body parts. As a result, all organisms have a role to play in this process and act as producers, consumers, or decomposers. Each is dependent upon the other in the process.

9-6 Erosion, Drought, and Deserts

1. a 2. b 3. b

Q. The author describes the soil as "the bridge between the inanimate and the living." What does he mean by this?

A. Answers will vary.

9-7 Nasrudin Hodja: The Man who Rode His Ass Backwards

1. c 2. a 3. a

Q. Why have Nasrudin Hodja Stories maintained their popularity over the years?

A. Nasrudin Stories have maintained their popularity because they depict wisdom that transcends both time and place.

9-8 Calamity in Vandervotteimittiss (Part I)

1. d. 2. c 3. d

Q. What is the purpose of this selection?

A. To describe Vandervotteimittiss. The author is describing a rather boring place. It is the beginning of a longer story.

9-9 Calamity in Vandervotteimittiss (Part II)

1. b 2. a 3. a

Q. Describe at least 3 characteristics of the physical appearance of the newcomer.

A. (a) dark in color (like snuff) (b) long hooked nose (c) small eyes (pea) (d) wide mouth (e) good teeth (f) smiling (g) mustache and beard (h) tight fitting black swallow-tailed coat (i) carrying a hat (j) sinister face

9-10 Was It Really Necessary to Use the Atomic Bomb?

1. d   2. d   3. c

Q. What conclusion did the author make concerning the use of the atomic bomb by the Truman administration?
A. The author felt the Truman administration was more concerned with how the bombs would be used and not on the moral question of whether they should be used. And, he felt they did not determine the long-term effects of the fall-out on future generations.

9-11 Energy Sources

1. d   2. d   3. a

Q. Why is it important for us to understand where our potential energy sources come from?
A. It is important to know about the various sources of potential energy in order to use and conserve them wisely. It is also important to continue research to find out the best ways to use the sources we have available.

9-12 Reflections on the Potato

1. b   2. b.   3. b

Q. How do the Filipinos view their identity?
A. They regard their identity as being static. That is, they feel they are fixed to an original identity of certain things upon which outside things have been added.

9-13 Rendezvous with Halley's Comet

1. a   2. d   3. d

Q. Why is it important for scientists to study events like Halley's Comet?
A. Scientists believe that comets consist of parts of the original building blocks of our solar system and that much information about the solar system's birth is frozen in there.

9-14 The Great Depression: Could It Have Been Avoided?

1. d   2. b   3. c

Q. What arguments did the structuralists make as to why the depression took place?
A. This group believed the depression took place because people had little money to spend, banks were not regulated, taxes were too low for the rich and corporations, and Wall Street needed to be regulated. Until these things took place, prosperity would not return.

9-15 America Creates a LIterature

1. d   2. c   3. a

Q. In your opinion, why did it take fifty years before America found its own literature and began to produce leading writers?
A. Answers will vary.

9-16 The Impact of Television

1. b   2. a   3. b

Q. Based on what you have read, what conclusions can you make?
A. Answers will vary.

9-17 What is a Newspaper?

1. b   2. c   3. a

Q. What are some commonly accepted characteristics of what constitutes a newspaper?
A. The following criteria are used to determine what is a newspaper:
   (1) must be published on a regular basis
   (2) must be devoted to the masses
   (3) must be available to everyone who wants it
   (4) must contain news, i.e., current events
   (5) must champion the interests of its geographic constituency.

9-18 Ecology and Ecosystems

1. b   2. c   3. c

Q. What factors determine the make-up of an ecosystem?
A. The factors that determine our ecosystem include organisms, populations, communities, ecosystems, and ecospheres. Our purpose is to see how all these interact with one another.

The Desert as a Way of Life

1. b   2. c   3. b

Q. How do the people of Niger adapt to the living conditions in the arid and semi-arid regions of the country?
A. The people of this region and their activity is dependent upon the existence of watering places, their entire life is focused upon how they will get water for themselves, live-stock, and for growing. In addition, their clothing and dwellings are adapted for the best climate as well as their diet.

9-20 The Articles of Confederation and the Constitution

1. b   2. a   3. c

Q. Why were the Articles of Confederation necessary at the beginning of our new nation?

A. This document made sense for the colonists who had just gotten out from under a strong central government. The agreement gave each state authority and local self-determination. Later, the need for a unified nation to deal with domestic and foreign affairs led to the development of the U.S. Constitution.

9-21 Crossing Paths With a Snake

1. c   2. a   3. d

Q. What specific techniques did you learn about treating snake bites from this article?

A. Answers will vary.

9-22 White Greed for Indian Lands

1. b   2. c   3. d

Q. Red Cloud of the Ogala Sioux said: "When the white man comes to my country he leaves a trail of blood behind him." Is this still true today concerning the American Indians?

A. One would hope not; however, the article would suggest that the American Indian has suffered greatly under the white man's control.

9-23 The Career and Life Planning Process

1. d   2. a   3. b

Q. Why is career and life planning important to you?
A. Answers will vary.

9-24 The World's Homeless Millions

1. d   2. a   3. c

Q. What have planners learned concerning how to improve and make housing for the poor more attainable?

A. They have learned that it is important to "help the poor to help themselves" by constructing buildings from less expensive but equally good materials, by building shelters that the poor can afford, and by mobilizing the savings of the poor to finance construction of their own homes. It is through this type of approach that adequate housing can be made a reality for the poor of the world.

9-25 Who Decides What is News?

1. a   2. b   3. b

Q. What are the major factors a journalist looks at to determine if a story is worth pursuing?
A. The two factors in selecting to do a story include (a) the availability of news and sources and (b) the suitability of the news to the audience.

9-26 An Energy History of the U.S. and the World

1. c   2. b   3. c

Q. What potential problem could the world community face in the coming decade concerning energy consumption?
A. The world has become dependent upon fossil fuels for its energy. This dependence is finite and the consumption of these fuels is a great concern. At present rates of consumption the world could be in difficulty in the coming decades if they rely on fossil fuels for their energy supplies.

9-27 Diversity in Ecosystems

1. c   2. a   3. c

Q. What factors determine the make-up of an ecosystem?
A. An ecosystem is made up of various living and non-living organisms. The more diverse the ecosystem the more stable it seems to be.

9-28 Protecting Tots from Drug Poisonings

1. c   2. a   3. d

Q. Why is it important to use child-resistant packaging for prescription drugs?
A. Children are poisoned every year because they get into prescription drugs left in easy opening containers. In order to prevent this from happening it is important to request child-proof containers for all prescripton drugs.

9-29 What Makes the Cascade Volcanos Hazardous?

1. c   2. d   3. d

Q. What are some indicators that a volcano may erupt?
A. Certain conditions may exist that tell scientists an eruption may be near. Some of the indicators are: (1) increase in thermal activity; (2) more sisemic activity; (3) gravity and magnetic measurements change; (4) gas and temperature monitoring increase; and (5) direct observations indicate changes.

9-30 Myths and Facts of Generic Drugs

1. c   2. b   3. b

Q. Why are your attitudes about generic drugs now that you have completed this passage?

A. Answers will vary.

9-31 Learning to Live

1. c   2. b   3. a

Q. What is the central message of this passage?

A. The main point of this article is that perseverance is a quality shared by all persons dealing with the drug problem throughout the world. This determination is fostered by the love and concern for those who have become dependent on drugs.

9-32 The Myth of Superabundance

1. a   2. c   3. d

Q. What was meant by the "myth of superabundance" during our early history as a nation?

A. Farmers assumed they would find new land when the old land became useless. At this time, it appeared that one could never use up all the land no matter how much was used. The same was true of forests and wildlife.

9-33 Was the "Relocation" of Japanese-Americans Defensible?

1. d   2. c   3. c

Q. Why did the Supreme Court agree to "collective ancestral guilt" for all Japanese-Americans during World War II?

A. Pressure from people living on the West coast and the hysteria of the times prompted the Supreme Court to make the decision of collective guilt for Japanese-Americans. All were considered treasonous.

Realize enough
existing
Half
answer
accepted
accept
newspaper